Literacy in Times of Crisis

T0190712

"The authors push the reader beyond simplistic understandings of literacy....
To my knowledge there is not another book that brings attention to our
national and international interdependence on individual and collective
literacy in a way that is as powerful."
Etta R. Hollins, University of Southern California

"Fresh, provocative, timely, and important, this volume extends the field of
sociocultural literacies in new directions. Covering an excellent range of issues,
populations, and geographical areas, what unites it is its attention to the ways
in which literacy practices serve people who face different kinds of challenges
in their lives."
Marjorie Faulstich Orellana, University of California,
Los Angeles

On the frontline of critical issues in education today, this volume covers new
ground for teachers and teacher educators for whom crisis is a daily part of
their work. It explores the relationship between crisis and literacy in order to:

- improve educators' ability to recognize, cope with, and avoid crisis;
- advance understanding of the dynamic relationship between crisis and
  cultural, historical, and political literacy practices; and
- contribute to a deeper theoretical understanding of literacy practices as
  they are situated in social practices.

The types of crises addressed are diverse, including natural disaster, cultural
and community disjuncture, homelessness, family upheaval, teen pregnancy,
and disability. Along with nine empirical studies, a teacher early in her career,
a veteran teacher, and a teacher educator share their perspectives in commentary sections at the opening and conclusion of the book in order to provide
applications to their specific fields.

Laurie MacGillivray is Professor of Literacy in the College of Education at
the University of Memphis.

Literacy in Times of Crisis

of Crisis

Practices and Perspectives

Edited by Laurie MacGillivray

Routledge
Taylor & Francis Group

NEW YORK AND LONDON

First published 2010
by Routledge
270 Madison Ave, New York, NY 10016

Simultaneously published in the UK
by Routledge
2 Park Square, Milton Park, Abingdon, Oxon OX14 4RN

Routledge is an imprint of the Taylor & Francis Group, an informa business

© 2010 Taylor & Francis

Typeset in Baskerville MT by Keyword Group Ltd

Library of Congress Cataloging in Publication Data
Literacy in times of crisis : practices and perspectives /
edited by Laurie MacGillivray.
p. cm.
1. Language arts–Psychological aspects.
2. Students–United States–Psychology. 3. Crisis intervention
(Mental health services)–United States. 4. Language arts
teachers–United States–Anecdotes.
I. MacGillivray, Laurie.
LB1575.8.L54 2010
428.0071–dc22   2009035374

ISBN 10: 0-415-87163-8 (hbk)
ISBN 10: 0-415-87164-6 (pbk)
ISBN 10: 0-203-86629-0 (ebk)

ISBN 13: 978-0-415-87163-1 (hbk)
ISBN 13: 978-0-415-87164-8 (pbk)
ISBN 13: 978-0-203-86629-0 (ebk)

Dedication
To Billy, Mom, and Dad for helping me collect life's
goodness and showing me how to share it.

Contents

Preface

This is a book about the importance of literacy in times of crisis. It explores the relationship between crisis and literacy across a wide range of people, places, cultures, and situations. Highlighting the complex interplay between crisis and literacy practices, it looks at how literacy plays many roles—facilitating communication, maintaining connection between survivors, expressing grief, shaping memories, providing information, and so much more. The questions at the heart of the book are these:

- What is the relationship between literacy and crisis?
- What literacy practices attenuate the impact of crisis?
- How do community literacy practices play a role in responding to crisis?
- What role does literacy play in the way families, schools, and communities respond to crisis?
- What is the relationship between school literacy practices and crisis?

As I began exploring these issues in my own research, working to understand the role of literacy practices in the lives of families living in homeless shelters (Chapter 4), I became aware of the practices they rely on that often go unrecognized by themselves and the schools. I began to talk with colleagues about the complex interplay between crisis and literacy they are finding in their own work, and learned about the research of others that examines the complex relationship between literacy and crisis. This book is the result of those conversations.

I talked with April Bedford and Devon Brenner about the ways that crises can heighten the need for certain literacy practices, as revealed in their analysis of the role of blogs and emails after Hurricane Katrina struck (Chapter 3). I learned about the ability of literacy practices to sustain one's self during difficult times such as evident in Gisele Ragusa's investigation of dialogue journals between parents and children during divorce (Chapter 5) and Kara Lycke's work with teenage mothers (Chapter 6). Also connecting literacy and crisis, Mary Thompson's work focuses on the way a troubled teen used blogs and anime to craft a new identity after her father was incarcerated (Chapter 7) and Gisele Ragusa's analysis of the reading habits of parents whose children have been newly diagnosed with a learning disability (Chapter 8).

I discussed with others about the ways that literacy can exacerbate or even cause a crisis. Loukia Sarroub has been studying how Yemeni refugee women can be forced to choose between marriage and learning English (Chapter 9). Rebecca Rogers and Kathryn Pole's work examined how the term "crisis" framed a school district takeover (Chapter 10). Susan Florio-Ruane's analysis of historical documents offers yet a different perspective on the relationship between crisis and literacy (Chapter 11).

These conversations continually raised concerns about the gap between school- and home-based literacy practices and about the ways that educators might better prepare young people to understand, adapt to, and avoid crisis. In light of this I was curious to learn about practitioners' perspectives on these issues. So I talked to Tracy Sweeney, a teacher early in her career, Jane Fung, a veteran teacher, and Elizabeth Moje, a teacher educator, about their reactions to the explorations of literacy and crisis (Chapter 12).

These chapters offer a deeper understanding of the dynamic relationship between crisis and cultural, historical, and political literacy practices. As a whole this book aims to contribute to a deeper theoretical understanding of literacy practices as they are situated in social practices, with the intention of helping communities—in and out of schools—improve our ability to recognize, cope with, and avoid crisis.

Key Features

Literacy in Times of Crisis includes the perspectives of a teacher early in her career, a veteran teacher, and a teacher educator. These three professionals provide commentary on the empirical chapters to examine applications to their specific fields. In the beginning of the book, the professionals introduce themselves, describe their experiences with literacy and crisis, and introduce questions which frame their reading of the chapters. At the close of the book, they reflect briefly on key aspects of the volume and share implications for their own work. The purpose is to offer insight into the cumulative knowledge of the text and its relation to teaching and teacher education, encouraging a focus on broader issues related to crisis, literacy practices, and teaching. We invite you to read their opening statements before journeying into each empirical chapter and to review their responses afterward.

Personal Prologue

I write sporadically throughout the three weeks in the hospital. Much of that time I sit next to his bed. In the beginning we talked, now I talk to him not sure how much he understands. Finally the reality of his dying has seeped in. The days are filled with harried nurses, jell-o, MRIs, and waiting. The nurses can't find his vein for IVs and I can't watch his silent grimaces.

My father is dying and I look to words. I write and read toward meaning. In the throes of losing him, I write poetry about the boy playing with a truck outside in the hall and our favorite doctor. I think I compose as a way to make sense of this and to also contain the emotions. My step-mother, Etta, and I read the many letters friends have sent. Some are brief condolences, others rich description of the ways dad had touched their lives. I try to read one of the Oprah books, but don't get very far.

The day after he dies, I write about the weight of his ashes on my lap as we drive home from the funeral parlor. We need to write his obituary right away and we don't hesitate. After so much sitting and wondering, Etta and I have a task with a deadline. We work pragmatically searching for obituaries that we can use as models. As part of this process, we discuss what we want to stress about who he was. We say, "He would want us to . . . ." Etta wants to focus on his recent causes rather than his earlier achievements. And I agree. My aunt requests we include the title of the book he wrote from his dissertation. Others suggest word changes. Mostly Etta and I pass the drafts back and forth. We craft his obituary; we craft our memories; we seek to craft others' memories too. In so many ways, words sustained me as I grappled with the crisis of my father's death. Free verse allowed me to focus on flow, meaning, words rather than format. I shared the poems with my step-mother as we sat together and with those who could not be in the room. Through those words, I explored feelings too melodramatic, grim, and revealing for conversation. In contrast to free verse poetry, the obituary had a format. After his death, the perimeters of the genre felt safe. We composed guided by both traditions and desires. And the letters I read offered pictures of my father as a teacher and prankster. They made us cry and laugh. They were evidence that others would also hold him in their hearts.

My memories demonstrate the importance of literacy in times of crisis and highlight the complex interplay between crisis and literacy practices. Literacy played many roles—facilitating communication, maintaining connection between the survivors, expressing grief, shaping memories, providing information, and so much more. As a literacy professional, I was able to stand back after the fact, and appreciate the ways literacy sustained me during those months. Reflecting on my own practices raised questions I could not answer alone. My quest to find answers has led to this book.

Acknowledgments

I've been lucky to have colleagues who are also my friends. The insights and support of Amy Ardell, Maria Barillas, Devon Brenner, Margie Curwen, Ana Martinez, Jenn Palma and Nancy Walker are with me regardless of the distance between us. Devon Brenner played a pivotal role in helping this book come to fruition through rich discussions, encouragement, and detailed feedback. She was a beacon throughout this process. I am thankful for the outstanding contributors and their commitment to addressing the complexity of crisis and literacy. The essays of Tracy Sweeney, Jane Fung, and Elizabeth Moje add a dynamic layer to the empirical work. I deeply appreciate their energy and insights. I am indebted to Richard James for broadening my understanding of crisis. Melissa Carroll, my GA, read through every page examining content and form. I am grateful for her diligence and attention to details.

I also want to thank Verizon's Friends and Family Plan which allows me to talk with Eve, my best friend, about the difference between organic and free range eggs while we walk our dogs in different time zones. She has been central to my life since I was eleven years old. Lastly, I'd like to thank the mothers and children who, in times of crisis, choose to thrive.

1 Introduction

Examining Crisis

Laurie MacGillivray and Devon Brenner

At its most basic level, a crisis is a turning point around which things change. Before the crisis, systems are functional, events are manageable. The existing social, capital, physical, and mental resources are sufficient for day-to-day living. But then along comes an event or series of events—an "identifiable stimulus or catalyst" (Collins & Collins, 2005)—that existing coping mechanisms cannot handle. An event becomes a crisis when it is perceived to overwhelm the systems that made things "work," that is, when it raises a problem that cannot be solved in the immediate future. Because the crisis cannot be solved, it stresses the physical, social, and psychological resources beyond the traditional ways of solving problems that have worked in the past. In this volume we are defining a crisis as time-limited. As opposed to long-term problems such as poverty or on-going illness, crises have both a beginning and an end. Eventually, systems recover. We develop relationships with new people who provide support, we find new resources that allow us response to the crisis, or we develop coping strategies that convert the unsolvable crisis into something we can accept. Stasis is reestablished—sometimes for the better, sometimes for the worse, sometimes both—and the crisis has passed (James, 2008).

The literature on crisis (e.g., Collins & Collins, 2005; Halpern & Tramontin, 2007; James, 2008; Ritchie, Watson, & Friedman, 2006) describes four domains of crisis—developmental, situational, existential, and ecosystemic. These domains refer broadly to the origins or site of the crisis. As we considered the power of these four domains to describe the crises that are analyzed in the chapters of this book, we began to develop a language for talking about the ways in which crises vary, including their origins but also other aspects such as impact and scale. Building from the literature on crisis and crisis intervention, we have identified the following six facets of crisis: scale, visibility, commonness, relative manageability/impact, expectedness, and perception.

These facets describe features of a specific crisis and are not mutually exclusive but overlap in complex and intertwining ways.

1. *Scale* The scale of crises varies widely. Crisis can affect an individual, a family, a community, or can occur at a global level. Scale refers to the number of people directly and indirectly impacted. Different events such

as a personal injury, an illness, the closing of a neighborhood school, and an earthquake may have quite different impacts (Halpern & Tramontin, 2007).

2.   *Visibility* Visibility refers to the degree of privateness of a tragedy. A tragedy such as a miscarriage is often barely visible to those not immediately affected. Thus, there is likely to be little external support. In contrast, there are crises that are public and visible. A house fire, for example, is a highly visible crisis.

3.   *Perceived Frequency* Some crises are common and regularly affect many people. For those crises, there are cultural understandings of "appropriate" ways to respond and rituals which can offer support. However, when a crisis is less common, there may be no existing rituals and others may not know how to respond.

4.   *Relative Manageability/Impact* The impact of a crisis is difficult to measure and is related to many complex factors. The scale of the crisis itself affects impact. Some crises are, objectively, more devastating than others, in terms of loss of life, property, financial resources, and the like. However, the impact of a crisis may have more to do with the victim's existing mental, financial, social, textual, and other resources than the actual precipitating event (Halpern & Tramontin, 2007). The combination of preexisting resources and the victim's emotional and psychological response determines the ultimate impact of a crisis.

5.   *Expectedness* Another dimension by which crises vary is in their level of expectedness. Some crises can be predicted well in advance, but many crises are completely unexpected and thus prevent preparation. Emotional, psychological, material, and financial resources can be readied which can diminish the effects of the crisis. The dimension of expectedness can affect readiness for and ability to respond to a crisis. The hypervigilence of being attacked, exemplified by our government, can cause a unique economic and social crisis of its own (James, 2008).

6.   *Perception* The dimension of perception has two main aspects that affect understanding of and attitudes toward a particular crisis. The first is whether the victim perceives the event as a crisis in the first place. An event is not a crisis unless it is perceived to be so. The same event may cause a range of reactions (Halpern & Tramontin, 2007). The second aspect of the dimension of perception is public perception. There are different responses for those crises that are viewed as a reflection of social ills than for those crises viewed as natural.

Literacy and Crisis

Literacy practices are intertwined with crisis. Literacy practices can be seen as a component of many of the six facets of crisis we have described above. For example, the visibility and perception of a crisis is related to the number, form, and content of texts read and created, such as newspaper articles that publicize an event. People may turn to books or websites to find out how others have responded and may find resources which make a crisis more manageable. Some may write in a journal in order to prepare for an expected crisis, or this very act may change their perception of the crisis. In any case, the ways in which individuals and communities use literacy in times of crisis are highly contextual, situated in the immediate context of crisis and response.

Situated Literacy Practice

An examination of the juncture of literacy and crisis is possible with an analysis which foregrounds context. Each contributor to this book examines the local, situated literacy practices of individuals, communities, and cultures as they experience particular crises at particular moments in time. According to Gee (2000), a look at situated literacy practices can be valuable because these practices provide insight into the complex relationship between beliefs, actions, cultures, and textual practices (see also Barton, 2000; MacGillivray & Curwen, 2007). The authors of this text assume that literacy practices represent "general cultural ways of utilizing literacy which people draw upon in particular situations" (Barton, 2001, p. 96). Literacy practices are always contextualized, embedded in larger social, political, and cultural contexts having complex, multiple purposes (Barton, 2000; Street, 2001).

Socio-Cultural Literacy Practice

A focus on literacy in context is grounded in a sociocultural perspective that focuses on culture, race, social class, religion, economics, politics, laws, and historical events. Literacy as social practice situates literacy events in the context of families, communities, institutions, curriculum, and policy. This perspective also attends to change, which is particularly relevant with new technologies and the speed of their evolution. "As societal expectations for literacy change, and as the demands on literate functions in a society change, so too must definitions of literacy change to reflect this moving target" (Leu, Kinzer, Coiro, & Cammack, 2004).

The chapters of this book examine literacy practices during crises in contrasting situations, including crises that vary in scale, visibility, commonness, relative manageability/impact, expectedness and perception. Since crisis characteristically disrupts the social order and involves agentive response, it makes available for study a range of interests, expectations, and activities not apparent within systems such as schools which may outwardly seem tightly ordered and impenetrable. The texts that people read and write during crisis, that sustain us during challenging times are varied, personal, and complex.

As educators, we have come to see that the texts that arise during crises are often not those texts that are welcomed at school or that "count" on official tests. From anime to free verse poetry, from graphic novels to text messages, the wider range of literacy practices used by the victims of crisis in these chapters invites educators to reexamine teaching and assessment policies and to build bridges between real-world and school-based literacy practices. By examining how learners "do" literacy (Magro, 2006/2007) during crisis, we offer an expansive view of literacy and challenge those trends that narrow school-based literacy (Heath, 1983; Hull & Schultz, 2001; MacGillivray & Curwen, 2007; Monkman, MacGillivray, & Leyva, 2003).

By examining a range of situations, this book deepens an understanding of the literacy practices that allow us to survive and even thrive in times of crisis. For example, literacy has been assumed to be an effective intervention against crisis. Within days of the Oklahoma bombing, teams of specialists had written materials for teachers to use to help children cope (James, 2008). Children were encouraged to write their stories and draft letters to rescuers to cope with the images of 9-11.

There are many ways in which literacy is an effective response to crisis. Herman (1997) for example, describes the ways in which sharing of moments, images, and stories of trauma can be a sign of recovery. Self-help books, discussion boards, professional resources, and blogs provide sources of information and comfort to survivors of crisis. Journal writing, text messaging, Bible reading, and letter writing can help victims to frame and reframe crises and to communicate their needs and responses to garner support. Several authors in this volume illustrate the very ways that literacy practices serve to diminish the scale and impact of a crisis, to create a sense of community and commonness after crisis, to alter perceptions of crisis, and to provide a variety of text-based mental and social resources for responding to crisis.

However, a sub-set of the authors in this volume challenge the notion that literacy is always a palliative for crisis, and present evidence that the relationship between literacy and crisis is neither straightforward nor always beneficial. In some cases, literacy exacerbates crisis. In others, it can and often does support victims of crisis. However, text can also be used as a tool to manufacture a crisis that does not exist or to exacerbate the impact of an otherwise relatively localized and inconsequential problem. And, because literacy and culture are intertwined and because cultural groups often clash on grounds of values, the mere acquisition of a particular set of literacy practices can be the very genesis of some crises.

Literacy and crisis share a complex and intertwining relationship. By examining ways that youth, families, and communities use literacy when in the midst of crisis, we explore that relationship and, in so doing, provide implications for both teachers and teacher educators. Listen to the voices of these three practitioners as they consider their own questions about the relationship between literacy and crisis in the next chapter.

References

Barton, D. (2000). Introduction: Exploring situated literacies. In D. Barton, M. Hamilton, & R. Ivanic (Eds.), *Situated literacies: Reading and writing in context* (pp. 1–6). London: Routledge.

Barton, D. (2001). Directions for literacy research: Analysing language and social practices in a textually mediated world. *Language and Education, 15*, 92–104.

Collins, B., & Collins, T. (2005). *Crisis and trauma: Developmental-Ecological intervention.* Boston, MA: Lahaska Press.

Gee, J. P. (2000). The New Literacy Studies: From "socially situated" to the work of the social. In D. Barton, M. Hamilton, & R. Ivanic (Eds.), *Situated literacies: Reading and writing in context* (pp. 180–196). London: Routledge.

Halpern, J., & Tramontin, M. (2007). *Disaster mental health: Theory and practice.* Belmont, CA: Thomson.

Heath, S. B. (1983). *Ways with words: Language, life, and work in communities and classrooms.* New York: Cambridge University Press.

Herman, J. (1997). *Trauma and recovery: The aftermath of violence—from domestic abuse to political terror.* New York: Basic Books.

Hull, G., & Schultz, K. (2001). Literacy and learning out of school: A review of research and theory. *Review of Educational Research, 71*(4), 575–611.

James, R. (2008). *Crisis intervention strategies.* Belmont, CA: Thomson.

Leu, D. J., Jr., Kinzer, C. K., Coiro, J., & Cammack, D. W. (2004). Toward a theory of new literacies emerging from the Internet and other information and communication technologies. In R. B. Ruddell, & N. Unrau (Eds.), *Theoretical models and processes of reading* (5th ed., pp. 1570–1613). Newark, DE: International Reading Association. Retrieved February 5, 2009, from http://www.readingonline.org/newliteracies/lit_index.asp?HREF=leu.

MacGillivray, L., & Curwen, M. (2007). Tagging as a social literacy practice. *Journal of Adolescent and Adult Literacy, 50*(5), 354–369.

Magro, K. (2006/2007). Overcoming the trauma of war: Literacy challenges of adult learners. *Education Canada, 47*, 70–74.

Monkman, K., MacGillivray, L., & Leyva, C. H. (2003). Literacy on three planes: Infusing social justice and culture into classroom instruction. *Bilingual Research Journal, 27*, 245–258.

National Institute of Child Health and Human Development (NICHD). (2000). *Report of the National Reading Panel. Teaching children to read: An evidence-based assessment of the scientific research literature on reading and its implications for reading instruction* (NIH Publication No. 00-4769). Washington, DC: U.S. Government Printing Office.

Ritchie, E., Watson, P., & Friedman, M. (2006). *Interventions following mass violence and disasters: Strategies for mental health practice.* New York: Guilford Press.

Street, B. (Ed.). (2001). *Literacy and development: Ethnographic perspectives.* London: Routledge.

2 Commentators' Introductions

Tracy Sweeney, Early Career Teacher, Rancocas Valley Regional High School

Biography

Tracy Sweeney has taught for five years at Rancocas Valley Regional High School in Mt. Holly, New Jersey. She has taught Journalism and Basic Skills, Heterogeneous and Honors English. In 2007, she co-authored an article on the reading habits of a refugee in and out of school which appeared in the *Journal of Adolescent and Adult Literacy*. She is active in literacy endeavors locally and nationally. Tracy received her Bachelor's in Secondary English in 2004 and a Master of Science in Curriculum and Instruction in 2007. She is currently pursuing a Doctorate of Education in Curriculum, Instruction, and Technology in Language Arts at Temple University. She is certified to teach English Education 7–12, English as a Second Language K–12, and is Nationally Board Certified in Adolescent/Young Adult English/Language Arts. Tracy lives in Philadelphia with her newborn son, Noah Dean, her husband, Eric, and her beagle, Albert.

Opening Essay

In 1963, my maternal great-grandfather with the help of a biliterate scribe wrote to the Consul of the United States in Ponta Delgada, São Miguel, Açores, in regards to his children's citizenship status. He resided in the United States with three of his eight children, but five were still in Portugal and wished to immigrate to the U.S. Since my grandmother was then married she was considered an independent and thus ineligible for immigration. However, a family crisis soon created her immigration opportunity. My grandmother's husband had a heart-attack at 42 years of age and my grandmother, widowed, was once again considered a dependant of her father in the eyes of U.S. immigration laws. Following copious correspondence between my family, the Foreign Service of the United States, and the American Consulate, my grandmother and her eight children moved to the United States in 1967.

Due to my great-grandfather's inability to write in English and Portuguese, only a thumbprint marks his participation. But our family history would be different if not for his understanding of the power of print to change lives. For me, the letters are artifacts documenting my family's crisis, granting me the opportunity to trace my maternal family's difficult journey. My grandfather's sudden death left his family in crisis. However, these letters, continuous written implorations on my grandmother's behalf, granted her access to the United States and a supportive extended family.

As a first generation American (U.S.-born) child raised in a bilingual family, I was afforded rich literacy experiences. Serving as a cultural sponsor for family members, I saw the struggles that resulted from illiteracy. This buttressed my decision to become an English teacher, and today, after five years of teaching, I am most passionate about teaching struggling readers and writers, both native English speakers and students for whom English is a new language. For many of my students, their lives and family histories have been affected by crisis, and the classroom has provided them with opportunities to speak, write, and read about their experiences. I invite my high school students to share indelible moments, and often, they choose times of crisis. I have had students write about moving, suicide, divorce, abortion, rape, running away, disease, death, and family exile for homosexuality. My students share these life-changing events willingly, and this leads me to question:

- How are students in crisis affected by literacy practices in my classroom?
- What is my role in fostering literacy activities for students in crisis?
- How can school literacy communities support students in crisis?

Especially since I am early in my career, it is easy to get caught up in the minutia of classroom life. This book is an opportunity to think about the big issues that brought me to teaching. I want to model literacy practices as powerful forces in facing and coping with crisis as my great-grandfather did for me. These three questions will guide my reading across multiple contexts and perspectives of the chapters. I hope it will scaffold my own understandings of the potential relationships between crisis and literacy and allow me to better support students who face crisis daily.

Jane Ching Fung, Veteran Teacher, Alexander Science Center School

Biography

Jane Ching Fung has taught for more than twenty-one years in Los Angeles public schools. She works with a diverse population including a large body of children living in poverty, speaking languages other than English, and newcomers to the United States. She is a teacher researcher dedicated to directly impacting the lives of her students, the education of teachers, and literacy at a local and national level. In 2002, she was recognized with a Milken Family Foundation National Educator Award, which selects teachers with outstanding student achievement and the ability to be a teacher leader. Although Jane is currently teaching kindergarten at Alexander Science Center School in urban Los Angeles, she is also active at a national level serving as a board member on the National Commission for Teaching and America's Future and on the Public Broadcasting Service Teachers Advisory Group. She has worked with the Center for the Future of Teaching and Learning, and was a fellow for Teachers Network Leadership Institute. Jane received her BS in Child Development in 1986 and her MA in Curriculum and Instruction, with a focus on Language Arts, in 2000. She is licensed to teach elementary education, Reading Recovery Certified, and National Board Certified in Early Childhood Generalist.

Opening Essay

Darius had been out for a week. When he returned to our kindergarten class, he handed me a letter from his mother and said, "My grandmother died, she had a hole in her stomach and she died." I could see the sadness in my young student's eyes, and his normally bouncy body was unusually still that day. Darius, the bright, outspoken, class clown, had suffered his first major loss. When he started to sob quietly in class, we let him do it. During Writing Workshop it was Darius that chose to write about what had happened to his grandmother. He drew a picture of her in bed with a hole in her body. He wrote, "My grandmother had a hole in her stomach. She died. My mom was crying." The class listened to him share his story in Author's Chair. He answered questions they had and listened as his peers reacted to his crisis by sharing their own experiences of loss with pets, grandparents, and distant uncles in another country.

Having taught young children for the past twenty-two years, I have seen how students, even emergent ones, use literacy as a way to understand and respond to a crisis or trauma in their lives. I remember the graphic illustrations used in stories Hanna wrote during the OJ Simpson trial. The media coverage had flooded the airways bombarding the minds of even the youngest children. After the chaos that surrounded our school during the Rodney King verdict, students drew pictures of burning businesses and people running in streets with television sets. I remembered student journal entries, "My mommy was scared," "We cannot go outside anymore," and "My uncle got a new TV."

Just like my students, I find myself using writing and reading, in my own life, to deal with personal crisis. All through high school and college, I kept a journal documenting moments in my life that were both memorable and painful. Now with technology, I have turned to emails, blogging, and online research to help me through times of crisis. When my son was having extreme behavior issues, I reached out to friends, family, and professionals for support through a steady exchange of emails and letters, including my pen pal of over 30 years. I started a blog last year and it has opened a new world for me. In a way, it is my journal, made public. I can write about happy things and I can also write down my feelings of fear and sadness. Although I am not writing to a specific individual, I find putting my life and times of crisis into words has been quite a liberating experience.

My personal and teaching experience with literacy in times of crisis leads me to wonder:

- What literacy experiences are most helpful to young students during times of crisis?
- What strategies can I use to promote home literacy practices in times of crisis?

When Laurie told me she was writing a book on literacy in times of crisis, I was intrigued by the topic. As a veteran teacher who has shared both personal and very public times of crisis with my students, I look forward to gaining more insights on ways literacy supports and helps us makes sense of the world in times of crisis.

Elizabeth Birr Moje, Teacher Educator and Researcher, University of Michigan

Biography

Elizabeth Birr Moje has spent twenty-five years as a teacher, some of those years working with young people and some with fellow teachers. As a teacher educator, she teaches courses on practices for engaging young people in reading and writing texts of the different secondary school disciplines. Her research focuses on urban youth culture, youth literacy, and content area/disciplinary literacy. As part of both her research and teaching, Moje often teaches in middle and high school classrooms and spends time with young people and their families outside of school. Her most recent work in Detroit, Michigan has spanned an eleven-year period, focusing on the funds of knowledge available to youth and teachers for building strong understanding of subject-area content and for building proficient literacy skills and strategies.

Moje is widely published in books and in top reading journals including *Reading Research Quarterly, Journal of Adolescent and Adult Literacy, Teachers College Record*, and the *Harvard Educational Review*.

Elizabeth received a BA in 1983, her MA in Reading Education in 1990, and her Ph.D. in Literacy and Language; Research Methodology, in 1994. She is certified to teach grades 7–12 with endorsements in History, Political Science, and Biology and is a licensed K–12 Reading Specialist.

In her spare time, Moje serves as chauffeur to her daughter, Avery, who attends middle school in Ann Arbor, and dances, plays piano and flute, and sews for recreation. Moje is married to John Moje, an accountant and technology consultant.

Opening Essay

Several years ago, for reasons I cannot recall, my mother-in-law shared with me a piece of text that her mother—my grandmother-in-law, if you will—had written to document the experience of her eldest son, Karl, being stricken with polio as a child. It was the 1930s, they lived in rural Nebraska, and my grand-mother-in-law—Minna—was, as one would expect a "stay-at-home mom." She was a working-class mother of seven children; her work was domestic, not academic. And yet, in a moment of crisis, Minna wrote an account of her experience, an account that appeared to serve no other purpose than to document the experience, absorb her fears, trumpet her relief, and sound a warning to others. No small purpose, indeed.

The writing was not eloquent in form or dramatic in tone. It was written in what one might call vernacular English, employing abbreviations, colloquialisms, and the occasional typographical error. Its form was not important to Minna; its purpose was. And the text is powerful, perhaps all the more so for its terse, matter-of-fact rendering of experience. As I read, I felt the need Minna must have had to "get this down," to pour her fear and relief onto the page, to make sure she did not forget, to let Karl know what had happened, or to warn others of the signs of the disease. And, as far as I know, Minna did not keep a journal or write to express herself. I will never know why she wrote about that time of crisis, but I do know that she did. In this moment, she wrote.

The power of literacy in that experience was not just experienced in the form of writing for self-expression or the documenting of experience. The substance of Minna's account reveals another act of literacy that played a critical role in this experience. At one point in the account, Minna noted that, when consulted, the town physician diagnosed Karl's illness as the "flu." Minna, dissatisfied with his diagnosis, sought other sources of information by consulting a medical dictionary that she kept in the house. She put the symptoms "fever," "nausea," "muscle weakness," and "headache" together and came up with polio. Minna then called the doctor again and insisted on another visit. On the second examination, the doctor concurred with Minna's diagnosis, and they raced to Omaha at "90 miles per hour." Minna describes the harrowing journey in relatively straightforward terms, and yet a mixture of anxiety and disbelief radiates through the simple words. Given my own experience in rural Nebraska, my knowledge of road conditions and automobiles of the time, and the terror I feel even thinking about my child suffering from a life-threatening illness, I could feel the terror still lurking in her words, despite the fact that Karl had been saved (but not without the consequences many children of the time experienced as a result of contracting polio).

As important as her expression of this event and what it meant for me as reader, a mother, and a scholar of literacy is the power of what Minna did with her literate skill in that moment. Minna's turn to text in a moment of crisis empowered her to question the doctor's diagnosis; it is equally important to note that Minna clearly felt a certain level of power apart from her literate skill—or perhaps because of it. She knew that she had other sources of information to use in this crisis. And she felt confident in questioning the doctor's authority (this was, after all, a different historical context, a time in which medicine did not have quite the status of "science" that it now has). Indeed, the role of power here is profound. Minna had the power to turn to text and the text further empowered her to challenge the doctor. Minna acted as an agent of change in this crisis, and literacy supported—if not enabled—her agency.

So what do we make of my rendition of Minna's story? What is important about it and how does it help us—as teachers, researchers, curriculum developers, policy makers, administrators, and/or parents—think about the role of literate skill in crisis and the role of crisis in shaping or constraining literate skill? What I find perplexing about this account is what happened when I tried to share it with a group of future educators. I was teaching a secondary "content-area" literacy course at the time that I was introduced to Minna's account, and I thought that it was a compelling way of illustrating the power of literacy in everyday life and the need to feel power in order to use literate skill, thus underscoring the need to teach literacy in every facet of secondary schooling and to provide opportunities for students to use their power. I read the piece to my class and then, when nobody reacted to my question about what makes this account interesting, stumbled through my ideas about why the piece was compelling, about what literacy meant to this working-class woman in rural Nebraska when she faced a personal crisis. Despite my eloquence as an orator, not one student in the class took up my idea. Nobody seemed moved by the idea that literate skill and text—in this case, written text—played two critical roles in this experience, one life-saving and the other, perhaps, soul-saving. My primary questions, then, for the authors of this collection are as follows:

1. How do we *convince* those who face daunting demands on their time, including following strict pacing guides and preparing students to succeed on tests, that considering how many children and youth in our schools face crises and trauma *is* part of instruction and that literacy teaching can play a role in that work?
2. In a related vein, what is the role of work on literacy in times of crisis in the upper grades? Does this work matter in physics class? British Literature from 1900–1960? Pre-calculus? Should we assume that students in such classes do not experience trauma or crisis? Or are they "mature enough" to handle their own crises?

3. How do we prevent a focus on trauma and crisis in children's and youths' lives from becoming voyeuristic? How do we avoid pathologizing the very children and youth we hope will be empowered by a literacy pedagogy that makes a space for the trauma and crisis of everyday life?

4. What is the role of power as literacy is employed in times of crisis and trauma? Can traumatized children and youth feel empowered? What will it take to develop a sense of agency when everything is crumbling around them? Does literacy confer power or is a sense of agency necessary for one to employ literate skill in powerful ways?

Part I

Reading and Writing in Times of Crisis

3 Making Contact in Times of Crisis

Literacy Practices in a Post-Katrina World

April Whatley Bedford and Devon Brenner

I'm fine. Tommy [son] and I are in South Lake at my brother-in-law's house and we're about to head to my mother's in Waco. Blair [husband] stayed behind and we were all really scared for a while, but he's fine, too. We lost our roof and a couple of windows, but it could have been so much worse! And of course, I'm married to a roofer. I'm not sure when he'll be able to get out and come to Texas or when we'll be able to go back home, but we are all safe. Thanks for checking in on us.

(Email from April Bedford to friends, hours after Hurricane Katrina made landfall in New Orleans)

On Saturday, August 27, 2005, two days before Hurricane Katrina struck her home in New Orleans, April evacuated to Texas. She packed enough clothes for three days, a few books, and her laptop and evacuated with her sixteen-year-old son, Tommy, and their new puppy. Her husband, Blair, stayed behind to secure their home. He planned to leave the next day—ahead of the storm—but when the levees suddenly rose, Blair became trapped before eventually hitch-hiking out of town one week later. The family was together for just two weeks, and then Blair returned to the Gulf Coast to begin recovery efforts. April and Tommy stayed in Texas until October 3, 2005. During their five-week exile in Texas, they stayed first with relatives and then in a hotel. While in exile, April employed a variety of new literacies—those literacy practices that have emerged as a result of rapidly changing informational and computer-based technologies (Cope & Kalantzis, 2000; Kress, 2003). Sometimes she did this in familiar ways such as maintaining contact with friends and family through email, and sometimes in ways she had never encountered before, such as blogs. After she returned to New Orleans in early October to begin rebuilding her home and life, April witnessed novel uses of literacy that arose in direct response to the Hurricane, such as spray-painted signs that spoke of rescuers' findings in abandoned houses and survivors' wry observations on the Federal Emergency Management Agency.

Hurricane Katrina presented a crisis of immense scale, unprecedented visibility and immeasurable impact. Literacy practices from this time help us understand how individuals adapt and respond to a crisis of this nature. In this chapter we provide a narrative portrait (Clandinin & Connelly, 2000; Lawrence-Lightfoot & Davis, 2002) and analysis of the major literacy practices April enacted and observed over the two-month period following the Hurricane. We analyze both April's experiences with literacy in response to the immediate crisis of her evacuation and literacy practices that arose in the very unfamiliar, post-Katrina environment in New Orleans. Narrative inquiry honors the stories of individuals and focuses on whole stories rather than fragmented bits of data. Portraiture, a complementary methodology, is a form of writing that attempts to bring stories to life for readers by providing vivid, detailed accounts of lived experiences (Lawrence-Lightfoot & Davis, 2002). In combining these two methodological approaches, we describe, reflect on, and analyze April's experiences with literacy practices in the aftermath of Hurricane Katrina.

We view literacy as a set of socio-cultural practices in which people engage (Resnick, 2000), that is, as ways of making meaning that emerge through people's needs to communicate with one another across time and space. A socio-cultural perspective on literacy practices recognizes that different communities, cultures, and groups employ literacy in different ways, and literacy practices are learned within and from larger discourse communities (Gee, 1989). To learn literacy is to learn an "identity kit" of a particular group (or groups), a way of "saying-writing-doing-being-valuing-believing" common to those who share a particular set of literacy practices. From this perspective, we recognize that context, function, and purpose shape literacy practice (Resnick, 2000) and that "any literate action, critical or not, is embedded in a particular socially constructed practice(s) in which texts serve specific purposes as they constitute social relationships and define the nature of knowledge about the self and the world" (p. 86). In particular, this perspective explains that there is not one monolithic "literacy" but that different communities employ linguistic practices and hence their values in different ways (Gee, 1996).

We also take a critical perspective toward literacy practices. A critical literacy perspective recognizes the inherently political nature of literacy practices (e.g., Ciardiello, 2004; Comber & Simpson, 2001; Edelsky, 1999). Not all communities of people have equitable access to literacy, and the literacy practices of different communities are valued in different ways. A critical perspective recognizes the complex and inequitable nature of the relationship between literacy and power (Lewison, Flint, & Van Sluys, 2002).

While we situate this chapter within the theoretical perspectives of socio-cultural and critical approaches to literacy, we also acknowledge that the construction of this narrative portrait is heavily dependent on memory. We analyze April's experiences from the perspective of the present, three years after the Hurricane. Not all events, thoughts, and feelings can be recaptured. We have relied primarily on email messages received and sent between August 29 and October 31, 2005 and photographs containing print messages taken during October, 2005. Emails and photographs serve as primary source documentation of literacy practices and as scaffolds for triggering additional memories and reflection.

This portrait is, by nature, partial. The literacy practices analyzed here represent only a small sampling of the myriad of literacy practices in which April and other residents engaged, with a focus on those practices that played a role in April's own response to and recovery from the crisis of Hurricane Katrina. In this chapter, we reconstruct and analyze April's experiences with literacy in a chronological manner, focusing on three distinct time periods: (1) the week immediately following the storm when April's major concern was whether her husband would make it out of the city alive, (2) the following four weeks while she was displaced from her home; and (3) her return to New Orleans. Experiences in each time period highlighted different literacy practices and revealed different aspects about the role of literacy in response to crises. The narrative is presented in first person and is written in an italic font.

Week One: The "Intolerable" Period

When I first evacuated in advance of the storm, I was apprehensive about the destruction the hurricane might cause, but I convinced myself that the damage would be minimal. The second day of evacuation, when I discovered that my husband would be remaining in New Orleans during the storm, I was furious that he allowed himself to be in that situation, but my anger was motivated by fear for his safety. In the hours in which the storm was pummeling the city (the third day of evacuation for me), my fear was overwhelming. On Monday, after the hurricane had passed, I spoke to my husband briefly by phone. He assured me that he was fine and that he had enough food and water to remain in New Orleans indefinitely but that it would be impossible for him to leave the city until the roads were cleared. At the time of this phone call, neither of us knew about the broken levees. Although I felt uneasy about the immediate future, I remained convinced that I would be returning home soon and that my husband would be fine until I did. Grateful for his safety, I drove from Dallas to my mother's house in Waco on Tuesday afternoon, but when I arrived I was immediately bombarded with anxious phone calls and ominous television coverage of the levee breaches.

For the next four days, all of my thoughts were focused on New Orleans. I barely slept. During this time, communication with my husband was limited. I dialed his cell phone number dozens, possibly hundreds, of times a day. Very rarely, less than once a day, he answered. While I would be relieved to discover he was alive, the few details he would tell me coupled with the news reports of the dire conditions continued to fuel my fears. My husband spent the four days he was stranded in New Orleans rescuing neighbors and passers-by in his small fishing boat. Many of these people he fed and sheltered in our home until they could be safely evacuated.

During this week, very few people knew where I was. My cell phone was not working. Although I was hundreds of miles away from New Orleans, cell phones with a 504 area code were transmitting calls very, very rarely. Colleagues who only knew my university email address were unable to make contact because the university server was not working. However, friends who knew my personal email address began sending messages, and email became the primary form of literacy in which I engaged immediately after Katrina. My friends wrote of their fears and worries: "I am hoping that this email reaches you and that you and your family are okay. I seem to remember that you have relatives in Texas? Perhaps you are there now?" "I've been worried about you. When you get a chance, would you let me know you're okay?" I know that I attempted to reassure my friends about my safety, and I remember feeling very comforted by their concern.

On Thursday of this week I spoke briefly with my husband. He told me he would be transporting an elderly couple in his boat, trying to find a way for them to evacuate, and I knew that he planned to return several miles to our house, alone and in the dark, that evening. When no one had heard from Blair by noon on Friday, I was frantic.

While I had cried many times each day over the experiences of so many on the Gulf Coast and the fate of my beloved city of New Orleans, I had not cried about the plight of my own family. However, on that Friday, September 2, I broke down in my mother's kitchen wailing, "We have to get him out of there." I was terrified at that time that my husband would not be leaving New Orleans alive.

I turned to my computer. In searching the Internet for anyone I might be able to contact to try to rescue my husband, I discovered a collection of blogs established on our local New Orleans newspaper website, arranged by neighborhood. Although I had heard of blogs, I had never encountered one before. After locating the blog for my own neighborhood, I posted a message asking if anyone had seen my husband or could go to our house to check on him. Immediately, I received several responses—all expressions of concern but none with news about my husband. Though I had not met her, one neighbor left the most comforting message. She invited me to email her privately and told me that when (if?) my husband was found, he could break into her house and use anything he could find there. I was overwhelmed by the generosity and support of this complete stranger. This support sustained me until I did receive a phone call from my husband's brother, about 1:00 Friday afternoon, that Blair was alive and (relatively) safe.

During this week, I remained supported by email messages from friends, acquaintances, and now strangers, until Blair and I were reunited on Saturday, September 3, one week after I evacuated. Throughout this time, my communication with my husband was very sparse. We spoke by phone only three times although he was sometimes able to make contact with friends or relatives who passed his messages along. The day after he reached Texas, we discovered that we could have been communicating by text-messaging, but while we both had access to our cell phones, neither of us was familiar with this new literacy practice. None of the friends and neighbors Blair helped knew how to use text messaging, either. Later, we discovered text messages sent by friends on his cell phone, messages Blair did not know how to access at the time they had been sent.

From the very beginning, new literacies played a primary role in April's response to the myriad of crises imposed by Hurricane Katrina. When traditional forms of communication failed to function, April maintained her social networks by connecting with friends and colleagues using email. In part due to the visibility of the Hurricane through near non-stop national news coverage, April received messages from friends, family, colleagues, and even strangers who knew she lived in New Orleans. Email provided April with a way to reassure most of her friends and family of her safety and to be comforted by their concern for her. April engaged in literacy practices that were not available even ten or fifteen years ago.

One of the salient features of new literacies is the way they change rapidly. Changing technologies afford new ways of communicating and novel ways of using text to convey ideas. At the same time, users of new literacy technologies rapidly develop ways of employing the technology to communicate in unfamiliar ways (Leu, Kinzer, Coiro, & Cammack, 2004). At first, April only used her computer to communicate in familiar ways—using email to recreate pre-existing social networks, to communicate, for comfort. However, as the severity of April's crisis increased while her husband was missing, April rapidly adapted her literacy practices. Though she had never read or written a blog prior to this time, her desperate search for information about Blair led April to her computer. Internet searches she already knew how to perform led her to the local newspaper's website, and once there, April quickly learned how to read, understand, and post blogs. Through blogging, April built new relationships with unknown neighbors and gained resources for her husband. As Leu et al. (2004) state, to be truly literate in the 21st Century involves "the skills, strategies, and dispositions necessary to successfully use and adapt to the rapidly changing information and communication technologies and contexts that continuously emerge in our world and influence all areas of our personal and professional lives" (unpaged). April's previous experiences with some new literacy practices and her disposition toward using them in a time of crisis enabled her to learn new skills and strategies that sustained her.

While these new literacy practices provided immense comfort and communication for April, her story highlights inequitable access to literacy practices (Luke, 1998). April, her neighbors, loved ones, and colleagues had access to a powerful set of literacy practices not available to all or even most of the evacuees and residents of New Orleans. This access was due in part to the fact that they owned or had access to a variety of technologies (computers, internet service, electricity) that supported literacy practices, but also because they already engaged in these new literacies on a regular basis—they knew how to conduct searches; form discussion groups; and compose, read, and forward emails. Due to the privilege she was afforded by being a well-educated, middle-class woman with a professional career, April was able to establish a wide network of support that enabled her, through these new literacies, to cope with the trauma she experienced as a result of Hurricane Katrina. Many residents of New Orleans, particularly the very poor, had little access to these literacy tools and practices. When Katrina struck, the city of New Orleans had a poverty rate of 23% with 103,000 residents living below the poverty line (Center for American Progress, 2005). The national poverty rate at the time was 13.1%. A Brookings Institution report says that 14% of the residents of the greater metropolitan New Orleans area did not have access to a vehicle (let alone a computer), including 36% of all poor people and 27% of Black residents

(5% of non-poor residents and 5% of white residents did not have access to a car) (Berube & Raphael, 2005). Nationwide, 32% of Black Americans owned a computer in 2000, compared to 51% of all Americans, and while 86% of Americans earning more than $75,000 owned computers, only 19% of those earning less than $15,000 a year were computer owners (U.S. Department of Commerce, 2000). Perhaps even more troubling, the city of New Orleans had a 40% illiteracy rate, and the high school graduation rate for Black students was only 50% (Flaherty, 2005). Clearly, many of New Orleans' residents were not able to access the literacy practices that sustained April. Literacy access is just one of the many features of economic and racial disparity exposed by the scale and visibility of Hurricane Katrina (Dyson, 2006).

However, just because most of these residents did not have access to computers, email, and blogs does not mean that they did not engage in a wide range of literacy practices in the immediate aftermath of the storm. Although cell phones did not work for traditional phone calls most of the time, they could almost always be used for text messages. Text messaging does not "count" as a literacy practice in many settings, particularly public schools where cell phones are generally prohibited. Text messaging is often denigrated as part of the presumed downfall of young people's ability to spell or speak in complete sentences. The crisis created by Hurricane Katrina causes us to take a second look at this and other new literacies that worry educators. Text messaging provided an important literacy practice to its communities of users before Hurricane Katrina, and the practice of sending text messages became even more powerful after the Hurricane when it was the only reliable way to communicate.

April and her husband would have been able to access this practice except neither of them knew how; because of their lack of familiarity with text messaging, they weren't even aware that this technology would have allowed them to communicate in the aftermath of the Hurricane. Neither did many of the members of their age, race, geographic, and socio-economic communities, apparently, since April received no text messages from colleagues or friends attempting to contact her. However, many New Orleans residents, particularly many young and minority residents, possessed this literacy practice. Surveys show that low-income, minority, and young people are increasingly more likely to own cell phones to the exclusion of land-lines (Pew Research Center, 2006). Because pay-per-use cell phones allow phone ownership by those with very low incomes and those without a permanent address, nearly one in five individuals with incomes less than $10,000 have a cell phone (Pew Research Center, 2006). Many users prefer to text message because texts do not use up minutes in a cell phone service plan. While text messaging was not a literacy practice which April could use at the time of Hurricane Katrina, this new literacy practice allowed many of New Orleans' marginalized citizens to use literacy for crucial functions in sophisticated ways in the aftermath of the storm.

Weeks Two through Five: Displacement
and Uncertainty

Though the first week of the aftermath was perhaps the most traumatic for April, its impact continued to be felt for several more weeks. April's narrative continues:

By the second week after Katrina struck, my husband was safe and my family was reunited in Texas. However, we were still displaced. The ground floor of our house had been flooded, the roof had blown off, and there was no electricity. Nothing about our futures was certain. Would we be able to return to New Orleans? Would we be able to salvage anything? Did we still have jobs? How would we pay our bills with no records of who and what we owed? Should Tommy, our son, start school in Texas? If so, where? The list of questions we faced seemed insurmountable.

Just as acquaintances had been frantic to find out information about me during the first week of evacuation, I was now desperate for news about all of the people I knew from New Orleans. Each day I would think of more people I hadn't heard from and send out messages trying to find out if they were safe. About ten days after the hurricane struck, a colleague from the University of New Orleans set up a discussion group on Yahoo to share news about the safety and locations of colleagues and students from our department. Another two weeks passed before all thirteen members of our department and various other colleagues had been accounted for. Because our New Orleans-based phone numbers and email accounts no longer functioned (servers at the University of New Orleans were down for months after the hurricane), it took a while for us to find each other. Of course, it was impossible to locate many of our students, and some of those who were found had harrowing stories to tell.

During this time, I read emails, but perhaps more importantly for my own recovery, I also wrote emails. I wrote to stay connected to my friends, to reassure them of my welfare, and thank them for their support with messages such as this one from September 10: "You are all great friends and colleagues, and I hope that you will all continue to stay in touch. Your tremendous support is what gets me through the day!" Our house and neighborhood had sustained tremendous damage and our lives were full of uncertainty, but I realize now that I constructed my messages to sound positive and upbeat. While I did express anxiety about the future, the tone of my messages was never as sad, afraid, angry, or conflicted as I actually felt at the time that I was writing them. Perhaps because I did have so much for which to be thankful, I didn't want to let anyone know that I was actually in crisis.

I also wrote because I needed to tell my story. One friend noted that she hoped my writing was cathartic for me, and several mentioned that my writing had "powerful voice." My writing was indeed cathartic, and if my voice was powerful, it was because I was writing about experiences that had a huge emotional impact on me. I wrote to record my own history. I actually began to do more of this and to save my writing at the prompting of a friend from Maryland, who wrote, "I know you'll save your emails, but your description is so powerful. It helps us understand in a small way what it must be like for you to recover your life."

Recovering my life was indeed what I was doing, and I was doing it, in part, through reading and writing. Looking back, I realize that I did not consciously turn to writing to deal with what I was experiencing. I planned to. I actually bought a journal within a couple of days after the storm and labeled it "The Katrina Diaries." I've kept journals all my life, but I just couldn't bring myself to write in the journal I bought. In the midst of dealing with the crisis, I couldn't face writing about it, too, at least not without the purpose of passing along information to others. I did realize at some point along the way that it was important and therapeutic for me to tell my story. At that point, I started keeping many of the email messages I wrote.

After the terrorist attacks on September 11, Probst (2001) wrote about the importance of this kind of writing, saying, "Stories will save us, if anything will" (p. 50). Probst describes the importance, for those working to understand and respond to crisis, of "articulating and reflecting upon their responses, and using them to think about what they were seeing and hearing" (p. 52).

April used her email audience to engage in this healing sort of writing and to preserve her responses and experiences for later reflection. In the past, others have used journaling and story-writing to do the same. The internet abounds with recommendations to let students and others tell and write their stories after a crisis or tragedy. The California Attorney General's Crime and Violence Prevention Center (2001), for example, recommends that teachers make time for journaling after a crisis. In April's case it was important not just to write, but to have an audience for that writing. April wrote to make sense of and convey her experiences to her friends and family. This audience of caring listeners prompted and responded to her storytelling. Email gave April a reason and purpose for writing and perhaps allowed her healing to happen more quickly and thoroughly than it might have otherwise. Writing her story as emails allowed April the opportunity to frame and reframe the crisis through repeated retellings. With each retelling, she increasingly portrayed herself as strong, capable, and even fortunate. April's access to literacy practices and membership in a literate community facilitated her recovery from crisis.

Literacy and Recovery amidst Displacement

By far, the greatest number of emails I received offered expressions of emotional support while I was in crisis. I received messages of support from friends and acquaintances in 21 different states and Canada. Their words definitely helped me cope with the stress I was enduring. Over and over, people viewing this highly visible and large-scale crisis from afar wished to contribute to the response, and asked, "What can I do?" I often felt guilty in receiving so much support because there were so many who had lost so much more, but the overwhelming kindness I encountered (almost always initiated through email) changed my life as profoundly as any loss I experienced as a result of the storm. In their messages, a number of individuals expressed how doing something tangible to help me lessened their own feelings of helplessness and frustration in response to the devastation of Hurricane Katrina.

On September 6, 2005, I received a message from a friend who wrote, "Maybe you would want to get involved with helping the children in the shelters once you get settled temporarily ... even just a 'story time'?" My own literacy community turns to books in times of crisis. We read to escape, to understand, and for the models that literature provides. Many of these friends had sent me books to help me escape the stress I was enduring, and I knew how much reading those books had helped me endure. I began to think about the children from New Orleans who were displaced without any possessions. On September 10, 2005, I sent the following message to all my "children's literature" friends:

> *I've been thinking about what I could do to help the evacuees here in the Dallas area ... I'd like to go to the schools or shelters and just read to the kids. Of course, I have no books. I also know that many of the children in the shelters have probably never had books before. So if you have any review copies that you would like to send, I will make sure that they find good homes.*

Immediately, books began pouring in, eventually totaling over 3,000 donated books. Like me, all of the senders believed that books would comfort children in crisis. Surprisingly, at first I had trouble even finding a school willing to take the books. This was because by the time I was able to organize the donations, children had been moved out of shelters and were being enrolled in schools too overwhelmed with creating spaces for this large influx of students to even answer my phone calls. Once I did identify some schools that evacuee children were attending, some of the school personnel were hesitant to give the books to individual children. They wanted to keep them for their under-resourced classrooms and libraries. Fortunately, I received enough books that I was able to distribute them to evacuee children as well as to donate some to classrooms and school libraries. Over a two-week period at the end of September, I visited four elementary schools and one middle school in Dallas, and at one school I met children from New Orleans, gave them books, and spent time reading with them, a day I will never forget.

Books were among the few items April brought with her when she evacuated to Texas. Through the lens of her own literacy practices, April assumed that giving children books to keep would be comforting. April and her colleagues believed in the inherent value of book ownership. School personnel, however, had more pragmatic and less sentimental views of the function and role of books. They seemed to view books as resources their schools could use and, though they did not explain why, were reluctant to put the books in the hands of displaced students. These contrasting views of the role of books and book reading help us to see that "all views of literacy have epistemological, cultural, and political biases that are dependent on the social, economic, and experiential viewpoints of their proponents" (Gallego & Hollingsworth, 2000, p. 4). The evacuated students were grateful to receive books of their very own after losing so much. April received many heartfelt thanks from students, as well as responses to the individual books they received and read.

October 3 and Beyond: Re-Entry

We learned that the university would be resuming via online classes and in off-campus buildings on October 10 and Tommy's school would re-open on October 17. My husband had already returned to the Gulf Coast to begin working in early September, and on Saturday,

October 1, he suggested that Tommy and I return as well. Before departing, I wrote about my plans to my email network. Part of that message said,

> *Right now we don't know where we'll stay .... Several friends have offered to either share their homes with us or let us stay in their homes until they return in a few months .... We may be sleeping in sleeping bags or making several transitional moves, but we are moving back so that our family will be reunited and we can help with the rebuilding efforts. I am, of course, just a little bit nervous. I so appreciate your continued thoughts and prayers. They have gotten me through the last month!*

Needless to say, I was more than "just a little bit nervous," but my son and I packed our car with the things we had acquired during five weeks of displacement, cases of bottled water and nonperishable food, and headed for the unknown.

Of course, our community as we knew it was completely changed. We tried but could not prepare ourselves for the damage—wind damage from the hurricane, water damage from the flooding, mold from weeks of deserted buildings being left to rot. But I was particularly struck by the print that I encountered everywhere. The day I arrived back in the city, the first type of print I noticed was the writing on houses and other buildings. In an email I sent to friends five days after I returned, I wrote:

> *The most eerie thing was the writing on the side of every house. Search and rescue teams had written on the outside walls to indicate that the houses had been searched and whether or not bodies were found. The SPCA also wrote about the findings of their search for pets. I'm not exactly sure what the codes mean, but you know that if any number other than zero appears on the right side of the inscription, a body was found.*

These inscriptions, which came to be called "Katrina tattoos," can still be seen today throughout New Orleans (see Figure 3.1). Many remain on houses that have been untouched for over three years while others adorn the houses of owners who decided to keep the writing as a memorial to the tragedy rather than paint over them when they renovated their homes.

These official writings were not the only messages I witnessed on houses and buildings. Many homes and businesses also had spray-painted messages recording who had taken shelter there and for how long. My husband took a photo of one such message on our own home. Two of the people he rescued, Helga and Willie, had spray-painted their own, my husband's, and our dog's name and the dates they had been stranded on the board my husband used to shield the window beside our front door (see Figure 3.2). People also wrote identifying information such as their birthdates and social security numbers on buildings where they took shelter. In some cases, these authors survived; in others, they did not.

Many of the messages I encountered written in the aftermath of Hurricane Katrina expressed warnings, mostly to looters. One message I photographed on the front of a business on St. Charles Avenue read, "Don't try. I am sleeping inside with a big dog, an ugly woman, two shotguns, and a claw hammer." Next to this message was another, dated September 4, 2005, obviously written a few days later. It read "Still here. Woman left Fri. Cooking a pot of dog gumbo." This was the first example I saw of someone using dark humor to express his frustration with his plight in the aftermath of the storm. Many more such messages appeared

Figure 3.1 Katrina tattoo.

Figure 3.2 Documenting those who sheltered inside.

Figure 3.3 Warnings and jokes about Hurricane Katrina.

Figure 3.4 Warnings and jokes about Hurricane Katrina.

throughout the New Orleans landscape as people began to return to the city and sought ways to manage their response to the crisis.

A more hopeful source of print in post-Katrina New Orleans included signs—sometimes hand-lettered, sometimes professionally printed—posted on the medians of streets (what we call the "neutral ground") and in yards. In my first email to friends when I returned, I wrote, "There are signs everywhere saying that different stores and restaurants are hiring. In fact, the presence of signs of all kinds, particularly handwritten ones on plywood, are a new addition to the landscape." These signs served a myriad of functions. They expressed hope, "Still alive and kicking." They let people know how to find each other: "Smiths, now at 512 Barton." They communicated information about access to city services and business openings and closings, and much more. Immediately following the hurricane, writing informed rescuers of individuals' locations and requested help. In contrast, messages written after the flooding told the public about results of home searches by rescuers; sought information about acquaintances; protested the official response to the crisis; notified the public about the resumption of community services; and expressed humor, frustration, and survival.

An unlikely source for writing material became the contaminated refrigerators people hauled to the curbs outside their houses that took weeks for the city to pick up. There were political messages spray-painted on rotting refrigerators on nearly every sidewalk. Abandoned refrigerators became such a prominent feature of the post-Katrina landscape and important means of communicating that there is even a Wikipedia page about "Katrina Refrigerators." The messages on refrigerators were often humorous but also pointed, including statements such as: "Smells like FEMA"; "Levee Board Victim"; and "Katrina Leftovers."

Figure 3.5 Katrina refrigerators.

The spray-painted signs that dominated the environment to which April returned ranged from official records of searches, to the dry wit of the refrigerator door, to announcements of hope and rebuilding on plywood signs. The signs people wrote after the Hurricane carried none of the connotation of vandalism tagging usually entails, and they also had none of the artistic features found in most graffiti. Instead, these were messages written by residents of New Orleans who had all experienced the event of Hurricane Katrina. However, as literacy practices, post-Katrina signs shared many of the same features of tagging identified by MacGillivray and Curwen (2007). Analysis of tagging and interviews with those who tag reveal that a primary purpose of tagging "is to sustain social relationships; it is a form of dialogue and conversation" (p. 360). Similarly, residents of New Orleans and the rest of the Gulf Coast used their spray-painted signs to communicate their hopes, fears, frustrations, and needs to the members of their community. Katrina signs were also like tagging in that tagging provides a means for its authors, typically marginalized youth with little access to traditional literacies, to make themselves known, to achieve some recognition for their struggles. Certainly all of the post-Katrina signs announcing "Still alive and kicking" performed a similar function for people with no electricity, whose paper and pens had all been ruined by the flood and who no longer had access to even the most basic city services. A third and crucial function of tagging is to provide an outlet for commentary on larger societal issues. Katrina signs also served this function, allowing the survivors to vent their frustrations about the effectiveness of the response to the crisis. A tagger who calls himself SABER described graffiti as "controlling the corporate realm" (SABER & Tyke, 2005, cited in MacGillivray & Curwen, 2007, p. 362). For those residents of New Orleans and the Gulf Coast most affected by Hurricane Katrina, the feelings of near-helplessness after the crisis were overwhelming. Using print literacy to communicate, however makeshift, allowed them some sense of control over the physical environment and their response to it. These signs are still prevalent in April's neighborhood and across the Gulf Coast, testament to the importance of literacy practices in the response to and recovery from crisis.

Analysis and Conclusions

These are just a few of the many literacy practices that arose in the aftermath of Hurricane Katrina. Analysis of these literacy practices provides important information for educators, counselors, and policy makers. The scale, visibility, and impact of this crisis reveal—in ways which more local, individual crises may not—the multiple ways that literacy practices can be engaged both during and after a crisis to make contact, to preserve connections to the known and the familiar, to make sense of the unexplainable, and to transform experiences of loss and despair into opportunities for healing and hope.

For April, and presumably for many others, responding to a crisis through literacy was "natural." April used reading, writing, and new literacies on a daily, even hourly basis, in a variety of ways immediately after and in the weeks following the landfall of the Hurricane. April used reading and writing to establish and maintain social connections, to distract herself, as sources of comfort, to reflect upon her experiences, to learn critical information, and to give help to others. Although the ways in which April employed literacy were enabled by her access to technology and electricity, she was not alone in turning to print to support her and give expression to her needs, concerns, and frustrations. Even those without the most basic literacy tools found ways to use materials in their environment to communicate and cope with crisis.

For the most part, the literacy practices that April, her friends, neighbors, and other New Orleans residents employed are different from traditional school-based literacy practices. Recent educational legislation, policy, and practices have increasingly led to a view of literacy as a set of discrete skills used in the same way in all situations (Resnick, 2000). Based on April's experiences, we are encouraged to view "non-school" forms of literacy as valuable (Hull & Schultz, 2001). In particular, new literacies played a prominent role in the aftermath of Hurricane Katrina, revealing the importance of teaching children both how to use these practices and how to adapt to them. Direct teaching (and valuing) of new literacy practices may also be important to close the digital divide. Many of the literacy practices that students use to maintain their social networks outside of school, such as text messaging, MySpace, and Facebook, are discouraged and even banned at school. However, in times of crisis, these networks may be especially important.

More and more of us have access to new literacies. In 2002, nearly 60% of all households had access to the internet (Lebo, 2003; as cited in Leu et al., 2004), and we are adopting the internet at a rate faster than any other technology that has come before, including telephones and television (U.S. Department of Commerce, 2002). But perhaps what we need to do in school is not so much teach specific new literacies (our students hardly need us to teach them how to use Facebook), but teach the skills and strategies of critique, adaptation, and innovation. One of the key features of new literacies is that they are not static but ever changing (Leu et al., 2004). When she needed to learn how to subscribe and respond to blogs, April was able to quickly do so. Even the preponderance of Katrina refrigerators and tattoos points to the crucial importance of being able to adapt literacy practices to existing contexts and resources in times of crisis. And yet when schools treat literacy practices as static and unchanging, we shortchange students from learning to adapt their literacy practices in response to changes in their lives.

April's narrative reveals the importance of teaching students to read and write in a myriad of ways. We cannot wait until crisis strikes. Only if individuals already engage in and value a wide range of literacy practices prior to a traumatic event will they be able to turn to and adapt these practices for comfort and sustenance when crisis happens.

References

Berube, A., & Raphael, S. (2005). *Access to cars in New Orleans.* Washington, DC: Brookings Institution. Retrieved January 25, 2008, from http://www.brookings.edu/metro/20050915_katrinacarstables.pdf

California Attorney General's Crime and Violence Prevention Center. (2001). *Handling a crisis teaches students important lessons.* Retrieved February 13, 2008, from http://safestate.org/index.cfm?navid=234

Center for American Progress. (2005). *Who are Katrina's victims?* Retrieved January 25, 2008, from http://www.americanprogress.org/publicsearch?text=katrina&x=0&y=0

Ciardiello, A. V. (2004). Democracy's young heroes: An instructional model of critical literacy practices. *The Reading Teacher, 58*(2), 138–147.

Clandinin, D. J., & Connelly, F. M. (2000). *Narrative inquiry: Experience and story in qualitative research.* San Francisco: Jossey-Bass.

Comber, B., & Simpson, A. (Eds.). (2001). *Negotiating critical literacies in classrooms.* Mahwah, NJ: Erlbaum.

Cope, B., & Kalantzis, M. (2000). *Multiliteracies: Literacy learning and the design of social futures.* London: Routledge.

Dyson, M. E. (2006). *Come hell or high water: Hurricane Katrina and the color of disaster.* New York: Basic Books.

Edelsky, C. (1999). *Making justice our project: Teachers working toward critical whole language practice.* Urbana, IL: National Council of Teachers of English.

Flaherty, J. (2005). Notes from inside New Orleans. *Znet.* Retrieved June 1, 2009, from http://www.zcommunications.org/znet/viewArticle/5491

Gallego, M. A., & Hollingsworth, S. (2000). *What counts as literacy?: Challenging the school standard.* New York: Teachers College Press.

Gee, J. P. (1989). Literacy, discourse, and linguistics: Introduction. *Journal of Education, 171,* 5–17.

Gee, J. P. (1996). *Social linguistics and literacies* (2nd ed.). London: Taylor & Francis.

Hull, G., & Schultz, K. (2001). Literacy and learning out of school: A review of theory and research. *Review of Educational Research, (71)*4, 575–611.

Kress, G. (2003). *Literacy in the new media age.* London: Routledge.

Lawrence-Lightfoot, S., & Davis, J. H. (2002). *The art and science of portraiture.* San Francisco: Jossey-Bass.

Leu, D. J., Jr., Kinzer, C. K., Coiro, J., & Cammack, D. W. (2004). Toward a theory of new literacies emerging from the Internet and other information and communication technologies. In R. B. Ruddell, & N. Unrau (Eds.), *Theoretical models and processes of reading* (5th ed.) (pp. 1570–1613). Newark, DE: International Reading Association. Retrieved June 1, 2009, from http://www.readingonline.org/newliteracies/lit_index.asp?HREF=leu/

Lewison, M., Flint, A. S., & Van Sluys, K. (2002). Taking on critical literacy: The journey of newcomers and novices. *Language Arts, 79*(5), 382–392.

Luke, A. (1998). Getting over method: Literacy teaching as work in "new times." *Language Arts, 75*(4), 305–313.

MacGillivray, L., & Curwen, M. (2007). Tagging as social literacy practice. *Journal of Adolescent and Adult Literacy, 50*(5), 354–369.

Pew Research Center. (2006). *National surveys not undermined by growing cell-only population: The cell phone challenge to survey research.* Washington, DC: The Pew Research Center for the People and the Press. Retrieved February 13, 2008, from http://people-press.org/reports/pdf/276.pdf

Probst, R. (2001). Difficult days and difficult texts. *Language Arts, 9*(2), 50–53.

Resnick, L. B. (2000). Literacy in school and out. In M. A. Gallego, & S. Hollingsworth (Eds.), *What counts as literacy: Challenging the school standard* (pp. 27–41). New York: Teachers College Press.

U.S. Department of Commerce. (2000). *A report on Americans' access to technology tools.* Washington, DC: U.S. Department of Commerce. Retrieved January 25, 2008, from http://search.ntia.doc.gov/pdf/fttn00.pdf

U.S. Department of Commerce, National Telecommunications and Information Administration. (2002). *A nation online: How Americans are expanding their use of the Internet.* Washington, DC: U.S. Department of Commerce. Retrieved February 13, 2008, from http://www.ntia.doc.gov/reports/anol/index.html

For Further Exploration

Brinkley, D. (2007). *The great deluge: Hurricane Katrina, New Orleans, and the Mississippi Gulf Coast.* New York: Harper Perennial.

Clark, J. (2007). *Heart like water: Surviving Katrina and life in the disaster zone.* New York: The Free Press.

Coiro, J., Knobel, M., Lankshear, C., & Leu, D. (2008). *Handbook of Research on new literacies.* Mahwah, NJ: Lawrence Erlbaum.

Lee, S., & Pollard, S. (2006). *When the levees broke: A requiem in four acts.* HBO Home Video.

The Information and Communication Technologies Digital Library: http://www.ictliteracy.info.

4 "Hallelujah!"

Bible-Based Literacy Practices of Children Living in a Homeless Shelter

Laurie MacGillivray

"It's our promise to God that we will read …," proclaimed ten-year-old Alysha during an interview at a homeless shelter when explaining why she read the Bible. Homeless children and families are a growing population. One and a half million children go to sleep each night without a home of their own (National Center on Family Homelessness, 2009). Many children without permanent housing live in homeless shelters. Mothers and their children live side-by-side with strangers and deal with constant change. Rules about when and where to eat, bathe, and sleep must be frequently negotiated. In contrast, religion can serve as a constant. This chapter analyzes the manner in which four children living in a homeless shelter discuss Bible-centered literacy practices.

Background

Over the last twenty-five years there have been many classic studies (for example, Heath, 1983; Moje, 2000; Taylor & Dorsey-Gaines, 1988) which have informed our understandings of literacy practices beyond school. They have captured how literacy practices are grounded in local practices, history, and culture. Specific attention focuses on how often teachers are not aware of and/or do not know how to build upon students' out-of-school literacy. This body of research offers a context for these practices, but they have a primarily secular focus (see Hull & Schwartz, 2001 for an overview of out-of-school research).

Religion and literacy are rarely addressed in the field of education (for exceptions, see Eakle, 2007; MacGillivray, Ardell, & Curwen, in press a; Norton, 2006; Sarroub, 2002). Even though religion can be central to identity and group membership, as literacy teachers and researchers we often stay clear of the subject (Eakle, 2007; Williams, 2005). Williams explains, "Although religion can be important in terms of identity and culture and a vital part of many students' lives, it is a subject we often shy away from in conversations about teaching writing and reading. We are more willing to talk about race, gender, culture, or even social class than we are to discuss religion" (p. 515). This avoidance is also evident in our research journals. For example, in fifteen years only two articles (Eakle, 2007; Sarroub, 2002) in *Reading Research Quarterly* contained the words "faith," "Bible," or "religion." Sarroub (2002) contributed to our understanding of literacy by examining the multiple uses of secular and religious texts across home, school, and community settings. She captured the way that textual interactions can serve a variety of purposes. Eakle (2007) also attended to religious texts with attention to the way they can create collective thoughts which serve to both unite readers and distance others (p. 504).

More information on religion and literacy can be gleaned from larger studies of family literacy. These investigations found that the purposes of reading the Bible are numerous and include inspiration, information, escape, group affinity, and to gain affirmation for a belief (Heath, 1983; MacGillivray et al., in press a; Purcell-Gates, 1997; Taylor & Dorsey-Gaines, 1988). As part of a larger study (MacGillivray, Ardell, & Curwen, in press b), we found that the Church offered a nurturing and rich context for identities. Mothers' expectations and demands to read the Bible framed the children's literacy-based religious practices. Interactions with mothers were integral to the children's conversations about religious beliefs. The mothers modeled literacy engagements through reading the Bible, belonging to a religious community, and talking about the Bible in relationship to their own lives. Through conducting Bible-study, sharing religious texts, and discussing the Bible, mothers also created bonds with others who presented themselves as Christians. They saw religion as a sign that other mothers at the shelter might be more likely to share their values, focus on their children's welfare, and be hopeful about the future.

In spite of the large and increasing numbers of homeless children in our classrooms, literacy professionals know very little about what life is like for children living in homeless shelters and even less about their literacy practices (Walker-Dalhouse & Risko, 2008). Studying children living in homeless shelters is increasingly important as numbers continue to rise. Although caused by a myriad of circumstances, homelessness and the act of moving into a homeless shelter is typically a crisis. It is often the point in which families face their own negative stereotypes of people who are homeless. No longer able (or willing) to live with friends and family, moving into the shelter represents a breaking point, a problem that cannot be solved in the immediate future.

For many reasons homeless children move frequently; in fact, they move three times more than even their low-income peers (Bassuk, Weinreb, Dawson, Perloff, & Buckner, 1997; Buckner & Bassuk, 1997). The crisis of residential instability often involves staying in emergency and transitional housing, in over-crowded apartments with family members and friends, or in a tent or car (Rivlin, 1990; Stronge, 1992; Stronge, 2000). Shelters have the potential to be "safe refuges" in the midst of crisis (Herman, 1997). Although perhaps a better alternative to the street, shelters bring with them several specific problems such as lack of privacy, rigorous guidelines and rules, shared bathroom facilities, and the taxing behaviors of other children and adults (Boxill & Beaty, 1990; Van Ry, 1992). The nature of shelter life often impinges upon families' ability to carry out all of their prior home literacy practices. For example, the space needed for books is limited and mothers who used to keep a journal can be hesitant due to a lack of privacy (MacGillivray et al., in press a; in press b).

Overall, the research on children living in homeless shelters is sparse as is the work on literacy and religion. It is not clear how children living in crisis might participate in literacy practices and how these might relate to membership in a religious community. This study offers a close examination and analysis of the ways children living in a homeless shelter talk about their Bible-based literacy practices.

Theoretical Framework

In this chapter, I position literacy practices within larger social practices as a way to attach meaning that is grounded in context. The attention to social literacy practices refers to the "general cultural ways of utilizing literacy which people draw upon in particular situations" (Barton, 2001, p. 96). This belief is nestled within socio-cultural theory, which examines literacy practices that "refer to the broader cultural conception of particular ways of thinking about and doing reading and writing in cultural contexts" (Street, 2001, p. 22). Embedded within literacy practices are specific literacy events which are the visible episodes of individuals' experiences mediated through text (MacGillivray & Curwen, 2007; Street, 2001). I also apply this concept to religious events. The meaning of observable literacy events, such as discussing a verse from the Bible, is rooted in larger religious practices. Taking notes during a Christian worship service can be viewed as pious, but the same act in a synagogue can be considered inappropriate.

Acting as a member of a community of practice enables identity claims. I conceive of identity as in flux yet continuous, coherent yet dynamic. Discourses foreground and/or background various claims of "I am …." (Collins & Blot, 2003; Wenger, 1998) which can be unconscious as well as conscious (McCarthey & Moje, 2002). For this study, I attend to identity claims related to both literacy and religion. The meaning of an event, such as reading the Bible, is dependent on larger shared understandings of what it means to be a person who reads and a person who is religious (Zee, Hermans, & Aarnoutse, 2006). The claims can serve to unite members of a community of practice (MacGillivray & Curwen, 2007). This attention to identity can highlight the ways children in crisis are creating meaning in their worlds and in the discourses from which they draw. Identity claims can be one way to affirm relationships and can cause isolation and conflict. These dynamics are particularly relevant for families in crisis who must live together in the close quarters of a shelter.

Identity claims occur within a space. Space, like identity, is shifting and fluid, includes all that a moment holds (Eakle, 2007). Rather than viewing a homeless shelter as a building with a geographic location and set number of rooms, the shelter is viewed as only one aspect of an event. The actors, their motives, the interpersonal dynamics, the movement and talk of the characters—all of these are considered (Eakle, 2007). In a homeless shelter, critical features of space include individuals' and families' emotional, mental, and physical health, the reasons they are homeless, the explicit and tacit rules of the shelter, their literacy practices, religious beliefs, and material belongings. Attention to space during data gathering and analysis allows for insights otherwise ignored. Homelessness is a menagerie of trials, upheavals, achievements, and disappointments; only a fluid and expansive notion of location can begin to capture the ever-changing dynamics.

Context, Participants, and Methodology

Safe Shelter (pseudonym), near downtown Los Angeles, was chosen to serve as a primary research site to offer a micro view of the realities of life in a homeless shelter. It is a non-profit shelter for homeless and battered women operating primarily on donations and private funding. Although many shelters are faith-based and require participation in church services, Safe Shelter does not. The shelter consists of three houses: one is an emergency shelter (residents are allowed to stay up to three months) for approximately half a dozen families. The other two are four-family houses that serve as transitional shelters (residents may stay six months to a year). In both kinds of shelters, the mothers and their children stay in one bedroom and share a living room and kitchen with the other families.

As part of a larger study (see MacGillivray, 2005; MacGillivray et al., in press a; in press b), I gathered data at the shelter while serving as a participant observer for four months, documenting how families utilized their literacy skills during evenings and on weekends. Besides many informal discussions, structured interviews were also conducted with nine children, five mothers, and two members of the shelter staff. The purpose was to extend and clarify information gathered during observations. In the interviews with children, topics included their perceptions of and purposes for reading and writing, their literacy habits and activities in-school and out-of-school, the reading and writing of those around them, and the details of shelter life.

This paper focuses primarily on a group interview with four children (see Norton's 2006 exploration on children as informants on family spirituality). Two of the children were staying in transitional houses (allowed to remain six months to a year): Alysha, an African American was in third grade and shared a house with Jackie, a European American, who was also in third grade. Steve, a second-grade European American and his older sister, fifth-grader Danelle, were staying in the emergency shelter (limit of three months). Although vast differences are often found in religious practices, this was not apparent among these four children. There was no explicit discussion of ethnicity or culture. All of the children had been in one or more shelters prior to their stay at Safe Shelter.

I told the children that I wanted to learn about their reading and writing and what it was like to live in a homeless shelter. The interview lasted approximately forty-five minutes and occurred one evening in the shared space of the emergency shelter where the children were waiting for their mothers to finish a shelter-mandated activity. The babies and preschool age children were sitting on the other side of the room watching television. I found the four older children huddled around a table playing crazy eights and chatting when they agreed to participate in a group interview. Although I asked rather traditional questions about literacy, such as what it means to be a good reader/writer and the reading and writing they saw occurring around them, the children repeatedly focused on Bible-based events.

By focusing on a single extended interaction, I seek to explore the realms of possible meaning occurring in a specific space. I am not claiming to know what was in the children's minds, but to offer insights into the way certain abilities and values were in the foreground during the children's talk. This is an examination of how their talk might claim membership. The findings drawn from a group interview were triangulated with and enriched by other interviews with the help of a research team and field observations for reliability. Field notes from my time as a participant observer and interviews with the four children's mothers will be cited when they are particularly relevant to the group interview.

Findings

Religion was the prominent theme in the group interview. This chapter examines this in three different ways. The first section offers an analysis of the overall interview as related to religion and literacy. The second focuses on an interactional style which the children used at times during the interview. And the third section attends specifically to the children's claims of membership in a Christian community.

Talking Religion During a Literacy Interview

A large percentage of the talk in this interview was related to Bible-reading and related activities. In response to my questions, there was talk of favorite books and classroom reading, but this differed greatly from the spontaneous talk surrounding religious practices. A brief look at frequency offers insight into this phenomenon.

The interview was composed of 364 conversational turns. In response to questions related to their favorite books, class activities, with whom they read, and through piggy-backing on others' comments, the children named eleven books—five children's books, three adolescent novels, one adult novel, the Bible, and an eleventh text which seemed to be a writing prompt used across classrooms. The children did not engage with one another about the children's and adolescent books; the conversational turns ranged from one to eleven and averaged four. For almost half of the books, I was the only one who responded with questions or comments. There were two exceptions: *A child called "It"* (1995), an adult novel by Dave Pelzer, and the Bible. There were forty-six conversational turns related to *A child called "It."* These were primarily by two children. Half of the fifty-six conversational turns related to Jackie's requests to borrow the book and for Danelle to give a detailed description of what it was about.

In contrast, eighty-six conversational turns, more than a fourth of the entire interview related to the Bible or being a Christian even though I never initiated these topics. All four children participated in these interactions. There were three points in the group interview where the Bible and Christianity were the focus: the opening in which children claimed a membership in a religious community, an extended conversation in the middle about reading the Bible, and near the end a brief interaction about reading and writing in church.

The children's talk around reading the Bible and its content occurred in four ways. First, the children commented on the content, such as Alysha's response to the mention of Revelations (the last book in the New Testament which is often recognized for graphic images). "It's scary, it's kind of scary." Second, they developed an idea, such as when Danelle helped describe a "Promise," "It's just, until just, just to keep reading it." Third, they shared a similar experience as when Steve chimed in, "My mom makes me [read the Bible] too." And lastly, Jackie, as she did with *A child called "It,"* asked questions. She followed up comments such as when she asked, "You read Revelations [Book in the Bible]?"

In contrast to the other books, the scriptures were the center of rich conversations. The children immediately moved away from the question-answer format to interact with each other. They fed off of each other in order to make claims about themselves as readers and Christians. Interactional style was one way they made claims.

Call and Response

At the opening of the interview, I asked the children to introduce themselves and say something about themselves as readers or writers. Even though the children did not know each other well, by the third conversational turn they had brought Christianity into the interview and shifted the focus to each other. Their religious claims and Bible-based reading practices were foregrounded. Here is an excerpt from the very beginning of the interview.

Jackie:	My name is Jackie from Sheridan Street School. It's Monday, March 15, 2004.
Steve:	Hi my name's Steve. I like to read books. Especially action books and I like to play cards. And that's one thing I'm good at.
Jackie:	And I'm a Christian.
Steve:	Me too!
Alysha:	Me too!
Alysha:	And I like to, and I like to (*pause*) how do you say it?

Jackie:	Read?
Alysha:	I like to read about the Bible and …
Steve:	Me too!
Jackie:	Me too!
Jackie:	And believe in the Lord.
Steve:	Me too!
Alysha:	Me too!
Jackie:	Hallelujah!
Alysha & Steve:	Hallelujah!
	(*Laughter*)
Jackie:	No, don't kid.
Alysha:	Huh?
Steve:	Huh?
Alysha:	Okay. And I like to read action books me too. And I like to read.

When the children began talking about being a Christian they responded to each other rather than me. Their interactions reflected a genre of communication called "call and response" which is deeply rooted in African American culture and often practiced during religious services. The audience becomes involved through repeating affirmations thus blurring the distinction between leader and listener (Smitherman, 1977).

This communication style offered a context for talk of religious practices. They were demonstrating how to be members of a religious community *as* they claimed membership. Cries of "Me too!" and "Hallelujah!" demonstrated their ability to be part of the religious community, reinforcing the power of statements such as "I am a Christian." There were twelve affirmations during the interview—ten "Me too!" and two "Hallelujah!" Eight affirmations were in the opening of the interview as reflected above. There was also a pair of affirmations at the end of the interview which served as book ends, reinforcing the participants' sense of unity and shared religious values. The children say, "Me too!" only two other times in the interview and each was said in isolation, acting more as a "this also happens to me," rather than a celebratory declaration.

The format also connected the children through a familiarity with the same communication pattern. This recasting of the interview quickly positioned them as a community with shared values. They were unified, sharing and affirming identity claims. The focus was on each other and their beliefs. They had quickly blurred the lines between interviewer and interviewees. Without realizing, I shut down the momentum of the children seeking to regain my role as an interviewer (and my power):

Laurie:	Guys, it doesn't help to keep saying "Me too."
	(*Pause and a bit of giggling*)
Jackie:	C'mon Danelle. We're waiting.

Jackie: What do you like to read about books?
Danelle: My name is Danelle and I like to read books.
Jackie: (*Interrupts*) What kind of books?

Even when I refocused the interview to a question-answer format, Jackie continued to ask questions to the other children, such as, "What do you like to read about books?" "Your promise? Yeah, you read Revelations?" and "You like it because he cusses?" Her questions reflect an interest in other readers' likes, the reasons for them, and their Bible-based reading practices. So her questions continued her identity claims as a reader and a Christian as well as maintaining a more participatory interview.

I'm a Christian

Although I did not ask about their religious affiliations, children volunteered that they were Christians at the beginning of the interview. They also made indirect claims to membership in a religious community in three ways. First, they talked of a commitment to learning about the Bible. The children claimed their participation in this tradition by describing their own commitment or promise to study a verse of the Bible everyday. Through overlapping speech, the children defined "a promise" and simultaneously declared their own practices. Danelle brought up promises as she explained the kind of reading she did with her mother. Steve explained to me, "Well, like my promise is Psalm 23." Alysha explained that she had to read the "Holy Bible," and elaborated on Steve's description by saying, "And we have to read that like everyday. It's our promise to God that we'll read." Whereas Jackie had initially chimed in on her mother's mandate to read the Bible, she was as curious as I was when the others brought up promises. We both asked what they were and then Jackie wanted to know why they chose certain verses.

Second, the children's talk about the content of the Bible reflected their ability to be Christians. These claims are demonstrated through familiarity with content and demonstrate an understanding of real life applications. This occurred in two places. The first exchange occurred as I was asking Danelle about her promise. Steve mentioned The Book of Revelations, and Jackie responded, "You read Revelations?" Two conversational turns later, Alysha inserted, "It's scary, it's kind of scary." The children's comments demonstrate their knowledge of the Bible.

In another instance, the children co-constructed an interpretation of Malachi, a book in the Old Testament. In this case, Steve shared, "Mine's [my promise is] Psalm. And my mom's promise is Malachi something." His older sister, Danelle, elaborated, "[Malachi is] about that God hates divorce." Steve clarified, "Like my mom reads this story under this Malachi and says that God hates divorces." Jackie jumped in, saying "It's the law. It's the law. You have to [obey]." The three participants were demonstrating knowledge of a specific verse.

Steve shares his mother's promise, Danelle describes the content, and Jasmine refines the point.

The third way children made claims about being a Christian was by talking of their membership in larger religious communities. Jackie talked of reading the Bible aloud with her congregation, Alysha wrote notes during church, and Steve and Danelle read with their mother. They situated their religious practices in specific congregations: the church of Alysha's grandfather, Jackie's church of seven people, and Steve and Danelle's ritualized Bible reading with their mother and in church. These communities appeared constant in spite of the families' recent moves. The pastor or another member from Jackie's church picked them up so they could attend service. This was also the case with Alysha and her mom. Besides transportation, other adjustments were made because of the current living situation. At times Jackie and Alysha, as housemates, prayed together or with their mothers before school. Alysha's mom was a part of a bible study conducted over the telephone (MacGillivray et al., in press a). Even though there were differences in their affiliations, they all shared the desire to be good Christians and situated this in the context of a faith community.

Bible study is the heart of Christianity for these children as it is for many who believe that the scriptures can be a way to know God. Their literacy practices enabled them to assert a religious identity. They reported a commitment to learning the Bible; they asserted their ability to comprehend the Bible through repeated readings, memorization of verses, and Bible study; and they discussed their participation in religious communities. Embedded in a religious context, the literacy practices reflected a dedication to the process of learning about the Bible and can be viewed as a necessary action of a Christian. Alysha even took notes during sermons and also wrote down recommended readings for the upcoming week. During the interview, other texts did not foster the same sense of community.

Discussion

The children's talk about their Bible-based literacy practices brought them together. In this interview, they created a mutually valued space, independent from location, in the midst of a constantly changing social landscape. Touchstone words "Hallelujah," "Malachi," and "promises" revealed their shared communities of practice in a way that discussing school literacy did not. Through the children's interactions, we see how they privileged the scriptures even though I kept asking questions about their favorite books and their interest in reading and writing. These children came together as Christians around the Bible as other religious groups attend to their pivotal texts. These narratives offer an identity and community to believers and seemingly an ability to weather crises. Religious texts can be the center of literacy practices as well as social practices, in the way few other secular texts can. Below, I seek to further explore the children's discussion of their Bible-based literacy practices by examining identity claims and juxtaposing the findings to the current conception of family literacy.

Identity

By repeatedly returning to their promises as pledges of religious fidelity, each child claimed an identity as a Christian. This had two consequences. First, this identity focused on their personal beliefs as located in a larger faith community. This served as a constant in what can feel like shifting sand in times of crisis. Consider, when coping with crises which contain change, many things typically stay the same: the residence with the familiar structure of the rooms, the neighborhood, belongings, amount of privacy, expectations for chores, and habits of religious practices. This contrasts sharply with the realities of frequent moves between others' houses and homeless shelters. The children must figure out the physical space, how people interact, with whom to speak, and numerous other explicit and tacit rules and expectations. They have much less control of their daily lives than most of their peers with houses. Through an identity claim of being a Christian the children also asserted their ability to be independent of their immediate conditions; they created a desirable space that was not tethered to where they slept.

Second, their identity claims of being a Christian positioned them as having resources. Their talk reflected an "owning" of a set of literacy practices and the ability to participate in social practices such as trying to improve one's life. This contrasts with their current situation of "not having" or "lacking." They are referred to as "homeless," rather than children without homes. They were in a shelter for "the homeless," given food and donations as "homeless families," and even interviewed by me because they were "homeless children." Self-identifying as a Christian was independent of their situation; it was a commodity which was especially valuable in crisis. It could not be lost or stolen and did not take up any space.

Reconsidering "Family Literacy"

Mothers were integral to the children's claims of being Christians. The children discussed reading with and for their mothers. Their mothers talked about reading their children's writing and listening to their talk about the Bible. The mothers drew upon the Bible to help manage the crisis. The Bible was central to their religious and literacy practices, rather than a residence. This raises issues around home as the de facto construct of family literacy. Location has been conflated with families doing literacy. There is a body of work that documents the differences of reading and writing practices across socio-economic, cultural, and ethnic groups, but there is still a tacit assumption of the status quo. An assumption that family literacy occurs within a relatively stable routine of school, work, food, and sleep inappropriately privileges structure over space. This study captures the children's claims of membership in religious communities based on their interactions with their peers, mothers, and congregations. It also shows how rich textual practices can maintain and nurture community independent of a stable residence. The children's comments describe a space in which they can claim identities as readers and as Christians and which is not reliant on location.

The children's repeated references to their mothers' role in their Bible reading practices reflect the way their mothers served as buffers. By supporting these literacy practices, the mothers emphasized Bible-based practices and scaffolded children's ability to claim membership. Mothers tended to reach out to other mothers who also read the Bible and presented themselves as Christians. This facilitated friendships for the children. Thus mothers helped create safe spaces for their children (Landow & Glenwick, 1999; MacGillivray et al., in press a; Rivlin, 1990) by enabling them to be a member of a Christian community.

Conclusion

Religion can be a way to "do" literacy. Scriptures serve as an anchor which contextualizes reading and writing. Rituals such as church services, prayers, and promises all draw upon the scriptures. Bible-based literacy practices are purposeful and gain meaning through their connection to social practices. The Bible can be integral to life regardless of what crises the family faces.

By examining religion, we can examine largely unexplored sites of literacy practices with rich familial, community, and cultural traditions. Literacy events situated within religious practices can reveal the ways reading and writing serve to sustain and nurture individuals and families during times of crisis. An assumption of a life-long practice frames the Bible as a text central to identity and community. Through reading and writing for this larger purpose, families can forge deep and sustaining bonds. For the children living without a home, it is a powerful conduit for connecting with strangers. In the midst of living in crisis, the ability to talk about the Bible served as a shortcut to developing friendships as well as an opportunity to claim competence as a reader and Christian.

There are children and mothers in crisis interacting in meaningful ways with texts outside of classrooms. The Bible can play a central role in families' lives. Even when school and classroom libraries are limited, this does not mean communities are without texts. Clearly, I do not want to downplay the need for additional resources for high-poverty schools, but by not recognizing community social practices we perpetuate a deficit model of families living in crisis and/or coping with long-term challenges such as poverty.

This study disrupts our notion of families in crisis. Increasing expectations and thinking beyond traditional contexts for literacy can serve families living without homes or in other states of crisis as well. Learning about homelessness in general and then how homelessness actually plays out for students is critical. During crisis, families may be in unfamiliar situations. Families might be in emergency shelters due to large-scale disasters or familial upheaval. Children may be living with a relative while parents deal with extreme illness, tragedy, or divorce. Giving children the opportunity to name and discuss the kinds of reading and writing practices which occur in their lives can help them make connections.

Implications

There are implications for research and education from this study. The findings from this study and the few others focusing on literacy and religion (Eakle, 2007; Heath, 1983; MacGillivray, 2005; MacGillivray, et al., in press a; Norton, 2006; Sarroub, 2002) reveal the power of familial and communal practices to shape literacy learning. Textual responses can contrast widely when highly valued by parents. Tapping in to the power of these connections can be a worthy challenge for schools. We do not need to bring the Bible into schools, but we can recognize and develop our understandings of the passion and significance which can surround a single text.

There are four educational implications. First, instructors of preservice and inservice teachers could explore the potential of religious practices to support literacy development. If teachers have not had the opportunity to consider reading and writing in schools and the relationship to religious texts, this will be difficult to do in their own classrooms. This chapter offers information about often ignored out-of-school literacy practices. Using this knowledge does not necessarily call for Bible in schools, but rather encourages a conversation about culturally responsive pedagogy and the role of texts when working with children in crisis.

Second, with an increased awareness of religious practices, teachers can be more explicit about connections between texts and across genres. Although in many classrooms non-fiction is seldom read (Duke, 2000), it and blurry genres such as *The Magic School Bus* series by Cole and Degen and Pilkey's *Captain Underpants* epic novels books are becoming more popular as self-selected texts with children. These offer opportunities to examine text features. Simply offering students a chance to talk about the way they go about reading different texts can enable them to make meaningful connections and also inform instruction. For example, religious texts are used as a reference within which extended narrative is found. The same verses are referred to repeatedly which contrasts with the narratives of storybook reading and chapter books.

Third, this work suggests the potential of religious practices as a space in which parents and children come together, even in the midst of crisis. When homework completion is difficult, there might still be reading and writing occurring in the family. Opening up an opportunity for parents to discuss these practices may allow teachers to learn about other avenues for developing literacy. Parents might also use home literacy practices to inform homework.

Fourth, in much of the work on out-of-school literacies (Barillas & MacGillivray, 2008; Colorado & MacGillivray, 2007; Heath, 1983;

MacGillivray & Curwen, 2007; MacGillivray et al., in press b; Moje, 2000; Taylor & Dorsey-Gaines, 1988) there is attention to ways that schools can build upon the strategies students use at home to navigate text. I would like to suggest that schools also attend to the ways that classroom strategies could inform and support out-of-school literacy practices. The more we realize the power of self-selected reading and writing and the role of family and communities, the stronger the case there is for reciprocity between in and out-of-school practices. This would mean that parent involvement goes beyond informing the teachers and curricula (Gonzalez, Moll, & Amanti, 2005) to include gathering information about how their family practices can be enhanced by the literacy practices which occur in schools. Teachers and parents could think together about how a strategy such as making predictions could be applied to the kinds of literacy activities which occur out of school.

In closing, literacy practices are often occurring in families and communities in nontraditional ways. School literacy practices could build upon these practices which are grounded in family, culture, and history. Children living in the crisis of homelessness deserve our attention. It is too easy to be blinded by assumptions that families living in crisis are not involved in print interactions. Learning about how the family is reading and writing across different situations helps educators to support the children's literacy growth. Reaching out to parents during times of crisis can help teachers better understand how the family is coping and how reading and writing are occurring in their current conditions. Being aware of Bible-based literacy practices can increase teachers' awareness of the ways reading and writing can be meaningful in times of crisis.

I'd like to thank Amy Ardell and Margie Curwen for working with me on this project and Devon Brenner, Marjorie Faulstic Orellana, Jenn Palma, and Anne H. Smith for many helpful conversations which developed my thinking and writing about these complex issues. I am very grateful to the mothers and children who in the midst of crisis took the time to share their lives with me. I also appreciate the James Randolph Haynes and Dora Haynes Foundation for generously supporting this work.

References

Barillas, M., & MacGillivray, L. (2008). For the family: One teen's self-selected digital literacies (Electronic version). *Language and Literacy, 10*(2), 1–9.

Barton, D. (2001). Directions for literacy research: Analyzing language and social practices in a textually mediated world. *Language and Education, 15*, 92–104.

Bassuk, E. L., Weinreb, L. F., Dawson, R., Perloff, J. N., & Buckner, J. C. (1997). Determinants of behavior in homeless and low-income housed preschool children. *Pediatrics, 100*(1), 92–100.

Boxill, N. A., & Beaty, A. L. (1990). Mother/child interaction among homeless women and their children in a public night shelter in Atlanta, Georgia. *Child and Youth Services, 14*(1), 49–64.

Buckner, J. C., & Bassuk, E. L. (1997). Mental disorders and service utilization among youths from homeless and low-income housed families. *Journal of the American Academy of Child & Adolescent Psychiatry, 36*(7), 890–900.

Cole, J., & Degen, B. (1990). *The magic school bus.* New York: Scholastic.

Collins, J., & Blot, R. (2003). *Literacy and literacies: Texts, power, and identity.* Cambridge, UK: Cambridge University Press.

Colorado, K., & MacGillivray, L. (2007, May). Siblings reading together. Paper presented at the International Reading Association, Vancouver, Canada.

Duke, N. (2000). 3.6 minutes per day: The scarcity of informational texts in first grade. *Reading Research Quarterly, 35*, 202–224.

Eakle, A. J. (2007). Literacy spaces of a Christian faith-based school. *Reading Research Quarterly, 42*, 472–510.

Gonzalez, N., Moll, L., & Amanti, C. (Eds.). (2005). *Funds of knowledge: Theorizing practices in households, communities, and classrooms.* Mahwah, NJ: Erlbaum.

Guerra, J. (1998). *Close to home: Oral and literate practices in a transnational Mexicano community.* New York: Teachers College Press.

Heath, S. B. (1983). *Ways with words: Language, life, and work in communities and classrooms.* Cambridge, UK: Cambridge University Press.

Herman, J. (1997). *Trauma and recovery: The aftermath of violence—from domestic abuse to political terror.* New York: Basic Books.

Hull, G., & Schwartz, K. (2001). Literacy and learning out of school: A review of theory and research. *Review of Educational Research, 71*, 575–611.

Landow, R. W., & Glenwick, D. S. (1999). Stress and coping in homeless children. *Journal of Social Distress and the Homeless, 8*(2), 79–93.

MacGillivray, L. (1994). Tacit shared understandings of a first grade writing community. *Journal of Reading Behavior, 26* (2), 245–266.

MacGillivray, L. (2005). When "home" is a homeless shelter. Final report for the James Randolph Haynes & Dora Haynes Foundation.

MacGillivary, L., Ardell, A., & Curwen, M. (in press a). Libraries, churches, and schools: Literate lives of homeless women and children. *Urban Education.*

MacGillivray, L., Ardell, A., & Curwen, M. (in press b). Supporting the literacy development of children living in homeless shelters. *The Reading Teacher.*

MacGillivray, L., & Curwen, M. (2007). Tagging as a social literacy practice. *Journal of Adolescent and Adult Literacy, 50*(5), 354–369.

McCarthey, S., & Moje, E. (2002). Conversations: Identity matters. *Reading Research Quarterly, 37*, 228–238.

Moje, E. B. (2000). "To be part of the story": The literacy practices of gangsta adolescents. *Teachers College Record, 102*(3), 651–690.

National Center on Family Homelessness. (2009). America's youngest outcasts: State report card on child homelessness. Newton, MA: National Center of Family Homelessness.

Norton, N. (2006). Talking spirituality with family members: Black and Latina/o children co-researcher methodologies. *The Urban Review, 38*, 313–334.

Pelzer, D. (1995). *A child called "It": One child's courage to survive.* Deerfield Beach, FL: HCI Books.

Pilkey, D. (1997). *Captain Underpants.* New York: Scholastic Press.

Purcell-Gates, V. (1997). *Other people's words: The cycle of low literacy.* Cambridge, MA: Harvard University Press.

Rivlin, L. G. (1990). Home and homelessness in the lives of children. In N. A. Boxill (Ed.), *Homeless children: The watchers and the waiters* (pp. 5–17). New York: Haworth Press.

Sarroub, L. (2002). In-betweenness: Religion and conflicting visions of literacy. *Reading Research Quarterly, 37*(2), 130–149.

Smitherman, G. (1977). *Talkin' and testifyin': The language of Black America.* Detroit: Wayne State University Press.

Street, B. (Ed.). (2001). *Literacy and development: Ethnographic perspectives.* London: Routledge.

Stronge, J. H. (1992). The background: History and problems of schooling for the homeless. In J. H. Stronge (Ed.), *Educating homeless children and adolescents: Evaluating policy and practice* (pp. 3–25). Newbury Park, CA: Sage.

Stronge, J. H. (2000). Educating homeless children and youth: An introduction. In J. H. Stronge, & E. Reed-Victor (Eds.), *Educating homeless students: Promising practices* (pp. 1-19). Larchmont, NY: Eye on Education.

Taylor, D., & Dorsey-Gaines, C. (1988). *Growing up literate: Learning from inner-city families.* Portsmouth, NH: Heinemann.

Van Ry, M. (1992). The context of family: Implications for educating homeless children. In J. H. Stronge (Ed.), *Educating homeless children and adolescents: Evaluating policy and practice* (pp. 62–78). Newbury Park, CA: Sage.

Walker-Dalhouse, D., & Risko, V. (2008). Homelessness, poverty, and children's literacy development. *The Reading Teacher, 62*(1), 84–86.

Wenger, E. (1998). *Communities of practice: Learning, meaning, and identity.* New York: Cambridge.

Williams, B. T. (2005). Literacy and identity. *Journal of Adolescence and Adult Literacy, 26,* 514–518.

Zee, T., Hermans, C., & Aarnoutse, C. (2006). Primary school students' metacognitive beliefs about religious education. *Educational Research and Evaluation, 12*(3), 271–293.

For Further Exploration

America's Youngest Outcasts: A State Report Card on Child Homelessness: http//www.homelesschildrenamerica.org.

National Alliance to End Homelessness: advocacy@naeh.org

NCFL: Family Literacy-Family Progress: http://www.famlit.org/site/c.gtJWJdMQIsE/b.1204561/k.BD7C/Home.htm

National Law Center on Homelessness and Poverty: Lawyers Working to End Homelessness: http://www.nlchp.org.

The National Center for Family Homelessness: http://www.familyhomelessness.org

5 Reactions to Divorce

Communication and Child Writing Practices

Gisele Ragusa

Introduction

> "I don lik the divors. I wich it was over .... "

Six-year-old Jonathon wrote this in his journal when his parents were fighting for custody. Antagonistic divorces, especially those played out in the court system can bring about an intense period of crisis for a family. As I was going through a divorce, journaling with my children was a positive experience as I found it to be with other parents dealing with divorce related crises. Yet, I could not find any research on the potential of children composing and divorce.

Divorce continues to be a significant social challenge in the United States. Studies predict that within the next five years, 50% of all marriages will end in failure. The greatest increase in divorce rates occurred between 1960 and 1990 with a sharp rise in the early 1970s. Currently, increases in incidence of divorce continue (National Center for Health Statistics, 2004). According to the National Center for Health Statistics (NCHS), in 2004, there were 7.5 marriages per 1,000 people and 3.8 divorces a year.

Family focused research has revealed that both individuals and groups are profoundly affected by divorce. Social science research has indicated that the effects of divorce not only impact children into adulthood, but they also affect subsequent generations of children, making this crisis rather large in scale (Amato & Keith, 1991). Nationally, children from divorced families drop out of school at twice the rate of children from intact families. Additionally, children whose parents divorce have lower rates of graduation from high school and college and also complete fewer college courses (NCHS, 2004). These children have poorer performance in reading, spelling, and math and repeat grades more frequently than children from intact two-parent households (Stack, 1998). Children younger than five years of age are more vulnerable to the emotional conflicts occurring during their parents' separation and divorce (Fagan & Rector, 2000). These alarming findings do not suggest that all children from divorced families are doomed to failure and dismay, as many people from divorced households experience success in life. The impact is mitigated by the family members' existing resources. Mental and social resources can be particularly relevant. Thus developing strategies to support children as they encounter this difficult situation can be powerful intervention.

This chapter explores the role that writing can play in mediating divorce related difficulties by telling the stories of two families' experiences with dialogue journals.

Theoretical Framework

The study uses a combined social cognitive, socio-constructivist theoretical frame to describe literacy events, learning, and social experiences associated with these events. Alexander (2007) describes social cognition as learning that occurs in a social context mediated by cognitive processes. Socio-constructivist learning refers to the process of constructing meaning using background knowledge and scaffolding by parents, teachers, or more capable peers in social situations (Ormrod, 2008). Applying the socio-constructivist approach (Vygotsky, 1962) to parent supported writing, the parent models effective writing inspiring the child to use models to maximize their writing capability. These combined theoretical perspectives relate to children's writing in that it is a developmental process informed by children's background knowledge. Writing development is exemplified by children's use of invented spelling and word approximations as they navigate the use of pencil and paper and are guided by their parents and others. Parental mediation and scaffolding provides support for children's writing development.

Early Writing Behavior

To fully understand the role of writing in managing divorce, we must first understand writing development for children in typical experiences unaffected by crises. Clay (1975) is a pioneer in analytical studies of children's writing development. She explored child writing behaviors and developed a set of distinct stages of writing. She purports that children gradually pass through each writing stage and that movement is mediated by experienced caregivers, teachers, or peers.

Other researchers have utilized stages to describe children's writing in their research. Sulzby (1988) developed an emergent writing scale with twenty-four levels of writing to describe children's writing behaviors. Modified slightly, this scale was utilized by Debaryshe, Buell, and Binder (1996) in their writing research. It includes eighteen sequential elements that demonstrate increasing capacity as a function of development. Debaryshe and colleagues' writing category schema provides a detailed account of the hierarchical progression of children's writing development.

Home Experiences Associated with Writing

Research has indicated that home experiences with print influence children's writing development. For greater than two decades, researchers have explored home literacy experiences and the role of the caregiver in children's writing development. Wollman-Bonilla (2001) conducted a study on the relationship between children and parents' informal written interchanges and the children's writing development. Wollman-Bonilla developed a coding schema for analyzing children's writing that includes two categories of parental writing responses: instructional scaffolding/feedback and modeling genres using a socio-constructivist theoretical approach. Wollman-Bonilla's results suggest that, although parents often do not engage in formal instruction in their home, they follow this practice when writing to and with their children. Consequently Wollman-Bonilla's schema was modified and used as one of two analytical schemas I use in this chapter.

Divorce, Stress, and Child Outcome

As is commonly acknowledged, divorce accounts for significant stress in children and families. It is important to note however, that stress associated with divorce is not isolated to the actual divorce process. Accordingly, Amato and Keith (1991) conducted meta-analyses of divorce studies and reported both short and long-term effects of divorce on adolescents post divorce. In the short term, the most significant effects of divorce are in psychological adjustment, self-concept, behavior and conduct, educational achievement, and social relations (Amato, 2001; Aseltine, 1996; Fagan & Rector, 2000). This constellation of difficulties underscores the significant impact of divorce on children, throughout their childhood years.

Researchers also recognize the "accumulation of stress" as it relates to divorce. Accordingly, divorce cannot be considered an isolated event but should be viewed as a process, beginning long before the actual divorce occurs and extending far beyond divorce proceedings. Studies reveal delayed effects of divorce. This was found particularly salient with the adjustment of adolescents (Wallerstein, Lewis, & Blakeslee, 2000). Wallerstein and colleagues referred to the delayed effects of divorce as "sleeper effects" which primarily result in emotional difficulties with peer and romantic relationships. So, although delayed effects were found, my focus is on the crises of custodial battles that can be one of a series of crises related to divorce.

Writing and Stress Mediation

Currently, no research exists that directly connects child writing with divorce recovery. There are, however, several studies that describe the role that writing plays in alleviating stress. Psychological and therapeutic research has identified writing as a useful tool for emotional expression and affect regulation (Kerner & Fitzpatrick, 2007; Pennebaker, 2004) and it improves health, psychological well-being, physiological functioning, and coping (Smyth & Helm, 2003). Research has indicated that writing about traumatic events can promote effective coping (Lumley & Provenzano, 2003; Pennebaker, Colder, & Sharp, 1990), decrease depression (Lepore & Greenberg, 2002), and promote positive development post trauma (Ullrich & Lutgendorf, 2002).

Writing about traumatic events is purported to be as useful as therapy in surfacing positive emotional responses and behaviors (Donnelly & Murray, 1991). Writing was also found to decrease psychological difficulties, particularly for individuals experiencing significant distress (Chan & Horneffer, 2006). Lyubomirsky, Sousa, and Dickerhoof (2006) analyzed the effects of writing, talking, and thinking about events post crisis. They found that writing was the most effective means to increased health, coping, and overall wellbeing post trauma. This finding suggests that writing is an effective intervention strategy for alleviating stress in crisis. Psychological and therapeutic literature does not target divorce related crises but it lends credibility to the use of writing as a means of communicating emotional stress. Composition can serve as a capacity building coping strategy for children and their families.

Journaling as a Safe Means of Communication and Coping

Journaling has been studied as a specific genre of writing in times of crisis. Journals have been used in therapy to induce reflection on the self and communication (Kerner & Fitzpatrick, 2007; Stone, 1998). In the therapeutic setting, journals are often organized around the emotional aspects of experiences and have been found to address difficulties associated with experiences (Alford, Malouff, & Osland, 2005). Because journaling is less personally invasive than face-to-face intervention, it can assist individuals with disclosure in emotionally difficult areas, providing a safe communicative environment between therapist and client. Writing about personally painful experiences in reflective ways has been found to help clients articulate difficult topics during interventions (Zeiger, 1994).

In the pages that follow, I describe a study in which journals between mothers and children are used to safely and reflectively communicate about divorce. I tell the story of two families who are deeply involved in divorce proceedings and the way that each family used dialogic journals to cope with and manage challenging events by communicating with one another safely and privately throughout the processes. As time progressed during the study, the children began to reveal many more emotive responses and it appears that they discovered ways to reflect on their responses and discuss real issues with their mothers in their own time. This is why I include the month of entry next to each excerpt that I present in the chapter.

In the Beginning: Erica Initiates the Writing Dialogue Process

These stories are situated amidst two child custody battles in a large state's divorce system. While divorce is becoming a relatively common occurrence with nearly 50% of all families experiencing it (NCHS, 2004), the particulars of the divorces are captured in the written interchanges between mothers and their children. Both families were deeply involved with court interfaces, but their contentions differed. One family was experiencing divorce across state lines while the other was involved in a within-state custody battle. Unfortunately, because of the children's ages, all were involved with the court proceedings to some degree. Accordingly, each child group had attorneys and all parties had to undergo psychological evaluations to determine fitness for parenting. The increased visibility and inclusion of strangers as the children's attorneys caused much stress for both the parents and their children.

Parent–child journaling arose from one parent's desire to communicate with her children while the children were staying with their father. One mother, Erica (a pseudonym), began having her children write about their day during the time that they were being cared for by their grandparents while she was working. After observing her son's first grade teacher using dialogue journaling she decided to try it. On one afternoon, the teacher shared the journal with her, and she noted that some of the entries that her son, Jonathon, submitted were divorce related. With this information, Erica decided that an in-home journal activity might assist her children in communicating with her during this emotional time. As a consequence of journaling, Erica began to recognize that much of Jonathon's written interaction continued to be centered on the family's impending divorce. He seemed to write freely, in spite of his developmental spelling, and he seemed to have a sense of peace after journaling. Accordingly, Erica began to encourage her daughter to share her feelings during her journal interactions. Shortly thereafter, she discussed what was happening in the journal process with a friend who was also divorcing and, consequently, her friend's family began to journal. What began as a simple informal writing activity mediated by common experiences, emerged as a dialogue journal interaction between both mothers and their children. The journal exchange with both families occurred during the period of the divorce proceedings and immediately post divorce for approximately six months. Journal exchanges were interactive and without writing prompts.

The Families

This study included five mother–child dyads in two single parent households. The children came from two mother headed families. Each child's dialogue journal was the unit of analysis for the study. Child participants were ages 6½ years (n=2) and 9 years of age (n=2). The mothers (Erica and Angela) were also study participants. The children's fathers were not included in the study as they were not participants in the dialogue journals. Table 5.1 (below) provides a description of pertinent demographics of the study families.

As indicated in Table 5.1, the two families share much in common. Angela and Erica are both educated mothers with children in similar age ranges. Both families have middle incomes. The primary difference in the two families is that Angela's ex-husband resides in a different state than his family. This factor made his visitation schedule quite different from Erica's visitation experience.

The Interactive Dialogue Journals

As previously described, the parent–child interactive dialogue journals were the primary instrument for data collection. Dialogue journals are informal written conversations between two or more people about topics of mutual interest (Fletcher, 1996). They provide individuals with a meaningful engaging writing activity because it involves context embedded exchanges and communication. These written conversations reinforce learning, but more importantly, facilitate the forming of bonds between individuals (in this case between divorced mothers and their children) that can provide a foundation for later cooperative activities, communication, and meaningful interaction.

Pulling It All Together: The Analytical Structures

During the journaling process, both Erica and Angela began to recognize the richness of their children's journal entries. The journals became a safe place for the children to communicate with their mothers about invisible emotional experiences during the divorce proceedings. The journal interactions served as both a means of communicating safely about highly emotional topics and as a means for increasing writing opportunities and practice. Accordingly, I began to consider analyzing the journal contents. I used two schemas to analyze the writing, one for structure and content and one for emotive related communication. Wollman-Bonilla's (2001) writing analysis

Table 5.1 Family characteristics

Family Names*	Age**	Socio-economic Status	Mother's Occupation	Father's Locale
Angela's Family	34	Middle income	Accountant	Out of state
Child no. 1—Michael	6.5			
Child no. 2—Karen	9.2			
Child no. 3—Caroline	10.5			
Erica's Family	32	Middle income	Educator	In state
Child no. 1—Jonathon	6.5			
Child no. 2—Julianna	9			

Notes
* Pseudonyms were used to protect child and parent anonymity.
** Age is recorded in the table as age at the onset of the study.

schema was modified and used to analyze the dialogue journals' form and structure. A category schema adapted from Wollman-Bonilla's research on instructional scaffolding and feedback was used to describe parental entries. Categories within parent related instructional feedback and guidance were: (1) *questions about message content*, (2) *acknowledgment of message impact*, (3) *acknowledgment of learning from child's messages*, and a fourth new category not included in Wollman-Bonilla's research, (4) *response to child's message—need for support*. I used an adaptation of Luterman's (1999) categories of coping with loss and change to categorize child initiated journal content as I acknowledged stress and coping in the journal content. These categories included: (1) *anger*, (2) *guilt*, (3) *vulnerability*, (4) *fear*, and (5) *confusion*. This second group of categories was utilized to illustrate the level and types of stress that were present in the families' journal exchanges. From the categorization, three themes emerged. They were: *communication, a safe place to write,* and *stress expression (putting it out there)*. These themes were interrelated and provided the structure for me to tell the story about the families' use of journals to cope with and manage divorce. The analysis focuses only on the parent–child written exchanges related to divorce.

Both mothers were involved with categorizing the data and choosing excerpts to be included in this chapter. I used a cognitive interview technique during the analysis process so the parents could assist me in analyzing and interpreting their children's journal entries and put them into meaningful familial context. Woolley, Bowen, and Bowen (2006) describe cognitive interviewing as having the individual discuss the message behind his or her responses. In this study, the mothers served as proxies for their children in the cognitive interview process, describing and interpreting meaning for their children's journal responses and reflecting on their own responses. This process occurred because, per Woolley et al. (2006), pre-adolescents encounter difficulties in articulating meanings for responses during cognitive interviews, particularly when abstract concepts including feelings and emotions are explored. The mothers provided a means for me to understand the message behind the writing, making it visible in many situations because they each knew their children's writing behaviors and were best able to decipher invented spelling, particularly with their younger children.

Dialogue Journals: Communication, a Safe Place to Share, and Putting It Out There

I found that the dialogue journals were a means by which the families engaged in deep, private, and somewhat invisible communication with one another. The journals allowed both Angela and Erica to communicate with their children while they were at work and while their children were in a relative's care. Angela and Erica reported greatly increased interaction once they began journaling with their children. Table 5.2 denotes the frequency and diverse categorization of each response between mothers and children.

Table 5.2 Frequency of entries in dialogue journals by categories Parents & Children

Parent's Entries	*f*	%
Questions about message content	5	6.6
Acknowledgment of message impact	9	11.7
Acknowledgment of learning from child's messages	4	5.3
Response to child's message—need for support	16	21.1
Total Instructional Entries	34	44.7

Children's Entries	*f*	%
Anger	13	17.1
Guilt	5	6.6
Vulnerability	4	5.3
Fear	9	11.8
Confusion	11	14.5
*Total Emotive Child Exchanges	42	55.3
TOTAL ENTRIES CODED	N= 76	100
NON-CODED ENTRIES**	N= 38	
TOTAL JOURNAL ENTRIES	N= 114	

Notes
* Some child entries were included in two emotive categories.
** Non-coded entries were those that did not contain any divorce related content.

As noted in Table 5.2, the children's exchanges related to *emotions* (55.3%) exceeded their parents' *instructional and guidance* exchanges (44.7%). This may be attributed to the finding that the children expressed mixed emotions during their exchanges, causing me to count an entry in more that one emotive category. Additionally, while the children often discussed their day's activities in the journals, they typically mixed emotion in with their accounts, particularly during the heated moments of the divorce. Related to the emotional exchanges, the parent entries were in response to the children's emotional communication. Accordingly, the highest frequency of instructional exchange came from the category, *response to child's message—need for support* (21.1%) suggesting that the parents were receptive to their children's need for support during their emotions focused interactions. An example of this occurred in Karen's journal entry and her mother's associated response (below).

Karen: I wish could rite all the words I want to say. I don't no how to spell them all. Those feeling words are hard.
Angela: Don't worry about spelling, Karen, I can tell what you mean. Just let the words get on the page as you think of them.

(Karen, month 4)

The frequency in the *response to child's message—need for support* category (21.1%) is far higher than the second most frequent response category under instruction, the category *acknowledgment of message impact* (11.8%). The most common category of emotive exchanges was the *anger* category (17.1%) with *confusion* (14.5%) closely following *anger* in frequency. An example of this is given below where both *anger* and *confusion* are noted in Michael's journal entry:

Michael: I not up der. I don. (Michael drew a picture of his dad and his house to accompany this entry)
Angela: Michael, are you sure you don't want to go see Dad? He loves you and wants time with you just like I do. Maybe it's just hard to go back and forth. We can help you with this.
Michael: Ok. I can.

(Michael, month 4)

At first glance, this entry appears to focus on *anger*, but when I dug deeper in my interview with Michael's mother, Angela, a different, less visible message emerged. According to Angela's cognitive interview, Michael wrote this entry after coming home from his dad's house. His mother confirmed that it was not so much about not liking to visit with his father. Rather, Michael was reacting to the fact that he had to transition between his mom and dad and could not have them together, a relatively invisible message embedded in his writing.

Interestingly, while the children expressed emotions often in their journals, their mothers' responses were not an expression of the same emotion, rather they were acknowledgments, labels, support, or redirections of the children's emotion. The exchange above reveals this pattern. The children expressed deep emotions in their journals, particularly as time progressed and they became more comfortable with journaling. One particular entry captured the impact of the emotion expressed by the children. Jonathon wrote:

Mom, it huts (hurts) way in my hart ... the divors. I don wan it. No no no.
(Jonathon drew a sad face with tears to accompany this entry)

(Jonathon, month 6)

When Jonathon's mother discussed this entry, we both cried. These few words and the accompanying illustration capture the depth of emotion that children often feel when divorce becomes a part of their reality and the invisible nature and impact of divorce. This crisis is "way" in their heart as Jonathon writes. Lumley and Provenzano (2003) describe writing as a means for helping parent and children cope with stress. This finding in their research is supported by the study presented in this chapter, specific to the relatively invisible pain associated with divorce processes.

The Messages behind the Written Words

While the overall frequency of responses in the dialogue journals is important as it relates to journal content analysis, nothing tells the invisible story behind the journal interaction better than the actual entries and the implied meaning behind them. In attempting to find meaning in the exchanges, three main themes developed during the six-month dialogue journal exchange. One theme that became apparent was that the journals served as means for *increased communication* between mother and child. This was evidenced both through review of the journal entries and through the cognitive interviews with the mothers. Communication was maintained in the journals on all accounts. As the following excerpt illustrates, the journals were interactive and communicative.

Caroline: I hate going between you. No can say it's a good thing to leave things at one place and the other. I don't think so. Mom, don't tell me it's a good thing to have two houses. I have friends in Montana and some down here. I don't get to go to parties when I'm with Dad, I miss Dad when I'm with you. This sucks so bad!

Angela: I am sorry this is so tough on you. I wish it could be different. What can I do to help make it better for you?

Caroline: I guess nothing mom. If I didn't go, I miss him. So that's the way it goes. I guess just hear to me. This is just like talking but I don't have to be in your face with it. It's better with my journal.

Angela: Sometimes its better for me too. I can think about what I'm going to say to you and write it down and change it if it doesn't come out right the first time if I'm sad.

Caroline: Me too.

(Caroline, month 6)

This illustrates *increased communication*, but it also touched on the safety issue (*a safe place to write*) in written communication, which was the second theme that emerged. Finding a safe and private place to communicate emerged primarily for the nine and ten-year-old children in the study. Divorce is crisis oriented and it causes much emotion to surface, increasing its visibility, as the frequency analyses of the journal entries reveals. Juliana wrote:

Juliana: It's a lot better to write about the divorce. When you come back from it (court), I know it and I want to talk to you about it but I know I could cry so I don't. I can write to you, I can do it in my room and you don't no when I'm done. Then when you write back and its hard … I can read it when I want to and hide if I want so no one bugs me. And no one sees me if I can't take it. I didn't like this thing you had us do but I think I do now.

Erica: Sometimes I feel the same way Juli. I have to think about what I want to say so I can be the best mom for you. I know it's hard for you guys. I wish I could take it all away but I can't. I hope you know that I would if I could.

Juliana: Yea, I know mom.

(Juliana, month 6)

In this excerpt, a description of *a safe place to write* emerges. Additionally, support and increased communication is illustrated. It is important to note that while three themes of writing content were present, they are interrelated, making it difficult to code data discretely and without overlap.

The third theme that emerged from the journals was *stress expression*. Both mothers reported deliberately minimizing their verbal discussions with their children about their divorces except when the children initiated the discussion topic. This practice occurred as a deliberate effort to minimize the stress that the children were subject to and essentially decreasing the crisis's visibility. Regardless of the parents' efforts, the children's journal discussion contained indications that divorce was on their mind forcing the crisis to become visible. One child, Michael (age 6,) wrote:

> Toda went to IMX (IMAX theater) ... fun. ... I don lik curt (court). To hard for me ... I wach the big TV ... big ants in mi fas (face).
>
> (Michael, month 6)

This journal excerpt reveals how thoughts of divorce slipped into Michael's writing even while he describes an enjoyable event at a school field trip. Michael's divorce reference occurs right in the middle of his IMAX description, suggesting that divorce preoccupied his thoughts. This pattern was not unique to Michael's interactions. Jonathon, the other six-year-old in the study, demonstrated similar journaling patterns. He describes a weekend visit with his father when he went fishing:

> Fish with dad is fun. Hot ... fun. Don wan a stay ther ... mom house is more confrtibl (comfortable) for me. *(Jonathon drew a picture of fishing with his dad to accompany this entry)*
>
> (Jonathon, month 5)

Additionally, it is evident from both boys' excerpts that they are in fact-stating mode in their entries. They appear to "live in the here and now" in their journals. This is characteristic of six and seven-year-old's writing and verbal expression patterns regardless of subject matter (Clay, 1975). Interestingly, the two younger children and the three older children in the study had different interactions in their journal particularly with regard to sentiment and structure. The younger children were up front and direct in their interactions and used few questions in their writing, while the three older children engaged in direct dialogue with their mothers, asking questions, passing judgment, and elaborating in their entries. The younger children included drawings in their entries as if to find ways to communicate that exceeded their writing capabilities. The older children rarely drew in their journals, focusing primarily on text.

Changes in Writing Behavior

Changes in writing behavior that emerged over time were an important analytical component of this study. In terms of journal content analysis, results revealed that invented spelling was salient, particularly with the 6½-year-old children. Additionally, diversified written vocabulary resulted from the journal experiences across children. As previously described, themes present in the journal entries were of an emotive nature. Accordingly, the children used descriptive words that they may not have used if they were not involved in the journal experience. Table 5.3 represents a timeline and describes changes in writing behavior over the course of the six-month study period.

Table 5.3 captures the significant changes in writing behavior over time for each child. As illustrated, each child's mean length of entry increased over time. Additionally, spelling ability improved and word usage and vocabulary increased. As an example, Jonathon began writing only a few words and progressed to more than fifteen words and word approximations in each entry. Interestingly, both younger children felt free to use invented spelling, illustrations, and word approximations throughout the study. This is likely to be a function of their mothers telling them not to worry about spelling, and as one parent stated, "just talk with mom" in writing. As previously described, the younger children illustrated their thoughts with drawings when they were unable to express their emotions with words.

With regard to writing structure, while all five children found ways to make their private ideas visible in their dialogue journals, the older children wrote using a diary-like style while the younger children described daily activities and inserted elements of the divorce in their journals. This critical difference in journaling practice could be developmentally determined representing a trajectory of writing behavior previously described by Clay (1975). While the focus of this chapter is not on writing growth, the cross-sectional nature of the study documents explicit writing growth as a function of age and experience. Table 5.3 illustrates the difference in the children's writing length in addition to the different types of writing that occurred as a function of their development. Additionally, Table 5.3 exemplifies how the children's writing patterns progressed over time. All five children increased their length of excerpt over the six-month period. Additionally, each child's style of writing changed as the study progressed. Overall, the children began as factual writers with limited exchanges with their mothers. However, over time, they developed questioning strategies and behaviors denoting a true desire to "dialogue" with their mothers. Additionally, the level of emotional sharing increased as the study progressed. The older children (nine-year-olds) became reflective and expressed significant depth of emotion in writing. This finding suggests that writing using an interactive structure and with the intent of using abstract words (emotions and feelings) increases (1) children's writing ability, (2) their ability to use abstract vocabulary, and (3) their writing confidence.

Table 5.3 Changes in writing behavior during the six-month period

Child/age	Month 1	Month 3	Month 6
Jonathon—6.5 through 7	Length—3–4 words plus illustrations Word usage—nouns, first person, occasional verbs Dominant characteristic/themes—fact stating, description, some emotions expressed, much inventive spelling	Length—3–5 words plus illustrations Word usage—nouns, verbs, some adverbial, friends and family members' names, descriptors Dominant characteristic/themes—fact stating, description, emotively based, inventive spelling, some questioning	Length—15–20 words plus illustration Word usage—verbs and nouns, emotional related words, friends and family members' names, repeated words from previous journal entries—correctly spelled from parent's model Dominant characteristic/themes—fact stating, description, much questioning, emotively based
Michael—6.5 through 7	Length—2–4 words plus illustrations Word usage—descriptors, nouns, his name and mom used often Dominant characteristic/theme—fact stating, description, articles missing, much invented spelling, emergent emotions	Length—3–8 words plus illustrations Word usage—repeats from previous journal entries, spelling more accurate Dominant characteristic/theme—fact stating, description, some articles missing, invented spelling, emotively based	Length—10–25 words plus occasional illustrations Word usage—repeats from previous journal entries, spelling relatively accurate Dominant characteristic/theme—fact stating, description, few articles missing, invented spelling, emotively based with some questioning
Juliana—9 through 9.5	Length—6–12 words plus occasional illustration Word usage—repeats from previous journals Dominant characteristic/theme—fact stating, descriptions, occasional invented spelling	Length—10–25 words Word usage—occasionally repeats from previous journals, abstract vocabulary, full range of word usage Dominant characteristic/theme—fact stating, description, questioning, some reflection, occasional multi-time exchange entries	Length—20–40 words Word usage—no limits, occasional spelling errors, full range of word usage, abstract vocabulary Dominant characteristic/theme—questioning, abstract thoughts, feelings based, multi-time exchange entries (2–3 plus)

(Continued)

Table 5.3 Cont'd

Child/age	Month 1	Month 3	Month 6
Karen—9 through 9.5	Length—10-15 words Word usage—Full range of word usage Dominant characteristic/themes—fact stating, description, questioning, emergent reflection	Length—15-25 words Word usage—original thoughts, full range of word usage Dominant characteristic/themes—reflection, questioning, two-three exchanges within a subject area	Length—25-40 words Word usage—full range of word usage, original thoughts Dominant characteristic/themes—questioning, rich interaction, multi-time (3 plus) exchange, reflection
Caroline—10.5 through 11	Length—6-10 words Word usage—full range of word usage, abstract words Dominant characteristic/themes—description, some resistance noted	Length—15-30 words Word usage—original thoughts, depth of conversation, full range of word usage Dominant characteristic/theme—rich interaction, emotion, reflection	Length—20-40 words Word usage—original thoughts, abstraction, full range of word usage Dominant characteristic/theme—rich interaction, reflection, emotion, multi-time exchanges (2 plus)

Interestingly, Erica reported that her son, Jonathon, went back through his journal and copied words that she used in her journal responses. She believed this practice strengthened his spelling and written vocabulary. One of Angela's children, Karen, wrote to her mother that she used her journal as a reminder of events and as a source of emotional support. She wrote:

> Sometime when I feel real bad I look at what you wrote to me and I feel better. I need to see that you love me and I can hold on to it.
>
> (Karen, month 5)

According to Angela, Karen took her journal along with her when she visited her father. Angela's children traveled across state boundaries to visit their father and mother. It appears from this entry that Karen used the journal as a constant when she transitioned from place to place, not unlike a young child uses a security blanket but more socially acceptable for a child in middle childhood.

Discussion

This study reflects the power of dialogue journals to aid communication in times of crisis while simultaneously supporting literacy growth for the children involved. The study emphasizes the diverse roles that writing and, in particular, dialogue journals can play in supporting families, development of coping and management strategies, and providing a safe place for emotively driven, often invisible communication between parents and children. Additionally, yet secondarily, dialogue journals can assist children in writing development informally and holistically. Figure 5.1 provides an illustration of the multi-dimensional supportive role that dialogue journals play for divorced families.

The children in my study grew in many ways, emotionally and developmentally, throughout the study period. Additionally, bonds increased tremendously through the journal interactions. The study results indicate that the children's writing styles changed as a function of the journal use. They began as short interactions and proceeded to longer interactions with abstract vocabulary use. The study provides a cross-sectional picture of five children's writing behaviors and documents the impact that dialogue journals have on writing depth, increased communication, and increased visibility of divorce related crises. Quantification of the journal content revealed that, in six months, with parental mediation, children's writing can improve significantly. Increased abstraction in journaling occurred as did increased length. This study confirms research that explores the role that parents play in teaching their children to write (Clay, 1975; Sulzby, 1988). The results also provide evidence that, while the cards may be stacked against children of divorced parents, written interaction opportunities can assist families in navigating through crises associated with divorce while simultaneously positively impacting children's writing achievement.

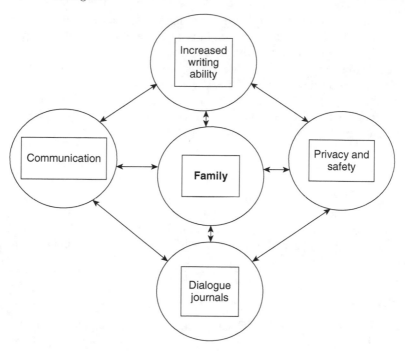

Figure 5.1 Interaction between impacts facilitated by dialogue journals.

Directions for Future Research

This chapter includes a review of the literature associated with written communication and divorce in addition to a description of a study in that context. This information sets the stage for the needs of diverse areas of research related to the role that writing plays in child development, child–parent communication, and therapeutic reflection through writing as a means of coping with divorce. I recognize that large-scale research is needed with a focus on interactive writing and children in therapeutic settings as the bulk of the research in this area is focused on adults. Additionally, longitudinal research on child writing practices during crisis is warranted so that a trajectory of change can be established. Further, research is needed on writing-based interventions for children in trauma that is particularly focused on divorce, because this is an area that is grossly under-published.

Recommendations for Practitioners and Parents

This chapter holds many implications for diverse groups including researchers, teachers, family therapists, and parents. I recommend that teachers regularly use dialogue journals with their children across grade levels with two purposes: (1) to increase communication and individualized attention between teacher and students, and (2) to improve students' writing via ungraded semi-structured written interaction. I also recommend that parents use dialogue journals with their children. The journals provide a comfortable means of interaction between parent and child and may increase communication amongst dyads. Parents can assist their children's writing growth informally through journaling. Additionally, I recommend that therapists utilize dialogue journals with their child and family clients. This technique extends therapeutic sessions beyond therapists' walls and provides a means for communication in between therapy sessions.

Conclusion

Divorce is a serious crisis that affects children and their families on multiple levels. Dialogue journaling can play a role in mediating this stressful process and provide a comfortable medium of communication between parents and children in addition to a mechanism for understanding, managing, and coping with divorce related stress. Dialogue journals provide a safety zone for youngsters' communication and can be utilized in diverse crisis related situations. Dialogue journals inspire child–adult communication, and also play a role in increasing children's writing development. While this study is limited by its size, it provides an example of the significant impact that dialogue journals can have on parent–child communication and on children's writing development. Writing has been under-utilized in child therapy. This study, while not focused on therapeutic intervention, provides an example of its potential in mental health intervention settings.

References

Alexander, P. A. (2007). Bridging the cognitive and sociocultural approaches in conceptual change research: Unnecessary foray or unachievable feat? (Special Issue on "Bridging the cognitive and sociocultural approaches in research on conceptual change") *Educational Psychologist, 42*(1), 67–73.

Alford, W. K., Malouff, J. M., & Osland, K. S. (2005). Written emotional expression as a coping method in child protective services officers. *International Journal of Stress Management, 12*, 177–187.

Amato, P. R. (2001). Children of divorce in the 1990s: An update of the Amato and Keith (1991) meta-analysis. *Journal of Family Psychology, 15*, 355–370.

Amato, P. R., & Keith, B. (1991). Parental divorce and the well-being of children: A meta-analysis. *Psychological Bulletin, 110*, 26–43.

Aseltine, R. H. (1996). Pathways linking parental divorce with adult depression. *Journal of Health and Social Behaviors, 37*, 133–148.

Chan, K. M., & Horneffer, K. (2006). Emotional expression and psychological symptoms: A comparison of writing and drawing. *The Arts in Psychotherapy, 33*, 26–36.

Clay, M. (1975). *What did I write? Beginning writing behaviour* (pp. 9–29). Portsmouth, NH: Heinemann.

Debaryshe, B. D., Buell, M. J., & Binder, J. C. (1996). What a parent brings to the table: Young children writing with and without parental assistance. *Journal of Literacy Research, 28*(1), 72–90.

Donnelly, D. A., & Murray, E. J. (1991). Cognitive and emotional changes in written essays and therapy interviews. *Journal of Social and Clinical Psychology, 10*, 334–350.

Fagan, F. P., & Rector, R. (2000). *The effects of divorce on America.* Washington, DC: The Heritage Foundation.

Fletcher, R. (1996). *A writer's notebook: Unlocking the writer within you* (pp. 64–109). New York: Avon Books.

Kerner, E. A., & Fitzpatrick, M. R. (2007). Integrating writing into psychotherapy practice: A matrix of change processes and structural dimensions. *Psychotherapy: Theory, Research, Practice, Training, 44*(3), 333–346.

Lepore, S. J., & Greenberg, M. A. (2002). Mending broken hearts: Effects of expressive writing on mood, cognitive processing, social adjustment, and health following a relationship breakup. *Psychology and Health, 17*, 547–560.

Lumley, M. A., & Provenzano, K. M. (2003). Stress management through written emotional disclosure improves academic performance among college students with physical symptoms. *Journal of Educational Psychology, 95*, 641–649.

Luterman, D. (1999). Grief: A parent's perspective. *American Annuals for the Deaf, 29*(3), 119–124.

Lyubomirsky, S., Sousa, L., & Dickerhoof, R. (2006). The costs and benefits of writing, talking, and thinking about life's triumphs and defeats. *Journal of Personality and Social Psychology, 90*(4), 692–708.

National Center for Health Statistics (2004). *Divorce and marriage.* Hyattsville, MD: Centers for Disease Control and Prevention.

Ormrod, J. E. (2008). *Educational psychology: Developing learners* 6th ed. (pp. 74–86). Upper Saddle, NJ: Pearson/Prentice Hall.

Pennebaker, J. W. (1997). Writing about emotional experiences as a therapeutic process. *Psychological Science, 8*, 162–166.

Pennebaker, J. W. (2004). Theories, therapies, and taxpayers: On the complexities of the expressive writing paradigm. *Clinical Psychology: Science and Practice, 11*, 138–142.

Pennebaker, J. W., Colder, M., & Sharp, L. K. (1990). Accelerating the coping process. *Journal of Personality and Social Psychology, 58*, 528–537.

Smyth, J., & Helm, R. (2003). Focused expressive writing as self-help for stress and trauma. *JCLP/In Session: Psychotherapy in Practice, 59*, 227–235.

Stack, S. (1998). Marriage, family and loneliness: A cross-national study. *Sociological Perspectives, 41*(2), 415–432.

Stone, M. (1998). Journaling with clients. *The Journal of Individual Psychology, 54*, 535–545.

Sulzby, E. F. (1988). A study of children's early reading development. In A. D. Pellegrini (Ed.), *Psychological bases of early education* (pp. 39–75). Chichester: Wiley.

Ullrich, P. M., & Lutgendorf, S. K. (2002). Journaling about stressful events: Effects of cognitive processing and emotional expression. *Annals of Behavioral Medicine, 24*, 244–250.

Vygotsky, L. (1962). *Thought and language* (pp. 124–139). Cambridge, MA: MIT Press.

Wallerstein, J. S., Lewis, J., & Blakeslee, S. (2000). *The unexpected legacy of divorce: A 25-year landmark study* (pp. 1–11). New York: Hyperion Pub.

Wollman-Bonilla, J. E. (2001). Family involvement in early writing instruction. *Journal of Early Childhood Literacy, 1*(2), 167–192.

Woolley, M. E., Bowen G. L., & Bowen, N. K. (2006). The development and evaluation of procedures to assess child self report, item validity and measurement. *Educational and Psychological Measurement, 66,* 68–87.

Zeiger, R. B. (1994). Use of the journal in treatment of the seriously emotionally disturbed adolescent: A case study. *The Arts in Psychotherapy, 21,* 197–204.

For Further Exploration

Cornell University (2007). *Cornell University Law School Divorce Resource Center.* Ithaca, NY: The Legal Information Institute. Available at: http://topics.law.cornell.edu/wex/divorce.

Johnston, J., Roseby, V., Gentner, B., & Moore, E. (2005). *A safe place to grow: a group treatment manual for children in conflicted, violent, and separating homes.* New York: Routledge.

National Institute of Health (2008). *Medline plus.* Washington, DC: Pubmed. Available at: http://www.nlm.nih.gov/medlineplus/divorce.html.

6 Reading and Writing Teenage Motherhood

Changing Literacy Practices and Developing Identities

Kara L. Lycke

Seventeen-year-old Elaine sits cross-legged on the floor with her 18-month-old son Marcus, a pad of construction paper between them; each is gripping a brightly colored crayon. Elaine points to the marks she makes and gently speaks to him. He joins her in marking the paper. After five minutes, Marcus' crayon is soggy from moving back and forth from the paper to his mouth. Elaine continues to encourage him to "write."

"I just love him too much .... It's funny though, he has changed my whole life around. Like before I had him when I was pregnant, I always knew I could do well in school but I didn't really try hard .... I wanted to go to medical school then, but I wasn't like really focused or dedicated to do it. And it's like, after I had him, it's like all right, it's not only about me any more, you know. [To her son] You have truly turned my life around."

(Elaine,[1] teenage mother, 17)

When Elaine, a high school student and teenage mother, learned of her pregnancy, she transferred to an alternative public high school with a child care facility and parenting classes and began focusing on her future. Her actions and words above illustrate one of many ways that her literacy practices changed after having a child. She began to read and write to her son. She suggests that a change has occurred in her identity. She dedicated her schooling to cultivating a professional career.

A teenage pregnancy could be described as a crisis, an "identifiable stimulus or catalyst" (Collins & Collins, 2005) that severely taxes a young woman's resources normally sufficient for daily life. As Chapter 1 of this book explains, crises occur in many dimensions and impact people's lives in complex ways. In the case of an unplanned or unwanted pregnancy, it is difficult to pin-point the exact crisis. Does it occur the moment a woman becomes sexually active, in the moment of conception, or when she discovers that she is pregnant? When a teenager decides to carry her fetus to term, she accepts nine months of an increasingly visible public crisis, one that may increase in its scope as she seeks or requires more assistance. The crisis is not resolved when the child is born since parenting is a life-long endeavor and a continual adjustment with the potential to spark other crises as time goes on.

Some teenagers become immobilized by the crisis of a pregnancy or their lives become seriously damaged, while others can pass through with minimal stress (Sandoval, 2002). Some young mothers are able to use the time of their pregnancy to recover or discover working resources, invent functional systems, examine and initiate changes in existing relationships, and develop new supportive relationships. They use new coping strategies to convert the crisis of teen pregnancy into a new way of life as a mother. I use two cases to examine the literacy practices and identity changes that can occur as a result of teenage pregnancy and early motherhood. The stories of both young women are of growth and opportunity as their literacy practices become tools for negotiating, supporting, and mediating accompanying identity changes.

Framing Teenage Motherhood

The national discourse that shapes the identity of teenage mothers situates them in the midst of a "failure of American society" (National Center of Health Statistics, 1992 as cited in Pillow, 2004). Popular images of teen mothers depict them as "stupid sluts," "children having children," "girls nobody loved," "welfare moms," "dropouts," and "neglectful mothers," and position them as "unworthy of public support ..., pitiable, yet incompetent to lead autonomous lives" (Kelly, 2000, p. 27). They are represented as educationally "at risk" (e.g., Chafel, 1994; Natriello, McDill, & Pallas, 1990; Small & Luster, 1994), personally irresponsible (Plummer & O'Neil, 1999), and sinners (Thompson, 1995).

The dominant view of teenage mothers assumes that parenting at a young age will have negative consequences. For many teens, having a child results in costs to their schooling and economic promise. In school, teenage mothers experience discrimination, alienation, decreased academic aspirations, and higher drop-out rates (Kelly, 2000; Zachry, 2005). The children of teen mothers are prone to failure as well (Neuman & Gallagher, 1994). Psychologically, teenage mothers face a changing sense of self as the responsibility of raising a child puts new demands on their time, severely constraining their activities and independence, and changing their relationships with family members, peers, and school personnel (Kelly, 2000; Luker, 1996; Pillow, 2004).

An alternative perspective on dramatic life changes, such as early parenting, views a crisis as a turning point on which one's life is irrevocably changed (e.g., Erikson, 1968; Sandoval, 2002). This perspective views the obstacles to one's goals and the tensions in one's life that arise from crisis as serious but *not necessarily* catastrophic. In accordance with this view, recent research on teenage mothers supports the idea that there may be more purposeful decision making on the part of young parents. Studies report that 22–44% of births by teenage mothers are the result of *intended* pregnancies at the time of conception (Frost & Oslak, 1999). In some cases, pregnancy and motherhood create a feeling of renewed responsibility, a more focused approach to education, and more positive experiences in schooling (Zachry, 2005).

Other research has examined teenage mothers' parenting practices and beliefs, specifically regarding how particular parenting practices can be taught and learned. Interventions in both teen parenting curricula and early childhood education substantiate those practices as assessment outcomes for developing teen mothers' ways of interacting with their children. A relationship-focused curriculum as part of parenting "training" helped teenage mothers to develop responsive, less directive, and more facilitative parenting skill (Deutscher, Fewell, & Gross, 2006). However, the research of Neuman and colleagues (Neuman, Hagedorn, Celano, & Daly, 1995) cautions us not to assume that teen mothers consistently share beliefs with school professionals about schooling and its desired outcomes. Luschen (1998) examined the tensions that existed in the hidden curriculum of one parenting program which focused on developing white middle-class mothering values at the expense of the teen's cultural values.

This chapter examines the ways in which two teens reconceptualized and adapted to the crisis of pregnancy and motherhood through changes in their literacy practices and shifting identities. For Elaine and Sheila, early parenting was a catalyst for changes in literacy practices directed at developing new relationships and making decisions about caring for their children. Teen motherhood, a new identity, was facilitated by and resulted in their changing literacy practices.

Literacy and Identity as Social Processes

The confluence of literacy and identity development can be studied in complex ways through socio-cultural and critical perspectives. Understanding literacy as a social process acknowledges the role of print and other symbol systems as central to literate practice, and also recognizes that learning and using symbol systems is mediated by and constituted within cultural practice (Heath, 1982; Street, 1995). This view takes into account that uses of non-print symbol systems support meaning-making with printed text. Street (1995) defines *literacy practices* as both the behaviors and ideological conceptualizations related to meaning-making with text.

Critical theories allow that literacy can be raced, classed, gendered, and politicized practices in which language (oral and written) is used to mediate and produce culture. Literacy is involved in the ways in which people use language for particular social purposes (Gee, 1989). It is not a neutral technology, but rather, an "ideological practice, implicated in power relations and embedded in specific cultural meanings and practices" (Street, 1995, p. 2). Defining literacy in socio-political terms allows us to examine the ways in which people interpret texts and how they use language to make choices about their identities.

Because literacy itself is cultural practice, literate identities are constructed within those practices. Just as certain cultural practices are valued more highly than others in particular contexts, certain literacy practices are valued more than others. Having access to valued conventions is vital to participating in any community and means having access to certain kinds of power. Adopting the valued literacy and discourse practices of a community allows individuals to enact identities that are appropriate or necessary for particular relationships and circumstances (Cope & Kalantzis, 1993; Gee, 2001; Moje, 2004; Moje, Overby, Tysvaer, & Morris, 2008). Teen mothers' access to and control of particular literacy practices define the ways in which they manage becoming mothers at a young age.

Research Design and Methodology

To better understand the connections between changing literacy practices and changing identities for teen mothers, I asked the following research questions: *How do Elaine and Sheila's literacy practices and their purposes for reading and writing change as a result of becoming mothers?* and *What is the relationship between their changing literacy and their developing identities as mothers?* The two cases presented here are part of a larger two-year ethnographic study which focused on the literacy practices of a group of teenage mothers as they enacted the multiple roles that made up their identities both in and out of school.

Research Site

The research site for this study was a Midwestern community that included a medium-sized city, a large university, Summit High School (SHS)—a public alternative high school, and the surrounding suburban and rural neighborhoods where the participants lived, worked, and raised their children. Summit, with a maximum enrollment of 125 students, was recognized for its award-winning Teen Parent Program which registered about twelve new students each year. The school required its teen parents to enroll in parenting courses and operated an on-site licensed child care facility for the students to use.

Participants

By taking advantage of an open enrollment policy in the district, students could attend Summit as a school of choice, and they commuted in from surrounding communities. The participants were recruited from the group of teen mothers attending Summit during the first year of the study. I began by holding a meeting with all interested young women enrolled in parenting classes. Of the twelve students who attended the meeting, either pregnant or already mothers, nine became part of the study. I told them about the multiple parts of the project: an after-school reading and writing group, interviews at several points in the project, and observations in school and selected locations and events outside of school. After participants signed a general consent form, data was collected in phases and personal kinds of data were collected only with their further consent.

The participants represented a range of social class groups from working poor to middle class. Their racial affiliations were as follows: one bi-racial (African-American/white), nine white, and two Latina/mixed-race. Of the nine regular participants, three were selected as focus participants, two of whom were Elaine and Sheila, the subject of this chapter.

Data Collection

Over the two years of the study I spent literally hundreds of hours observing and interacting with the participants, both with and without their children, across a variety of contexts. These contexts include parenting and children's literature courses, Summit's child care center, their homes, prom, doctors' offices, and community events. I planned, facilitated, and participated in an after-school reading and writing group which met two to three times a month. I hosted several weekend get-togethers which included their children, at the teen mothers' request, to examine and practice reading children's books. The participants engaged in the activities of the research to varying degrees; Elaine and Sheila were among the most active participants.

Field notes were taken and video/audio tape recordings were made as was appropriate to the context. I conducted both extended semi-structured and *in situ* interviews with the participants, their teachers, and their parents.

Data Analysis

Data analysis emphasized the changes in teen mothers' literacy practices and identities as they negotiated changing demands on them as students and as family members in their new role as mothers. Methods for analyzing data included a constant comparative method involving open, axial, and selective coding (Strauss & Corbin, 1990) and critical discourse analysis. For open coding, I generated categories for looking more deeply into, for example, discussions of texts in particular contexts, school literacy practices, identities, and genres of text. In order to examine these emerging themes more closely and to create axial codes, I wrote analytic memos to create coding paradigms, to ask questions about the codes and to note contrasts in and connections between their content (Merriam, 2002). Finally, during selective coding, with the help of the analytic memos, I reviewed themes and rewrote them for clarity of definition and to assemble the big picture under analysis. The conceptual model that I built in this process was structured for each case study by the following categories: *established literacy practices, emerging and changing literacy practices,* and *changes in identity.*

I used Labov's (1982, as cited in Merriam, 2002) linguistic approach to discourse analysis with longer interviews and discussions in order to examine stories the participants created in particular contexts and for particular purposes. Through summarizing the events and sequence of the narratives and considering the particular social contexts where the narratives were created, I was able to critically analyze the social and political meanings of their stories.

By combining the meanings made through the constant comparative method and discourse analysis, I systematically explored the relationships between literacy events (discursive practices, interactions with texts), wider social structures (Fairclough, 1995), and identities.

Focus Participants

Elaine

When I first met Elaine, she was seventeen years old, and her son Marcus was twelve months old. She presented herself as a self-directed high school junior who "likes to talk," and indeed her participation in classrooms and after-school meetings was substantial, if not dominant, and her semi-structured interviews often lasted for over two hours. She spoke candidly and comfortably on a range of topics. She talked openly about her bi-racial identity, calling herself "mixed," African-American and white. She said her struggle to fit in "was harder" for her than for people who identify with one racial category. She named school as a location where she had been racially categorized; it was a place where her racial identity mattered in her relationships.

Elaine did not represent the mythological poor, oversexed, black, teenage mother (Hallman, 2007; Pillow, 2004), but her identity more closely matched images of the white middle class. Her middle class status, determined by her parents' professional jobs and post-secondary education, positioned her as a good "girl next door" who was in need of help (Pillow, 2004). This status also brings with it an expectation of cultivated experiences and sophisticated language practices allowing her a measure of institutional entitlement, a privilege her working class and poor white peers did not enjoy (Heath, 1982; Lareau, 2003). Elaine was viewed by others as a leader, and she had close ties to the people in her family, church, and neighborhood. She especially enjoyed supportive friendly relationships with both of her parents and her older brother and sister. She lived with her mother, father, and son Marcus in a small city about ten miles from Summit High School in a modest home in a middle class residential neighborhood. Her parents were regular and consistent care providers for Marcus for which Elaine was grateful and satisfied.

Sheila

Fifteen-year-old Sheila was a sophomore in high school, and she was attending the parenting program at Summit primarily because her local school did not provide child care for her six-month-old son Drew. She planned to return to her hometown high school for her senior year, which she did after the completion of the study.

Sheila lived with her mother in a small rented house on the edge of a mixed social class, mostly white suburban neighborhood in proximity to several large farms. Often Sheila's mother was unemployed during the time of the study, and Sheila usually had part-time employment or was looking for it.

Sheila required a job within walking distance of her home or located conveniently for others to give her rides since she did not have regular access to a car. Sheila depended on me for rides on project activity days which she eagerly and regularly attended.

Sheila indicated at the beginning of the project that she was close to her mother, yet in several conversations throughout the project she revealed some turbulence in their relationship. Topics that raised conflict in their relationship over time included abortion, her mothering style, her education and employment—current and future, and her son's daily schedule. Sheila explained that she learned everything she knew about parenting from babysitting, parenting classes, the research project, books, magazines, and information on the internet.

Through Elaine's and Sheila's cases, I will discuss their *established literacy practices*—literacy practices that were learned and maintained during home and school literacy events; *changes in literacy*—literacy practices that evolved in response to becoming pregnant and having a child; and *identity changes*—developing ways teen mothers (re)presented themselves and the ways others represented them. These identity changes emerged out of their experiences and conceptualizations of themselves as mothers and resulted in or supported changes in literacy practices.

Elaine's Changing Literacy Practices: A Family Matter

Elaine used her established and changing literacy practices to authorize her emerging identity as a mother. Her literacy served her in family and school reading and writing activities and conversations about texts.

Established Literacy Practices

Elaine's established literacy practices were part of her family's personal/cultural knowledge (Banks, 1996) both before and after becoming a mother. These practices included sharing literacy experiences and reading multiple genres of texts for practical purposes and for pleasure.

Sharing Literacy Experiences

Literacy was infused throughout Elaine's everyday activities. She read independently and to Marcus, shared a daily devotional with her father, referenced books in conversations with family members, and kept in her home numerous books on various topics. Elaine named her grandmother and father as the most prominent of her family's "big readers," and it was they who "passed on" the importance of reading to her. When she was a child she and her father looked up a new word in the dictionary and read aloud from the Bible every day, and as a teenager much of her reading included books about faith that circulated among family members. Her family sought and shared information from magazines and the internet. Literacy shaped the customs in this household where decisions were often based on a synthesis of multiple sources of information. This perspective was also evident in Elaine's approach to school work, parenting, and relating to her son through literacy. Marcus' care was steeped within a literacy-rich household, as was Elaine's when she was a child.

Multiple Texts for Practical Purposes

Elaine and her family read a variety of popular literature and technical resources in the form of books, magazines, and internet information when deciding, for instance, where to shop for organic foods and what combination of foods make up a weight-loss diet. When Elaine took parenting classes at Summit, she and her sister Karla, a twenty-something single mom and former teenage parent who lived in a neighboring state, regularly exchanged parenting information via fax machines. Karla once faxed Elaine a section of a book relating the problems with toddlers eating shrimp. Flexible literacy was a family affair for Elaine.

Literacy for Pleasure

Before she became pregnant, Elaine enjoyed most of the reading and writing she was assigned in her school subjects. She was especially fond of the "free expression" she was allowed in her creative writing course at her neighborhood high school. She enjoyed leisure reading outside of school, and critiqued her own reading material choices. She disliked the book *How Stella Got Her Groove Back*, by Terry McMillan, because it was "predictable." "I don't like really boring books where I just read the first chapter or two, and it's like, okay, I don't want to read any more." She stated a fondness for Christian books, and a recent favorite was a Christmas gift, *Just Like Jesus*. She explained that the book tells the reader, "God loves you just the way you are but he refuses to leave you like that. He wants you to be ... just like Jesus."

Changes in Literacy

Elaine continued to read and write for multiple purposes and across genres after becoming pregnant. She continued to read for information, for school, for her religion, and for pleasure. As a mother, her literacy practices changed as she included Marcus in her literacy practices, and focused her school literacy on informational text.

Including Marcus in Literacy Practices

An established literacy practice of Elaine's family's was oral reading, and as a mother she increased and broadened this practice. Elaine established a pattern of reading with Marcus, as her father had done with her, when she was still pregnant.

She read aloud Christian books, medical books, popular magazines, her home-work, and C. S. Lewis' *The Lion, the Witch and the Wardrobe*. She and her parents continued their oral literacy tradition after Marcus was born by "always read[ing] before he goes to sleep." She held that if Marcus heard about a world of ideas through multiple forms, his potential for vocabulary growth and meaning-making with texts would expand. Elaine derived great pleasure from participating in and tracing Marcus' developing literacy. She described his excitement about books in this way: "If he recognizes something, he points it out. He gets all excited .... Some days he'll just read a couple of pages, put down his book and get another one. Go back and forth. He likes reading." She saw her family's passion for reading in Marcus and hoped that it would persist as it had in her own life.

When Elaine discussed her own reading and writing, she often connected it with Marcus' emerging literacy, thereby continuing the line of family literacy that extended from her grandmother. Elaine rejected the stereotyped images of a teenage mother when she described the importance of a literate life. She said, "I want [Marcus] to have, like, the widest vocabulary in the world. I believe that a child should always be better than their parents. It's like, your parents have done this, they have taught you that, and then you go on to the next step and do more. I don't want [him] to have to struggle in life because he doesn't have a lot of knowledge." A teenage mother in this family is not a failure, but her responsibilities increase to include a new family member into their literacy practices.

School Literacy Focused on Informational Text

After transferring to Summit, Elaine's reading and writing became more focused on non-fiction genres. While she still enjoyed reading and writing fiction, infor-mational text became increasingly important to her. She explained, "I like papers. I like reports and finding information . . . , like, why is this happening, what is the cause of it and stuff like that." She viewed expository writing in her courses as connected to her preparation for her career in medicine.

Identity Changes

Elaine's changing literacy practices were supportive of several changes in her identity. Her evolving (re)presentation of herself as a mother changed her relationship with family members and her role as a student. Specifically, her adolescent status was evolving into adult status, and she focused her literacy activities increasingly on her vocational interests.

Evolving Adult Status

When Elaine became a mother, her status among her family and peers changed. Because her family collaborated in Marcus' care, they began to respect Elaine as a capable parent. For example, when Elaine struggled with breast feeding, she, her mother and her sister shared print and electronic documents to discuss the challenge. Though her mother and sister strongly resisted Elaine's inclination to bottle-feed her baby, she decided to practice both methods until she became more adept at nursing at which time she would switch to that method exclusively. Though her mother and sister disagreed, they had no choice but to acquiesce and watch as Elaine's plan was implemented successfully.

Career Focus in School Literacy

Elaine's purpose for reading and writing in school was changing along with her status as an adult. She enjoyed many of her classes and felt intellectually challenged by nearly all of them. She aspired to become a medical professional—a physician, radiologist, or pediatric nurse—and she had plans to begin her college education at the local community college where her mother worked or at the state university where her father earned his Bachelor's degree. After becoming a mother, her coursework became more self-directed. She actively shaped her reading and writing, when she had the option, to develop her knowledge about healthy living and a potential career in medicine. She enjoyed psychology class assignments for which she analyzed the film *Rain Man* and researched autism and AIDS because she viewed this literacy work as connected to her career plans.

During one school term at Summit, Elaine was required to take a keyboarding class. She said, "We were kind of pushed more into taking Office Skills. I really didn't want to take it because I am not going into taking any secretary's job or anything like that." She believed the requirement resulted from a stipulation associated with a grant for job training. She explained that the school "get[s] a lot of money [for] the teen parent stuff." This policy decision that existed outside of her needs positioned her as someone who would need basic employment skills like keyboarding. As teen mothers like Elaine work "to describe and assign meaning to their own lives, [they] struggle against … the many competing discourses about the 'teen mother' identity" (Kelly, 2000, p. 3). The perceptions school policy makers have of teen mothers as a general category sometimes force teen mothers to enact multiple and competing identities (Hallman, 2007).

As an active family member and student, Elaine's established and changing literacy practices supported her evolving identity as a mother. As her literacy practices were increasingly used for constructing meaning from/with texts, her status increased.

Sheila: Managing Parenting through Literacy

The changes in Sheila's literacy practices were directed at managing her daily life as a mother, daughter, and full-time student. Sheila's model for raising children could be described as an "accomplishment of natural growth" (Lareau, 2003), where, in the home, children are given unstructured time and space to discover, learn, and make decisions largely without adult direction. Lareau found this parenting model prevalent in working class and poor families. While there are benefits to this model (e.g., collaborative skill development among peers), it can be partly characterized by hierarchical relationships between parents and children. By contrast, Elaine's middle class "cultivation" (Lareau, 2003) prepared her to interact on more equal terms with adults in her family and at school. Before Sheila had a child, she occupied a subordinate position to her mother and other adults in her life and experienced schooling through distant and hierarchical relationships. After her son Drew was born, however, Sheila did not follow the child rearing practices of natural growth or continue in subordinate roles. Instead, she began to enact a middle class value system in order to customize her education and her son's developmental experiences. When she transferred to Summit, she practiced with Rachel, her parenting teacher, a transformative active approach to learning. Rachel explicitly adjusted her curriculum to respond to her students' needs and interests in topics such as paternity, childbirth practices, disciplining children, and children's literacy. She coached her students to advocate for themselves and their children.

Established Literacy Practices

Before she was pregnant, Sheila's out-of-school literacy practices were almost exclusively private and expressive. She read poetry, romance novels, and mystery novels; she wrote poetry, diary entries, and letters she did not send. Her school literacy was motivated by following directions and completing assignments to get credit for her work. In keeping with her mother's parenting approach as an accomplishment of natural growth, Sheila practiced literacy for others or privately.

Changes in Literacy

Transferring to Summit and participating in the research project were two decisions Sheila made that led to major changes in her perspectives on literacy and on herself as a mother. In both settings, she used her literacy skills to learn about parenting within a community of young mothers and caring adults who could confirm or reject what she was learning from reading on her own. "I was somewhere else trying to figure it out .... I wanted to know that it was the right way and whether I need to fix something or to hurry up and teach [Drew] something." As a young mother, she developed more relationally and personally affirming literacy practices to substitute for her private, hierarchical practices. She used reading and writing as a tool for organizing her thinking and making decisions, directing her own and others' actions, and for presenting to her son a different kind of literacy than she knew as a child.

Organizing Thinking

Once Sheila came to terms with the idea that she was going to have a baby, she began reading voraciously to prepare herself for what she could expect for the remaining three months of her pregnancy and for her child's infancy. "When I was pregnant, I read lots and lots of baby magazines and books, but mostly magazines. If I read something more than once [in different texts], then I'd think, well that's probably right." She verified what she was learning by reading across resources to which she had access. "Um, [magazines] have lots of charts and stuff out. Like even just for crawling or motor skills ..., like zero to three months they'll do this, ... and I'll just look and see where he should be."

Sheila explained that after she became a mother she had no time for her former literacy practices and instead read and wrote for important practical purposes. She read "directions or maps," to "learn how to do" a variety of tasks, and she began making lists. She said, "I make lists for like the littlest things like, so I don't forget to brush my teeth or something." She said the act of writing helped her memory even if she never looked at the list again. Lists were a way for her to "align" information in her head that would otherwise be "floating around."

Directing Action

Sheila described a day when she left her son Drew in her mother's care so she could work a six-hour shift after school. She left a detailed plan, a list, for her mother that outlined important activities and when they should occur, such as when to start dinner and when to feed Drew, when to give him a bath, and when to put him to bed. The list was designed to help the baby stay on his regular week-day schedule since he would be going to daycare at Summit with Sheila in the morning. In spite of her clear list, Sheila seethed, "things don't get done." "I asked my mom to give him a bath and she's watched him for six hours 'cause I worked six hours. He took a two hour nap so that means she had four hours. He didn't get a bath. I was like, mom, I'm not gonna take him to childcare. He's got a swollen eye and he's dirty. They're gonna be like okay, that kid's abused, I don't want to watch that kid." It was important to Sheila that her son was well cared for in her absence, and she desired to present herself as a competent mother at school.

Sheila also attempted to negotiate Drew's care when it was in the hands of his father Dallas or Dallas' family. Dallas, not regularly present as a father, would occasionally take Drew on Saturdays when Sheila worked, and Dallas' mother and sister insisted on regular visitation with Drew, all of which was a source of great stress for Sheila. She worried about whether Dallas' family viewed her as a good mother and about the care Drew would receive with Dallas' family. As she did with her own mother, she wrote out detailed instructions for Drew's care when he was with Dallas' family.

Presenting Literacy to Drew

In Sheila's view, Drew's literacy development was key to his success and happiness. "Smart people read .... I want him to like to read, 'cause if you like to read it's probably ... something that you're good at." Because she wanted him to enjoy reading, she made sure as a toddler he was read to every day. Sheila described how he was "starting to memorize the things I say in books." When they read *Good Night, Moon*, Drew would say to Sheila, "Where's the moon? Where's the moon?" and then, "There it is, Mommy."

Modeling and imitation were important parenting tools for Sheila. She modeled for Drew methods of talking about books and ways to interact with books independently. She described his literacy development through examples of the ways in which he repeated her actions. When they read children's books together Drew pointed to or "smack[ed] the pictures" and said "woo," or kissed a picture of a crying baby as Sheila had previously demonstrated. Sheila encouraged Drew from a very young age to hold crayons, though they usually ended up in his mouth. He also "smack[ed] the paper with them," which Sheila explained was a sign of beginning writing. When he got older, they drew together and put their creations on the refrigerator with Drew commenting, "Ooh, perty!", the same expression he used to admire Sheila's handwritten words.

Identity Changes

As her literacy practices changed to serve relational and practical purposes, Sheila's identity changed for similar purposes. Her experiences at Summit and her involvement in the research project supported her actions as a competent decision-maker for her child and she began advocating for her own needs. She changed her reading material from romance and mystery novels to parenting resources and children's books she shared with Drew. She began to write for public purposes such as when she wrote a letter to a legal advocacy group Friend of the Court to "get child support going." She also wrote a letter to a creditor initiating delayed payment on a bill.

Sheila explained that learning about parenting became her primary purpose for reading, both in and out of school. She used parenting texts to validate the choices she was making and to question the advice others offered. She found that parenting magazines were a reliable source of information to which she directed other teen parents for advice on potty training, getting a workout when strolling your baby, and putting a child to sleep in his own bed. She cautioned other teen mothers to check information sources against one another and not indiscriminately heed the advice of people they knew.

> Relatives, ... just because they say something doesn't mean it's right and
> if [young mothers] have a feeling that that's not the way they want to

raise their baby then, they don't have to listen to them. But they don't have to get into an argument with them, just be like, ok, yep, and then, you don't have to do it.

She endeavored to maintain her established literacy practice of journaling and continued to view it as private. Journaling, though comprised mostly of lists since she became a mother, was her personal expressive space. Her journal was an archive, a representation of her activities as a mother. She discovered an old list in a journal she was keeping. "I was looking for paper to write something down, like what I need to buy with my [pay]check, and I saw a list. I wrote down Drew's schedule when he was a tiny little baby." In the absence of time to write regularly in her journal, the lists became a record of her activities as a new mother and her son's development through infancy.

Discussion and Conclusions: Responsive Literacy Learning and Teaching

Not every young woman in the study successfully navigated the crises she faced as a teen parent. Becoming teen mothers had devastating consequences for some as they struggled emotionally, relationally, and academically. Elaine and Sheila, on the other hand, began their pregnancies with different sets of established literacy practices and identities, yet their experiences as mothers enriched their literacies and identities.

The support system provided by Elaine's family smoothed her literacy and identity transitions; many of the changes she experienced as a result of her pregnancy deepened or broadened her established family literacy practices and accelerated her apprenticeship into adult roles. Having a child at this point in her life was not what she or her family anticipated, or even wanted, but they modified their existing literacy traditions to embrace him.

Sheila's literacy and identity transitions were much more acute since she enacted a largely new set of literacy and identity practices as a teen parent. While she set aside many of the private literacy pleasures she had established, motherhood afforded her a view of literacy as a relational, practical, and political tool. It became necessary that she develop her list-making skill beyond a record of her thinking into a way of asserting her parenting capabilities into her relationships with her mother and Dallas' family. In addition she began using literacy as a broad socializing and educational tool with Drew. Through literacy, she hoped to develop her son's intelligence, share mutually pleasurable attachment experiences, and fashion a kind of family literacy that Sheila did not know as a child.

The results of this study—which indicate that teenage women will modify or radically change their established literacy practices as a result of becoming mothers—point to four important conclusions. First, in both cases presented here, the participants had firmly established, meaningful ways of interacting with texts for multiple purposes before they became pregnant. This point is important in light of educational practice and policy that responds to popular beliefs that teenage women become mothers at least partly because they do not value education (Zachry, 2005), and that they do not cultivate literate lives outside of school. This research supports, however, that teen parents' beliefs about schooling can be highly compatible with those of school professionals (Neuman et al., 1995). They value educational achievement, independent learning, and information that enhances their lives. For teen mothers, the context of those values includes their children's learning and development. Elaine and Sheila sought a customized education for themselves, and they demonstrated clear notions of their own and their children's changing literacy needs.

Second, having a child does not necessitate hindered learning for teen mothers, but instead can enhance it. As Elaine and Sheila grew into their identities as mothers, they sought to amend their existing literacy practices and create new forms of literacy, both in and out of school, in order to adapt to their emergent learning needs and to provide quality care for their children. Because teen mothers' lives are significantly different from the lives of non-parenting teens, however, they require inclusive public schooling that is both the same and different from their peers' education. Otherwise, teen parents must choose separate "alternative" education programs which may be beneficial in numerous ways but also perpetuate a climate of segregation and hierarchy. Many teen mothers who leave school do so because of rigid policies that exclude pregnant and parenting teens, or because they experience pressure to attend special schools (Kelly, 2000; Luker, 1996).

Third, teen mothers require flexible educational support as both their literacies and identities are changing in their new roles as mothers. They require scaffolding that supports sophisticated and purposeful literacy development in the service of their parenting needs and practices. In Elaine's case, her education incorporated pedagogical strategies that were congruent with her family's beliefs and practices. Reading and writing to sustain her interest in health care supported her identity as a competent mother and as a potential medical professional. Sheila's literacy and identity changes required different kinds of instructional and relational support because she entered into less familiar literacy and parenting activities. In both cases, responsive pedagogical approaches to literacy and parenting education were important.

Finally, there is a critical reciprocal relationship between teen mothers' forms of literacy practices and their children's emergence into literacy. Coaching approaches may be an effective intervention strategy for helping young mothers understand and enhance the literacy experiences of their children (Neuman & Gallagher, 1994). My research suggests a similar approach may help young mothers make sense of and enhance their own literacy experiences as well. Teen mothers' awareness of their own and their children's changing literacy practices evolve together, as does their belief in the power of their own and their children's literacy. Supported by and constituted within their literacy practices, Elaine and Sheila both took on identities of committed students and competent young mothers. Their literacy practices took on new dimensions and purposes as they transitioned into new ways of life. Their efforts propelled them toward recovering from crisis and into equilibrating their own needs with those of their children, their identities as mothers with multiple other teen identities.

Note

1 The names of people and places are pseudonyms.

References

Banks, J. (1996). *Multicultural education, transformative knowledge, and action: Historical and contemporary perspectives.* New York: Teachers College Press.

Chafel, J. A. (1994). Meeting the developmental needs of young children of teen parents: A critique of social policy and implications advocacy. *Child and Youth Care Forum, 23,* 297–314.

Collins, B., & Collins, T. (2005). *Crisis and trauma: Developmental-Ecological intervention.* Boston, MA: Lahaska Press.

Cope, B., & Kalantzis, M. (Eds.). (1993). *The powers of literacy: A genre approach to teaching writing.* Pittsburgh, PA: University of Pittsburgh Press.

Deutscher, B., Fewell, R. R., & Gross, M. (2006). Enhancing the interactions of teenage mothers and their at-risk children: Effectiveness of a maternal-focused intervention. *Topics in Early Childhood Special Education, 26*(4), 194–205.

Erikson, E. (1968). *Identity, youth, and crisis.* New York: Norton.

Fairclough, N. (1995). Critical language awareness and self-identity in education. In D. Corson (Ed.), *Discourse and power in educational organizations.* Cresskill, NJ: Hampton Press.

Frost, J. J., & Oslak, S. (1999, 1/31/2000). *Teenagers' pregnancy intentions and decisions,* [web page]. Alan Guttmacher Institute Occasional Report. Retrieved January 31, 2000, from www.agi-usa.org/index.html.

Gee, J. P. (1989). Literacy, discourse, and linguistics: Introduction. *Journal of Education, 171*(1), 5–25.

Gee, J. P. (2001, December). Reading in "new times." Paper presented at the National Reading Conference, San Antonio, TX.

Hallman, H. L. (2007). Reassigning the identity of the pregnant and parenting student. *American Secondary Education, 36*(1), 80–97.

Heath, S. B. (1982). Questioning at home and school: A comparative study. In G. Spindler (Ed.), *Doing the ethnography of schooling* (pp. 102–131). New York: Rinehart & Winston.

Kelly, D. (2000). *Pregnant with meaning: Teen mothers and the politics of inclusive schooling.* New York: Peter Lang Publishing.

Lareau, A. (2003). *Unequal childhoods.* Berkeley: University of California Press.

Luker, K. (1996). *Dubious conceptions: The politics of teenage pregnancy.* Cambridge, MA: Harvard University Press.

Luschen, K. (1998). Contested scripts: The education of student-mothers in childcare schools. *Educational Studies, 29*(4), 392–410.

Merriam, S. B. (2002). *Qualitative research in practice.* San Francisco: Jossey Bass.

Moje, E. B. (2004). Powerful spaces: Tracing the out-of-school literacy spaces of Latino/a youth. In K. Leander, & M. Sheehy (Eds.), *Spatializing literacy research and practice* (pp. 15–38). New York: Peter Lang.

Moje, E. B., Overby, M., Tysvaer, N., & Morris, K. (2008). The complex world of adolescent literacy: Myths, motivations, and mysteries. *Harvard Educational Review, 78*(1), 107–154.

Natriello, G., McDill, E. L., & Pallas, A. M. (1990). *Schooling disadvantaged children: Racing against catastrophe.* New York: Teachers College Press.

Neuman, S., & Gallagher, P. (1994). Joining together in literacy learning: Teenage mothers and children. *Reading Research Quarterly, 29*(4), 383–401.

Neuman, S., Hagedorn, T., Celano, D., & Daly, P. (1995). Toward a collaborative approach to parent involvement in early childhood education: A study of teenage mothers in an African-American community. *American Educational Research Journal, 32*(4), 801–827.

Pillow, W. (2004). *Unfit subjects: Educational policy and the teen mother.* New York: Routledge Falmer.

Plummer, W., & O'Neil, A. (1999, October 11). Revisiting "The Baby Trap". *People,* 54–76.

Sandoval, J. (2002). *Handbook of crisis counseling, intervention, and prevention in the schools.* Mahwah, NJ: Lawrence Erlbaum Associates.

Small, S. A., & Luster, T. (1994, February). Adolescent sexual activity: An ecological, risk-factor approach. *Journal of Marriage and Family, 56,* 181–192.

Strauss, A. L., & Corbin, J. A. (1990). *Basics of qualitative research: Grounded theory procedures and techniques.* Thousand Oaks, CA: Sage.

Street, B. V. (1995). *Social literacies: Critical approaches to literacy in development, ethnography and education.* London: Longman.

Thompson, S. (1995). *Going all the way: Teenage girls' tales of sex, romance, and pregnancy.* New York: Hill & Wang.

Zachry, E. M. (2005). Getting my education: Teen mothers' experiences in school before and after motherhood. *Teachers College Record, 107*(12), 2566–2589.

For Further Exploration

Davis, D. (2004). *You look too young to be a mom: Teen mothers speak out on love, learning, and success.* New York: Perigee.

Healthy Teen Network, Baltimore, MD: http://www.healthyteennetwork.org.

Honnold, M. (2005). *More teen programs that work.* New York: Neal-Schuman Publishers.

Young Mommies Help Site: http://www.youngmommies.com.

7 When Daddy Goes to Prison
Examining Crisis through Fanfiction and Poetry

Mary K. Thompson

"My family, we ain't like it was," shared Lo, an adolescent female describing her family crisis of her father's absence due to a life sentence for committing a heinous crime. While Lo does not use the word "crisis" here to describe the events leading to her father's life sentence she writes about her life as a before and after sequence in her poetry and fanfictions. Fanfiction refers to writing using the media as a jumping off point where a fan might extend the characters and plot. Lo's writing is divided by before "it" happened and after creating a chasm that permeates much of Lo's writing and thinking about what it means to have her father absent from her life. As a self-described "daddy's girl" and the eldest daughter in a large family, Lo is hit hard by the hole created by her father's crime and his sudden absence in her tightly knit family. Lo used to identify culturally and linguistically as both Southeast Asian and Native American but since her father's arrest and prison sentence she has tried to forget her Southeast Asian roots. Lo is ashamed of her father and her deep rooted connections to him culturally and linguistically. She feels deeply hurt and ashamed of his crime and what it has done to the family.

This chapter documents Lo's experiences as a fanfiction writer, poet, and artist as she learns how to deal with her resentment, frustration, and distrust in the American legal system. She watches her father disappear from her life leaving behind a family deeply affected by his crime. Drawing from a theoretical perspective that examines literacy as an identity making process, I explore how Lo uses her fanfiction and poetry and art to constructively deal with her frustration and anger toward her father. It is in this space where Lo is able to negotiate, create, and explore other ways to think about her family's predicament and the struggles they face economically and emotionally. In doing so, I ask: (1) How does Lo construct an alternative identity in her time of crisis? and (2) How does Lo use various literacy practices to create a safe space in her time of crisis?

I worked at a community center two days a week helping teens publish their artwork and prose in a local community paper where I met Lo and her friends from the anime affinity group, Inuyasha Central (IC), called Mai and Ava. When I met her, Lo identified as both Native American on her mother's side and Vietnamese on her father's and was the shyest in IC. I met Lo and her IC friends who also love to write, read, and draw everything Inuyasha at the local community center at the start of their eighth grade year. As fanfiction writers of the popular anime series the girls do what Jenkins (1992) refers to as a "borrowing of popular media texts" to produce stories and interact with others with like interests. The Japanese anime series and their shared Southeast Asian heritage in a predominantly African American community is what brought the friends together.

Lo reluctantly began to see me as a trusting adult only after her friends Mai and Ava encouraged her to talk to me about her poetry. It is in this setting that I learned of Lo's famous writing notebook on the internet where Lo wrote most of her poetry and fanfictions. Lo was highly respected as a fan writer in IC as well as a writer and artist online in the affinity space devoted to others who shared an interest in everything Inuyasha. Lo began sharing her poetry long before her fanfictions fearing that adults might not understand fanfiction as a worthy endeavor.

This chapter is informed by four major theoretical perspectives that situate my thinking about Lo as an agent in her time of crisis. Lo is labeled as struggling and difficult inside of school while also being a prolific writer outside of school. Lo's writing becomes even more prolific when her family crisis becomes a central focus. Each perspective accounts for the ways social languages within particular contexts are spoken, negotiated, and contextualized in a dialogic manner. I briefly examine each below to explore the conceptual framework underlying this chapter. The four perspectives are: 1) Moving from language as linguistic representation to language as social representation, 2) Exploring socially situated identity, 3) Investigating movement between Discourse spaces, and 4) Examining Lo's positioning as it relates to the text.

Situating the Four Perspectives: A Sociocultural Framework

Adopting the new Literacy Studies view that literacy is a diverse set of social practices (Alvermann, 2002; Barton & Hamilton, 2000; Gee, 2000, 1996; Hull, 2000; Hull & Schultz, 2001; Street, 1995), this chapter takes ideological practices into account to challenge who participates when literacy is opened up and infused with a dynamic set of possibilities. Literacy accounts for the ways social languages within particular contexts are spoken, negotiated, and contextualized in a dialogic manner. For Lo, this is key to understanding how she incorporated various literacy practices into her life to negotiate her identity in meaningful ways. I briefly examine each below to explore the conceptual framework underlying this chapter.

Perspective 1: Moving from Language as Linguistic Representation to Language as Social Representation

Language as linguistic representation differs from language as social representation. Language as social representation is composed of a myriad of different styles and registers, but this view also recognizes that language is a way to enact a particular socially situated identity. To illustrate, there are ways of speaking to show membership as anime viewer, adolescent girl, hip hop singer, and so forth. Each of these identities highlights a particular "kind of person," or socially situated identity, through the use of a given social language. Bakhtin's (1981, 1986) perspective of social languages allows for a fluid understanding of how English language learners like Lo conform to different contextual spaces within and around powerful discourses. These discourses sometimes intersect and collide to create social language spaces unique to immigrant students like Lo who has a home language different from that used at school. These spaces also can limit or inhibit "safe" spaces where social languages can be acquired or used. For Lo finding a safe space to deal with her anger and frustration was paramount for her to regain her sense of self and dignity when the family was in turmoil. A Bakhtinian perspective also emphasizes that languages belong to no one; we speak from hearing others speak, we understand our perspectives from reading others' words; we use language in all manners to interact with the world. It is within these complex interrelationships that we form our own understandings of who we are in relation to how others see us. This is a helpful heuristic for making sense of Lo who is cognizant that she is read as "his daughter"—the man sent to prison and seen by the community as shocking.

Perspective 2: Exploring Socially Situated Identity

Second, socially situated identity is informed and shaped by specific contexts and activities. In looking at Lo's literacy identities through anime and poetry, I strive to better understand how identities change across context, and how this affects how she attended to various groups in her time of crisis. As Holland, Lachicotte, Skinner, and Cain (1998) affirm, "Identities are improvised—in the flow of activity within specific social situations from the cultural resources at hand" (p. 4). This negotiation of context specific identities and their social languages complicates affiliation for immigrant youth (Skilton-Sylvestor, 2002). That is youth like Lo are constantly negotiating their identities and status in relation to an unstable family, and other socially sanctioned spaces in their everyday lives. For Lo learning how to negotiate her identity with the pressure of her father being sent to prison as well as learning the complexity of a system of laws and courts that directly affects the family.

Perspective 3: Investigating Movement between Discourse Spaces

Gee's approach (1996, 1999) comprises a set of "tools of inquiry" that expose the ways in which language simultaneously creates and reflects its social, cultural, historical, and material contexts of use. Each tool of inquiry (situated meanings, social languages, cultural models, and Discourses) allows the study of a specific layer of meaning-making in talk and texts, showing, too, how these layers combine to create larger meanings, and ultimately, certain kinds of people engaged in certain kinds of activities. The larger discourses at work in Lo's life directly affect her understanding of how these powerful institutions can have a direct impact on her family and how her family, while not directly involved, are impacting her ways of knowing and being. Thus, Lo is shaped by forces larger than herself as she reads the world and words (Freire, 2000) around her to make sense of a father she thought she knew and a society ready to send him away for life.

Perspective 4: Examining Lo's Positioning as it Relates to the Text

In the last perspective, van Langenhove and Harré (1999) provide a lens to critically think about how we are positioned as writers and speakers in various discoursed spaces. This lens offers a way to consider how Lo interacts both in her real and fantasy spaces and how she is in a constant state of positioning and being positioned as she creates a context and a shared identity around her fanfiction writing and characters online. van Langenhove and Harré state:

> [P]ositions can be understood as the discursive construction of personal stories that make a person's actions intelligible and relatively determinate as social acts and within which the members of the conversation have specific locations (p. 397).

Drawing from this, positioning theory offers a way to locate and understand the way power is distributed among members as "storylines" are narrated and linked to ongoing reading and writing of one another in conversations and fanfiction. This is particularly salient because Lo incorporated other storylines and texts to position herself in critical ways to voice her views of events through a lens of crisis.

Pulling Perspectives Together: Reflections on Bakhtin, van Langenhove, and Harré

Drawing from the perspectives of language as social, identities as social, and Discourse spaces enables me to ask new questions about how Lo positioned herself in relation to herself and her family crisis. I use Bakhtin's ideas of dialogism along with van Langenhove and Harré's notion of positioning to understand how Lo relied on various social languages (texts) to situate her identities inside her anime and poetry. Moreover, I hope to understand how she was being viewed by others during her family crisis but more importantly how she could write herself differently even when things in her real life were in disorder (Bakhtin, 1981; van Langenhove and Harré, 1999). Lo was able to successfully navigate varied voices to enact the varied communicative and written practices constituting her worlds (Hanks, 1996), and these practices involved varied symbolic systems and material technologies.

This view of practice as a landscape of varied voices allows me to articulate the processes of enactment occurring in Lo's life as she deals with her father's absence through her fanfiction and pain in her poetry. Furthermore, these stories take on added significance when they become places of collision and inclusion as Lo becomes misunderstood in her peer group and family, thus reflecting the multi-voiced and dialogic nature of the IC girls' interactions. Bakhtin (1986) reminds us that the living voice (word) is not only a semiotic system but also an ideological and lived perspective on the world. While most of us recognize and have experiences of being included/excluded from a peer group or a community setting, this perspective addresses the challenges and identity constructions of immigrant youth such as Lo.

Moreover, through writing Lo positions her identities in the contexts she must traverse every day. Through her written stories and poems, she constructs new social worlds and interacts with them in ways that provide social capital within her peer group. This is central to how Lo's peer group constantly negotiate their identities in these fantasy online spaces as they relate to one another in real time. This complex interplay between the real and the fantasy allowed Lo to see outside her crisis to create a space where she could negotiate and play with her anger in proactive ways to distress. Most importantly it helped her not lose sight of her own relationships with her friends and family despite the many hardships. It is this divergence where positioning as a framework allows for a more nuanced look at how new identities were formed and reconstructed in the process.

Methodology

Context

This study comes from a larger ethnography exploring the in- and out-of-school literacy practices of Southeast Asian adolescent females. Lo and I first met in an after school program for teens struggling with school. In the after school program I worked as a tutor in the "teen room" for homework help. When I first met Lo I told her about my work as a researcher and how I wanted to learn more about youth growing up with languages other than just English. Lo was not an enthusiastic participant at first and was more interested in spending time with her IC friends—Mai and Ava. It was Mai who paved the way for Lo and me by inviting me to listen to Lo share her first short story and in doing so gave me insight into Lo's interest in anime art. Lo and I began sharing anime art as I also enjoyed anime as an adolescent growing up in Japan. When Lo learned I spoke Japanese our relationship blossomed as we had much to share in the after school program.

The after school program at a nearby community center offered Lo a sanctuary from school and home—a place where she and her IC friends could interact and play with language differently than they could at home or school. It was in this space that Lo spoke most openly about her writing and emotions related to her father. The girls were largely left alone at the center and were allowed space and time to be creative. Taking Lo's lead I became acquainted with her Inuyasha peers, Mai and Ava, who shared an affinity around the series and their collective writing practices of taking on the identity of a character from the series. Inuyasha is a popular anime series from Japan where feudal battles take place between feuding clans to decide the fate of the kingdom. Lo's character Inuyasha is also the name of the lead character in the series who battles with his dog-demon and human self. Lo is intrigued by Inuyasha's half breed identity and much of her fan writing centers on this struggle. I followed Lo as she navigated her eighth grade year, documenting how she and her Inuyasha friends incorporated various literacies both in and out of school.

Lo likes to visibly hide in her favorite hooded grey sweatshirt and baggy jeans and has a "don't mess with me" demeanor at school that she had long before her father's crime. Lo is proud of her tough talk and only uses it when necessary but gives the impression that her words can lead to fists if necessary. Lo once explained to me, "You gotta give the impression you'll follow it out no matter—and that's what I be doin."

Data Collection and Analysis

Data were collected over a one-year period to examine Lo's writing practices during her time of crisis. I specifically examined Lo's writing as it related to her understanding of her father's crime, her role as daughter, and her feelings and beliefs about her own personal identity crisis. I also wanted to understand how she changed as her father's role in her life changed. I examined events that Lo deemed important through her writing and talk to unpack the ways in which Lo was making sense of her world. Data sources included field notes, interviews with Lo and her family, interviews with Lo's teachers and Lo's writing both in and out of school. I spent time in the community center, Lo's home, and at school to understand how each space intersected in different ways in Lo's life. In following Lo both in and out of school I spent time in Lo's classes going with her to each class two or three times per week throughout the school year and as a guest in her home spending approximately two or three hours per visit and visiting sometimes twice a week and at other times going only once a month depending on the circumstances at the time. My home visits totaled sixteen throughout the year. All data were analyzed using discourse analysis methods (Fairclough, 1992; Gee, 1996) to unpack how Lo framed her understanding of her family crisis through various events that occurred over the year data was collected. Events included but were not limited to her brother's night in jail, her mother's new job, and Lo's time at a camp for Native American girls. Each event shaped Lo's understanding of her family's crisis in different ways, ultimately helping Lo make sense of the myriad of feelings and beliefs she had about her father's life sentence. I now examine three themes in Lo's writing practices as they relate to her crisis and her personal struggle. Each theme denotes Lo's way of describing and naming her crisis in personal ways.

Crisis Leads to Coping: Writing Safe Places

In doing so, as I mentioned earlier, I examine: (1) How does Lo construct an alternative identity in her time of crisis? (2) How does Lo use various literacy practices to create a safe space in her time of crisis? The three themes are: "Life sucks a big one," "Native girl fights back," and "Pent up anger."

Theme 1: *"Life sucks a big one"*

The above was spoken by Lo to Mai and Ava on the way to school. Lo later shared the conversation and it became an IC joke over the course of the week to see whose life could suck a bigger one. The three girls sometimes walked to school from the community center where they occasionally ate breakfast before school. That morning Lo shared a fanfiction she had written the night before. Most of Lo's fanfictions read like a serial storyline. This fanfiction is new but requires the reader to know that Lo published her work in short one-page installments and each begins where the last fanfiction ended. This is a common practice in the fanfiction community where the media text often leaves the viewer hanging on for the next installment. Lo follows this pattern in her own writing style as well. The previous piece ended with Inuyasha fighting with Miroku, a friend and warrior, on their way to fight Inuyasha's full-demon brother Sesshomaru. The underlined parts of the story highlight the theme of half-breed mutant that is common to Lo's writing after her father leaves the family in crisis. She wrote:

> <u>Inuyasha sits all quiet. I wish I had someone like me to talk to about being a half demon.</u> Something hits Inuyasha hard on the head. He goes into a sleep and feels like he is spinning super fast. He sees all his friends and some of bad people too—people who might be out to hurt him. He wake up and sees that he is by a different tree and next to the tree is Wolverine [character from X-men movie]. Inuyasha sees Wolverine and be all afraid cause he be looking like his brother Sesshomaru. Wolverine says he be hiding. They walk and talk. Inuyasha thinks Wolverine is funny and nice. <u>Wolverine says he is a mutant. Inuyasha thinks it be like him a mutant too cause he feels different and lonely.</u> They walked again. They go to a lake and sit. It is dark but they don't sleep. Inuyasha waits and waits. He sees something swim and there be a girl. She is super pretty and has long hair. She is Mystique [another X-men character]. Wolverine kisses her. Inuyasha hides and sees Miroku. Miroku be watching too. They go back

to the camp and talk. <u>Inuyasha thinks about Kagome but she will never understand what it means to be mutant like</u>. She left him a song. Inuyasha and Miroku listen to the CD.

> Bandanas to Barettes (uh, uh)
> Daisy Dukes to Spandex (all that good wit me)
> I like 'em G-H-E-T-T-O
> Now believe me she got to go (uh, uh)

The song goes on but Inuyasha goes. <u>He sits alone and thinks about the bad people more. He wants to be like others but they can never understand his pain. He be ripped up in little pieces hurt real bad. He can't get out always be mutant halfbreed.</u>

In the above fanfiction Lo combines three media texts to tell her story including X-men characters Wolverine and Mystique and a song by Lil' Bow Wow. She places these outside characters and themes alongside the original media anime characters Inuyasha and Miroku. This hybridization of several popular texts showcases Lo's skills as an avid watcher of media and her ability to combine shared themes of loneliness and identity into one storyline. This was not present before her father's crime and became a new focus for Lo's writing. Lo questions her father's heritage as being part of her own. Inuyasha is a dog demon on the series and struggles with the fact that his brother Sesshomaru (referenced in Lo's fanfiction) is a full demon and more powerful and adored as a result. Wolverine shares a similar identity as a mutant human. Lo often discussed in her IC group feeling like a mutant and shares an identity with these characters in her writing and thinking about no longer wanting to share her father's cultural heritage. She explains:

> Inuyasha he be a half-breed you know he is a dog demon and human—that's his weakness. I'm half-breed too—half Asian and Native. I want to forget my Vietnamese roots—they belong to daddy and they feel dirty now.

As a result of Lo's sense of feeling tarnished being related to her father Lo begins to re-examine her half-breed identity through the character Inuyasha from a different perspective. It is in this writing space that Lo begins to rewrite the text in a powerful way to deal with her pent up anger and frustration. In this rewriting Lo is positioning herself as distant from her father as she can no longer claim to be "daddy's girl" within the crisis that has claimed the family. In the above fanfiction Lo wrote, "<u>Wolverine says he is a mutant. Inuyasha thinks it be like him a mutant too cause he feels different and lonely.</u>" This showcases Lo's feelings of abandonment and her need to distance herself from her father.

While all the girls at some time enter as themselves in the fantasy world of Inuyasha, they are always present within the anime characters themselves.

But even in this multi-voiced characterization they strive for a stance that sometimes reflects "I am the character" (self-as-other positioning) and at other times may reflect "I am like the character" (self-in-other positioning). While subtle, these are important differences in how Lo constantly negotiates her position in the IC peer group through her identity as an anime character in the Inuyasha series. This multi-voiced characterization of being in dialogue with oneself and the anime character simultaneously takes on a complexity and significance in IC that is difficult to grasp. It conveys a meaning beyond the media text and enables Lo to share her half-breed identity without needing to name what is behind it in facing the new realities of her family situation.

The significance of being both (self and other) concurrently is important to Lo's relationship within the peer group and she is able to perform and transform herself as the series, the text, and her lived realities change. This dialogic self creates a new forum in which to think of the authoring "I." While the collective experience creates and negotiates this "I," it is never singular; rather it is both a singular "I" and a multi-voiced "I." That is the use of the indexical pronoun "I" encompasses the voice and traits of her character in real life while also taking her lived realities to the text as a storied character of the Inuyasha series.

Theme 2: "Native girl fights back"

The spring semester of Lo's eighth grade year could not have been harder. Lo was failing. As a struggling student, Lo was fed up with "schoolish practices" and refused to perform for the sake of pleasing her teachers. It is important to take note that the neighboring community near the school was well aware of Lo's family situation. But the crisis was invisible to the teachers and administrators, partially because none of them were living or active in the neighborhood where Lo lived. This is central to the teacher's misreading Lo's anger as being about school when it was more about everything that was happening outside of school. Even though the stakes were high with senior high school the following year, Lo did not see the point in doing well when the things she was asked to do were in her words, "silly things teachers make up cause they be mean."

By talking to Lo's teachers and seeing her record, I discovered that Lo was misdiagnosed in her kindergarten year with mental retardation (term used by teacher and records) because the school did not know that Vietnamese was Lo's first language. Lo spoke both Ojibwa and Vietnamese at home with her family and it was not until all Lo's siblings were school aged that English began to seep into their home. In short, Lo's anger with school did not begin with her father's absence but intensified as a result of her frustration and anger at home.

Thus, Lo began her last semester of her eighth grade year in a dark space. Her teachers suspended her for everything from bad mouthing a teacher to throwing a chair when her anger and frustration fumed out of control one day in her Read180 (Scholastic Reading Program for students reading below grade level). Lo explains why she couldn't take it any more:

> Them teachers be hatin me since I was little. I think the whole world be hatin me this year. I can't stand listening to them read and me repeatin stupid stuff back just so they can check on me reading. I read all the time. They be thinkin I am stupid—I know it. Stupid girl—stupid girl— [mumbling under her breath.]

This outbreak in Lo's reading class led Lo to be considered for home community schooling with some anger management sessions. It was soon learned that the community supported program in Lo's neighborhood was full and no room would be open for more than a month. The social worker intervened and signed Lo up for a Native American girl's camp experience during the school year for a month instead of serving her in house detention at the local community center. Lo remembers:

> I thought they would send me out to the woods to kill me or something. Who knows who these crazy's are takin kids away to a woods an' call it camp. I mean I was cryin when my mom said she thought the social puker [worker] was right and was makin me go. I thought she was gittin rid of me for sure.

Spoken in the past tense Lo remembered the event a month after returning home. As a researcher, I was not allowed to visit Lo at the camp so I am only privy to Lo's description of the time she spent there. When she returned Lo had changed considerably. Her reading teacher describes Lo before and after her camp experience:

> After the chair incident I was relieved to know that Lo was going somewhere besides the community center for school. She had been very angry and there didn't seem to be anything anyone could do. Her mother never returned my calls so I never quite knew what was going on. When I heard Lo went to a Native American girl's camp I was surprised. I never knew Lo was a Native American. She hung out with Mai and Ava so I assumed she was Asian like them. It has never occurred to me Lo was Native American. When Lo came back the first thing she did was apologize. I was so surprised I cried and then Lo started crying. We hugged and it was the first time I think we had ever touched.

The teacher's comments reflect how guarded and untrusting Lo was before camp. While the teacher had made several overtures throughout the school year to try and connect it was not until Lo returned from camp that their relationship began to take shape. While the teacher later learned that Lo's personal life was affecting her school work, the school year was almost over and time was now focused on events leading up to graduation. While the teacher had never connected Lo's cultural heritage as being Ojibwa, events from the year began to take on new significance as the teacher reflected back on things that triggered Lo inside the classroom for no apparent reason at the time. The teacher remembers:

> Knowing what Lo has been through this year—there are some many things that make more sense now—like when we were watching the film by Sherman Alexi [*Smoke Signals*] in the spring and Lo was outraged at it. I had no idea why but she hated the portrayal of the dad and refused to watch or write about it. I think it really hit a nerve for her. She just wasn't ready yet—but as her teacher I couldn't help her sort that out because I had no idea.

Lo returned from camp ten pounds lighter as she reported, "the food sucked so I had to" and she was a little less fearful of life. Lo wrote a lot while away and the biggest change was in her depictions of Inuyasha. Her pre-camp Inuyasha contrasts with her post-camp rendition. It is here that Lo began to embrace her Native American heritage and look more closely at what it meant to be both Native and Vietnamese. In the opening scene of this chapter Lo was working on another post-camp Inuyasha and commented on the change, "See he lookin' more native now. I mean he was just too Asian before—too anime—but now he's like-like real—ya know."

The pre-camp Inuyasha closely resembles the original media text and the Japanese style of drawing common to the manga. In contrast, the post-camp Inuyasha diverges considerably from the text and recreates an Inuyasha dog demon that more closely aligns with a Native American styled mythical creature. I asked Lo to describe the difference in detail but she only said, "He is more like me and he understands. He is like a truth teller and that's what I wanta be."

While I cannot explain what Lo means by her term "truth teller" her writing of Inuyasha changes to reflect a different, more assured Inuyasha and one that differs dramatically from her lonely half-breed Inuyasha. In her fanfictions Lo begins to position herself more and more as a hero and less and less as a lonely half-breed by assuming a more powerful position to speak to her IC peers. It is in her writing we first see evidence of a shift in how Lo perceives her crisis publicly. Her persona as a self assured warrior demon highlights Lo's adaptability during her family's crisis and shows how resilient she has become as a result. Below is an example of fanfiction that resembles many of the new themes in Lo's fanfiction writing.

> Inuyusha is hiding <u>waiting patiently</u> for Naraku to appear. Inuyasha hears perfect and listens as others whisper. Look. I know he is one afraid dog!! everybody knows those spiders in the haunted forest are super poison and he could die! Let him. Inuyasha waits. He wants to <u>jump and surprise him</u>.

Inuyasha walks sooooo still. <u>Waits and waits.</u> <u>Everyone expects him to be</u> <u>dead. He learned spiders are good friends</u>. He has their power now. <u>Naraku will come and he will get even. He will show everyone. Inuyasha</u> <u>will tell them that good can win. Inuyasha knows Naraku's bad and when</u> <u>he is in power he will fight to save the world from all ugly ways.</u>

In this excerpt and many others Lo creates an Inuyasha who waits to get even with the evil Naraku (the name means "hell" in Japanese). It is here that Lo creates a confident Inuyasha who is unafraid of hell. The themes of getting even, waiting patiently, and good prevailing over evil are common in Lo's fanfiction and are well received by her IC peers who are pleased to have their friend back after a long absence. This piece again showcases how Lo builds her relationships with her peers through writing about a part of herself as the character Inuyasha (self-as-other positioning) allowing Lo to be like her anime friend Inuyasha and at times be him in a way that allows her to escape her everyday world and be more than just Lo whose daddy is in prison. Inuyasha and Lo are at times one and the same. Lo speaks of herself as an Inuyasha-like character and as Lo takes on her Ojibwa roots after camp so too does Inuyasha in her drawing. Her poetry meanwhile remains a place for Lo's anger and resentment. Lo confidently shares with me the difference between the two genres:

Fanfiction is more more how do I say it for lots of people and Ava and Mai like my stuff better when it is like the show more. They get it better. But my poetry is like all mine—mine and it be like a place to be like all me. I can say like anything and I don't like haveta care what like anybody be thinkin.

In her own way Lo has made a perfect distinction between public and private writing. Her fanfiction has resumed a public place in her community of IC friends but her poetry remains something personal and private for Lo to share with a distinct few. Thus she positions herself in a way to keep her public and private personas separate. This powerful use of literacy highlights Lo's ability and creativity as she authors herself in a manner that bridges the comfort level of her peers while still affording herself an outlet to be angry and hurt in her poetry.

Theme 3: "Pent up anger"

While Lo was away at Native American camp coming home to see the same sadness was not easy. Lo shared this poem with me the week after she returned:

My stupid Ass Bro
He be stupid

How stupid nobody know
Last night my mommy gotta pick him up
He spent the night drunk in jail
Got into a stupid fight
Over what he don't remember now
Gotta pay a fine for being dumb
Momma be so mad with him
Stupid men
Hope my stupid ass brother don't kicked out
He be close
Momma told him one more stupid thing and he be out [referring to being
kicked out of the house]

The poem describes Lo's eldest brother who had dropped out of school and
taken to "livin around," as Lo described not sleeping at home but "sleeping
wherever he land." With a busy mother working at the casino to make ends
meet, Lo sees her brother dealing with her father's absence in a destructive
way. After sharing the poem Lo remarks:

My daddy would kick his ass if he knew he was drinking. That is the one
BIG rule in the house. No drinking. I can't believe B [name of big brother]
do this to mommy after all she been through. He needs a kick in the ass.
A big one. We don't have money for his legal shit. Momma had to borrow
money to get him out. He don't say nothing. It ain't her fault. He need a
big kick in the ass.

In another poem Lo writes about her feelings on her return home. It reminds
Lo that the home she returned to is not the same since her father's absence.
She writes:

Piss me off
Ain't the same no more around here
We all be done crying and yelling
It quiet now but in a bad way
No talk all pain
He piss me off
 real bad
What he did is shame
Shame cause he ruined a good thing
Good thing we all had
Mom crying in her room at night when nobody be listening but me
She's back to work at the casino
Trying to keep the bill man away
Workin late and sleeping all day
She is never be here

He piss me off
Ain't gotta my momma too busy
All alone
Pissed off

Lo returns to a house where it appears everyone is in their own private mourning. She feels lonely and seeks solace in her words. Poetry begins to consume more and more of Lo's time and she begins bringing her poetry work everywhere leaving fanfiction for Mai and Ava. Lo sits nearby writing frantically about her feelings of hate, her wishes and wants for a better world.

ONE DAY
One day all good then
BOOM
Everything be different
Everything about me different too
I am no longer daddy's girl
I grown
 a woman
Momma says I can't trust like her
I gotta be strong stronger than a man
I gotta use my hate for good
Make it
You gotta make it
Don't depend on nobody
They let you down
I gotta depend on me
Depend on me makin it

The poem "One Day" was written after Lo talked with her mother about her feelings for the first time since her father's departure. Their conversation became the inspiration for the poem and how she needed to grow up and see the world the way it really is. Lo explained the poem "One Day":

Mommy told me can't rely on nobody. I think she be right. After what daddy did how can you trust nobody. Daddy did wrong—and he hurt us. All of us. Mommy wants my life to be different. I got be one of those judges to make the big decisions. Change it all. They looked at daddy and all they see was a bad man not my daddy.

On her return, Lo talked endlessly about her camp time to the point that her friends wanted to hear nothing more about it, as Mai put it sarcastically, "how great it was that Lo got to talk about her feelings and stuff." It was in this tone that Mai and Ava were ready for Lo to move on and put her family crisis behind her. Lo became more distant from her IC group as the school year wore down seeing herself as different and not wanting to play in what she referred to as "their silly girl games."

At school Lo was more distant and quiet than ever before. She did not outwardly rebel against her teachers requests but was resigned to sitting and doing as little as possible. Most of Lo's energy went into writing poetry, rather than fanfiction, as an outlet for dealing with her family's predicament. A few weeks before the end of the year Lo received a formal letter informing her she had mandatory summer school in order to enter high school the following school year. I was at Lo's house when the letter came. Lo numbly remarked:

> It ain't that big a deal. I mean so what summer school is better than doin nothn' round here. It'll keep me outta trouble for sure. Last year I was so bored there be nothing to do all day. Now I gotta go to this all day but I failed eighth grade cause I'm stupid.

Resigned to calling herself stupid, Lo feared going back to school to fail again. Most of Lo's poems were written after her father left the family for good. Neither writing practice was given space inside of school. Lo felt that her literacy practices did not matter. On asking her why she did not share any of them with teachers Lo explained: "My fanfic don't count—they'd laugh Mai and Ava don't either. We all think the teachers be thinkin' we're silly doing that. My poetry is mine. It ain't for them." While Lo uses writing to constructively deal with her crisis in a proactive manner, she is unable and unwilling to make the move to showcase her talents as a fan author and poet in school. It is evident that Lo is angry and frustrated at the turn of events in her life but she is also positioning herself in ways that allow her to vent anger in ways that give her voice in her own terms and in her own way. Lo has learned that writing has the potential to be a powerful tool but she has also learned that school might co-opt and ruin the one space that she has successfully defined and created for herself. It is because of this, I believe, that Lo successfully hid her writing to keep herself and her words safe from the very people who hold power.

Conclusion and Implications

Examining Lo's literacy practices around Inuyasha and poetry through a wider literacy lens is of critical importance. Drawing from the perspectives of social languages, identities, and Discourse spaces allows educators to question how youth position themselves in relation to their communities, schooling, and themselves. Using Bakhtin's ideas of dialogism and Harré's notion of positioning we understand the complex interrelationships Lo took as she authored her identity through the anime character, Inuyasha, to understand her daily lived experiences in relation to her crisis.

Literacy as a Tool for Crisis

Lo wrote to understand, to know, and to redefine her relationship with her family, friends, and even herself as she saw the world as an ugly place when her daddy was sent to prison. Using literacy as her tool for knowing and reflecting, we gain an image of an adolescent successfully directing her anger, frustration, and loss through words. In her fanfiction Lo navigates an identity through Inuyasha, a character Lo describes as resembling her own fractured sense of self as she and Inuyasha each struggle with their heritage and upbringing in two different cultures. Through poetry Lo learns to vent her anger on the page rather than to lash out at others in destructive ways. She discovers that writing provides her a special space to redefine in her own terms what it means to be in crisis.

Creating Safe Spaces for Youth

The after school space provided Lo with a safe haven to write and create without inhibition and fear that she and her work would not "measure up." In contrast the classroom appeared to limit Lo in her abilities and created what Leander and Sheehy (2004) argue is the difference between thick and thin learning space. Lo's writing practices were situated in a context that allowed for fluid and flexible moments for learning and socialization. Lo's writing was meaningful in the after school context because it was collaborative, social, and purposeful. It helped Lo redefine herself and her crisis, and as a thin space gave her opportunities to redefine what it means to use writing for identity making purposes.

The classroom, in contrast for Lo, was a thick space and unsafe because it was designed for a monologic flow of information between teacher and student. In this context there was no space for Lo to creatively express her frustration and anger about her father's crime and her family's hardship. She was limited and forced into a production model of activities and assessments. Students in a thin space, however, "are not focusing on the object in order to reproduce it ... rather they are claiming their own object, expressly to situate themselves in specific power relations"(p. 100). Lo claimed her fanfiction and poetry in the thin space of the after school program and was able to design an identity around her crisis that was both productive and creative. As educators we can learn from after school spaces and other third spaces in youth lives to design safe havens that can assist students like Lo to find innovative ways to understand the power of literacy in their lives.

As educators it is critical to learn from Lo's crisis about how the classroom has the potential to be an identity making space. All learning is an identity making endeavor. By accepting students' needs and interests we can create safe havens. Lo taught me to rethink what we mean by safe spaces—spaces where youth can be themselves and feel free to express what they know and see. Lo learned the power of language on her own—imagine if the classroom provided yet another outlet for her to negotiate her crisis privately and publicly?

References

Alvermann, D. (Eds.). (2002). *Adolescents and literacies in a digital world*. New York: Peter Lang Publishing, Inc.

Bakhtin, M. M. (1981). *The dialogic imagination: Four essays by M. M. Bakhtin* (C. Emerson, & M. Holquist, Eds.), (M. Holquist, Trans.). Austin: University of Texas Press.

Bakhtin, M. M. (1986). *Speech genres and other late essays* (C. Emerson, & M. Holquist, Eds.), (V. W. McGee, Trans.). University of Texas Press Slavic Series, no. 8. Austin: University of Texas Press.

Barton, D., & Hamilton, M. (2000). Literacy practices. In D. Barton, M. Hamilton, & R. Ivanic (Eds.), *Situated literacies: Reading and writing in context* (pp. 180–196). London: Routledge.

Fairclough, N. (1992). *Discourse and social change*. Boston, MA: Blackwell Publishers.

Freire, P. (2000). *Pedagogy of the oppressed* (M. Bergman Ramos, Trans.). New York: Continuum International Publishing Group.

Gee, J. P. (1996). *Social linguistics and literacies: Ideology in discourses* (2nd ed.). London: Falmer Press.

Gee, J. P (1999). *An introduction to discourse analysis: Theory and method*. New York: Routledge.

Gee, J. P. (2000). The new literacy studies: From socially situated to the work of the social. In D. Barton, M. Hamilton, & R. Ivanic (Eds.), *Situated literacies: Reading and writing in context* (pp. 180–196). London: Routledge.

Hanks, W. F. (1996). *Language and communicative practices*. Boulder, CO: Westview Press.

Holland, D., Lachicotte, W., Skinner, D., & Cain, C. (1998). *Identity and agency in cultural worlds*. Cambridge, MA: Harvard University Press.

Hull, G. (2000). Critical literacy at work. *Journal of Adolescent and Adult Literacy, 43*(1), 648–665.

Hull, G., & Schultz, K. (2001). Literacy and learning out of school: A review of theory and research. *Review of Educational Research, 71*(4), 575–612.

Jenkins, H. (1992). *Textual poachers: Television fans and participatory culture*. New York: Routledge, Chapman and Hall.

Leander, K., & Sheehy, M. (Eds.). (2004). *Spatializing literacy research and practice*. New York: Peter Lang.

Skilton-Sylvester, E. (2002). Literate at home but not at school: A Cambodian girls' journey from playwright to struggling writer. In G. Hull, & K. Schultz (Eds.), *School's out: Bridging out of school literacies with classroom practice* (pp. 61–90). New York: Teachers College Press.

Street, B. (1995). *Social Literacies: Critical approaches to literacy development, ethnography and education*. London: Longman.

van Langenhove, L., & Harré, R. (1999). Introducing positioning theory. In R. Harré, & L. van Langenhove (Eds.), *Positioning theory* (pp. 14–31). Malden, MA: Blackwell Publishers.

For Further Exploration

Inuyasha fanfiction: www.inuyasha-fiction.com.

Working with Children of Prisoners: ncfy@acf.hhs.gov.

Native American Youth: www.hud.gov/offices/pih/ih/codetalk/planet/index.html.

8 Disability Identification

Shifts in Home Literacy Practices

Gisele Ragusa

Introduction

> "We didn't read, we didn't play much, I just couldn't. I was a basket case, and maybe, so was she [Kelly, her daughter]. I feel really bad about this now, and I suppose I did then but, I just could not cope!"

These were the words Kelly's mother used to describe her life immediately after receiving her daughter's autism diagnosis. This chapter focuses on the crisis experienced immediately following identification of childhood disability. The effects of this crisis are multi-scaled and are experienced in full force by the affected child's parents and their extended family. This study was inspired by my experiences working specifically with a resource center for families of children with disabilities and more generally with families of children with disabilities in diverse urban settings (Ragusa, 2007).

The Social Context of Disability in the United States

The incidence of disability in children is on the rise nationally, making this a large-scale crisis. Estimates derived from the National Center for Health Statistics (NCHS, 2004) between 1983 and 2004 indicate a significant increase in childhood disability, with incidences increasing from 5.8% to 6.8% of the non-institutionalized population under age 21. Survival from a wide spectrum of diseases and childhood traumas has improved phenomenally because of innovative medical advances, however these advances have left many fragile children significantly disabled (NIH, 2008). Disabling conditions across the spectrum dramatically affect family functioning, family mental health, and, ultimately, children's mental and physical health.

Research has indicated that family members are profoundly traumatized when their child receives a disability diagnosis. Significant psychological reactions resulting from these diagnoses (Colobro, 1990) include stress, depression, anxiety, and a host of other mental health reactions associated with this crisis. Shifts in parenting practices and familial routines also result from diagnoses.

In particular, familial home literacy experiences are significantly altered during the process (Turnbull & Turnbull, 1997). While Turnbull and Turnbull studied this phenomenon, their work focused specifically on supporting parents in the identification process rather than focusing on the specific role that literacy can play in mediating stress during the identification process. Accordingly, literacy practices are affected by factors including socioeconomic status (SES), social capital, support structures, and educational structures (Portes, 1998).

Theoretical Framework Associated with Crisis in Child Disability Identification

This chapter describes the changes in home literacy practices occurring when families receive a child disability diagnosis. It is informed by a combined social cognitive and sociocultural theoretical frame connected to two additional perspectives: (1) a theory of hope and (2) a need for social capital to describe literacy events and familial learning associated with disability diagnoses. Using these interconnected socially connected frames as tenets, Alexander (2007) describes theoretical approaches to learning and associated experiences as being epistemologically grounded. Figure 8.1 illustrates how contemporary learning theories are situated epistemologically in multi-dimensional spaces in families' lives.

Figure 8.1 provides the theoretical lens that informed my review on family crises research related to disability and the analyses of the data in the study that I present in this chapter. Accordingly, research has indicated that parental reaction, accommodation, and coping with identification of disability

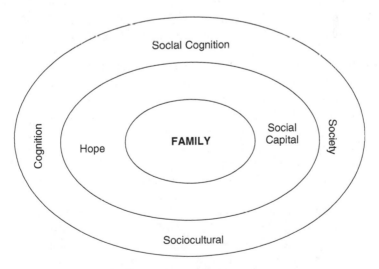

Figure 8.1 Theoretical schema: Reactions to disability identification.

is socially situated in the context of family development. Additionally, the sociocultural contexts of families inform the way disability identification affects literacy experiences in the home and the role that literacy experiences play in crisis related coping.

Currently, no research has been conducted that focuses on changes in home literacy patterns as a function of disability identification. Additionally, no research situates literacy in parental coping strategies and management of having children with disabilities. Further, there is no research available that informs parents about increasing resiliency during the disability identification process through particular literacy practices.

The Theoretical Link between Home Literacy Practices and Child Outcome

Much of the literacy research supports the perspective that literacy development is connected to social interactions occurring via literacy experiences, a social cognitive perspective on development. Vygotsky (1962) theorized that human development is directly connected to the degree and quality of interaction between the child and the assistance of a primary caregiver. Vygotsky's perspective purports that assisted performance is embedded in the everyday interactions between caregiver and child through the natural order of daily events. Utilizing this perspective as a guide in a home literacy study, Teale (1986) examined home background influences on young children's literacy development. Teale was interested in understanding how cultural background affects children's home literacy experiences and how that in turn affects literacy development. Teale's research indicates that children are diversely involved in literacy at home during the course of everyday experiences. There was a considerable range in quality and organization of social structures of literacy interaction. Parental knowledge and experience with literacy at home were better predictors of literacy development than socio-economic status (SES).

Similarly, in her study of literacy interaction with low-income families, Purcell-Gates (1996) identified social structures between parents and children in home literacy practices. These structures included literacy practices related to: work, religion, daily living routines, entertainment, participation in information network, storybook time, interpersonal communication, school/program related activity, literacy for the sake of teaching, and learning literacy. Purcell-Gates qualitatively analyzed the literacy mediated social structures in homes and found that low-income families engaged in diverse social structures around literacy.

Both Teale's and Purcell-Gates' studies described families in everyday routines without any significant crisis identified. The social structures identified in these two studies provide a typical baseline for home literacy practices in families. The study described in this chapter employs these structures as baseline comparisons for families and explores changes that occur in home literacy practices resulting specifically from encountering disability identification.

Risk and Resilience in Families Whose Children are Identified with Disabilities

Research on stress, coping, and resilience in parents of children with disabilities has yielded variable findings. Rahman, Harrington, and Bunn (2002) indicated an association between depression and stress in mothers. Children had an increased risk of delay after being identified with a disability. Family poverty and challenging behavior in the disabled child exacerbate parent stress (Singhi, Goyal, Pershad, Singhi, & Walia, 1990).

In spite of the stress related to the crisis of child disability identification and associated aftermath, many families demonstrate relatively significant resilience and coping abilities post identification (Hartshorne, 2002; Horton & Wallander, 2001; Smith, Oliver, & Innocenti, 2001). The need for information, knowledge of disability management, and support from professionals have been identified as management strategies that parents develop during child disability identification (Behr & Murphy, 1993; Chen and Simeonsson, 1994). When parents are effective in using these strategies, their resilience increases, allowing them to manage the crises that they encounter. Accordingly, they are able to move forward within the disability crisis and, ultimately, help their child. This phenomenon may be attributed to increased social capital in the disability arena (Portes, 1998). By this I mean that families who have social capital, or the knowledge and support to navigate informational and support systems, may manage disability related crises at a faster pace and with greater efficiency.

In a study related to familial coping strategies and reaction to disability identification, Behr and Murphy (1993) presented a model of "cognitive coping" and its role of adaptation to disability identification. In their Family Perception Research Project, cognitive coping patterns were measured in parents experiencing child disability identification. Three interrelated cognitive coping themes emerged: (1) gaining mastery and control, (2) searching for meaning or purpose, and (3) enhancing self-esteem. Within these cognitive coping themes, processes or coping strategies and associated beliefs or perceptions were embedded. This schema was utilized in my disability related research to codify coping strategies associated with child disability identification directly connected to changes in family literacy practices (Ragusa, 2007).

In related research on parent reaction to disabilities, Dunst and Dempsey (2007) revealed that professional support assists parents of disabled children in developing strategies that promote family empowerment. These strategies include: information seeking, control, and collaborative goal setting. Dunst and Dempsey identify help-seeking (or information seeking) as a strategy that leads parents from crisis to empowerment. While Dunst and Dempsey do not directly address literacy as an avenue of parental help-seeking in their research, they purport that through help-seeking and information gathering (which are often achieved through reading informational materials), parents are able to better cope with child disability identification.

The research on child disability identification is diverse. Coping strategies and family support have been found to positively influence family resilience during this crisis. Cognitive coping strategies including information seeking and professional support provision have helped parents to cope with the crisis of child disability identification. The role of literacy to serve as a medium for these strategies has not been examined. The study I present here examines disability identification, accompanying changes in family literacy practices, and strategies that parents have found helpful in managing this crisis.

Methodological Approach to Identifying Family Literacy Practices during Child Disability Identification

I used a mixed design, case study approach to examine the changes in home literacy practices of parents who have recently learned that their child has a disability. Parent interviews and semi-structured home observations served as sources of data. This study answers the following research questions: (1) What is the nature of the home literacy experiences in families when their children are identified as having a disability? (2) What factors associated with having a child with a newly identified disability affect the child's frequency and types of home literacy experiences?

The Families

The study participants consisted of seven families with children between the ages of four and eight who recently received a disability diagnosis. All families in the study had low incomes. The focal children had diverse disabilities ranging from developmental delay (significant functional delays) to autism. Table 8.1 describes the participant families' disability type, ethnicity, SES, and family constellation.

I used a purposeful sampling procedure of recruiting families who had recently received their child's diagnosis and had visited a resource center for families of children with disabilities for study participants. I selected families whose children had diverse and highly representative disabilities in the general population. This sampling procedure was applied in an effort to explore differences in family constellation and disability type and the role that these differences played in literacy practice changes occurring during child disability identification.

Table 8.1 Family constellation

Child's Name*	Ethnicity	Number of Adults	Number of Siblings	Total Number of People	Disability Type
Christiano	Hispanic	3	1	4	Devel. Delay
Karly	European American	1	2	3	Cerebral Palsy
Kelly	European American	2	1	3	Autism
Kevin	Hispanic	1	3	4	Fragile X
LaRhonda	African American	1	0	1	Devel. Delay
Lauren	European American	1	0	1	Deafness
Michael	Asian	3	0	3	Autism

Note
* Pseudonyms were utilized.

The Parent Interviews

At the beginning of the study, I conducted a conversational style interview in each family's home. This allowed for free flow of interaction and maximized the opportunity for open information sharing. I began by asking the parents to identify critical issues that emerged once their child was identified with a disability with attention to: 1) how their lives changed as a result of their child's disability, 2) the events that occurred during and immediately following their child's identification, 3) the literacy practices that they engaged in before, during and after their child was identified and 4) changes in these home literacy practices that may have been a function of the child's disability.

The Home Observations

The interview information guided me in selecting exemplary opportunities for conducting home observations that included literacy interactions. I explained that I wanted to capture as much information as possible associated with their in-home reading practices, but that I wanted the families to maintain their typical daily routines. I attempted to limit my participation while observing, however, occasionally the families interacted with me and included me in their routines. As an example of this, one family had a nightly routine of everyone reading individually so I brought a book and read alongside them.

Pulling the Crisis Together—Making Sense, Documenting Trends

In an effort to systematically capture the families' story, I coded, compiled, and categorized the interview and observational data using closed set qualitative techniques to document the unique home literacy experiences of children with disabilities and their families using a combined schema that I derived from Luterman's (1999) research on parents of children with disabilities and adaptations of categorical analyses from Teale's (1986) and Purcell-Gates' (1996) research. The emotive categories that I adapted from Luterman's research included: *inadequacy, anger, guilt, vulnerability,* and *confusion.* These categories were used to code the data as they best fit the descriptors that the parents provided during their interviews and some observational anecdotes.

The codes that I used to categorize the literacy related data from the interviews and observation combined social categories from Teale's work (*parent–child, child alone, parent alone, reference to stress when discussing literacy practices,* and *information seeking*) and Purcell-Gates' mediated literacy events, (*work, religion, daily living routines, entertainment, information network, storybook time, interpersonal communication, school related,* and *literacy for teaching*). I compared the data from field notes and interviews so that a comprehensive description of the home literacy experiences and factors associated with the experiences of a family with a newly identified disabled child was accurately portrayed. I wanted to present a comprehensive picture of the families to fully capture the story of the role that literacy plays in mediating disability crisis. Once each data set was analyzed, I engaged in cross-family pattern-matching to highlight similarities and differences in home literacy experiences across the participant families. I used HyperResearch 2.7 (a computer-based qualitative analyzer tool, 2007) to complete the data analyses and to "quantify" the coded results as frequency distributions so that the saliency of particular elements of the data could be illuminated. In the pages that follow, I describe the ways in which the parents described their experiences during their child's disability diagnoses. Each family had unique yet interrelated experiences to share during their times of crises.

My observational data collection focused on family–child interaction, literacy artifacts, social structures, and mediating factors related to literacy experiences. Evidence for each home visit description came from more than 28 combined hours of home observations. In terms of timing of my visits, I observed the families as closely after their child's identification as possible. The observational process and protocol from which I recorded my field notes contained elements of the methods used in studies conducted by Teale (1986) and Purcell-Gates (1996) as previously described in this chapter. Attention was directed toward family–child interaction and engagement in literacy using Purcell-Gates and Teale's "typical" literacy social constructs, because I sought to compare typical home literacy experiences to those in families who recently received their child's disability identification.

Hearing their Voices—the Ebb and Flow of Emotions: Hope and Fear, Vulnerability and Confusion

Hearing the parents' voices underscored that having their children identified with a disability was emotional, stressful, and impactful. Accordingly, I had pages and pages of emotion laden transcripts to analyze post interviews. These transcripts were rich with feeling based details of the identification process. In the pages that follow, I have included interview excerpts that paint a picture of the intense emotions experienced by each family. The excerpts are but a few examples of the emotive, coping, and resilience related responses that the parents made to the interview questions. The responses illustrate the perceived impact of the crisis associated with having a newly identified disabled child. One interview excerpt captures much of the flavor of what the parents shared during the interview data:

> My heart sunk when I sat in the doctor's office with Karly in my lap. I clung tightly to her as if she was gonna help me through it. I didn't want her to see me cry cuz I thought it would scare her, so I pulled her against me and leaned forward with my head in my knees. I just stayed there till the pain passed.

This mother's description illustrates the immediate shock and pain that the parents described when hearing their child's diagnosis. It also exemplifies their immediate efforts to manage the information and their attempts to protect their child from the pain that may follow the diagnosis.

Karly's mother was not the only mother who discussed her vulnerability and pain. Michael's mother described her visit with the pediatrician when her child's diagnosis was announced similarly. She said:

> I just knew something was up. He didn't look at me. We would go to the park or to his cousins, and he just didn't play like the other kids. At first we were happy, he kinda entertained himself. It was kinda like he didn't like his toys. He liked opening and closing doors and hitting himself on the floor. It really scared me. When we went to the doctor, I almost didn't want to know. But I had to. Then he dropped the bomb. He had it. But I didn't want to know it. I felt so raw, like I was so open to everyone.

Michael's mother discussed her immediate vulnerability and the confusion she experienced. She also talked about "not wanting to know" but knowing that a diagnosis was inevitable.

As I listened intently to the families, I noticed distinct patterns and trends in their descriptions. I attempted to categorize their responses, to recognize patterns among the participants. This led me to decide that using an analytical schema of categories and codes would be useful in organizing and painting a picture of the data intensity (See Table 8.2). In the information that follows, I provide exemplars of each of the emotive categories that surfaced during the interviews.

In the days immediately following receiving their child's diagnosis, parent responses included: "I felt like I had been stabbed in the heart." "I felt frozen in time." "I was so weak, and so emotional .... no control at all." I categorized these responses in the category, *vulnerability* (Luterman, 1999) as the parents who described these feelings indicated having little control over their emotions. When asked about their feelings about their child's disability diagnosis, one parent stated that she believed that she "was being punished." This comment was categorized as *guilt*, a term which has appeared in the literature on child-hood disability as a common feeling that parents experience post diagnosis (Turnbull & Turnbull, 1997). During an interview, another parent commented that she felt "ready to burst" after her child was diagnosed. She described "snapping at everyone." These parent comments were categorized as *anger* from my emotive schema. *Anger* has been identified in literature on grief related to disability identification as a common process that parents cycle through post diagnosis (Moses, 1987).

When I asked what the parents did to cope with the disability identification, one parent said that she "slept" because she "couldn't do anything right anymore." This comment was categorized as *inadequacy* from the schema. *Inadequacy* is also noted as a common feeling associated with the early stages of grief during the process of disability diagnosis (Turnbull & Turnbull, 1997). One parent discussed feeling "clueless to the diagnosis" during her parent interview. This comment was categorized as *confusion*. I posit that *confusion* may be closely related to and a precursor to *information seeking*, a pattern identified in the literature in previous studies associated with disability that noted that parents sought information as a means for resolving their *confusion* about their child's diagnosis.

The parents' discussions of literacy practices reinforced my expectations of changes in practices associated with disability identification. In an effort to connect the parents' report of changes in home literacy patterns to descriptions of these practices, I asked the parents to describe the kinds of reading and writing that occurred in their homes post diagnosis. *Stress* (Luterman, 1999) emerged as a primary limiting factor related to literacy experiences. As one parent described:

> Well …. I think I would like to read, most of what I read comes from Michael's therapist. It's about him, it makes me sad … and mad. I can't always hang with it … I want my old life back. The world can't only be about the big A [autism]. There must be more out there. The hard thing is that I never see or read anything good about autism. It's a doomed picture.

This quote illustrates the complexity of feelings and impact of *stress* that accompanies the disability diagnosis. Interestingly, the parents continued to make reference to *stress* and preoccupation with their feelings about their child's diagnosis (38.2%) as a rationale for why their literacy experiences were minimal, altered, or absent post diagnosis. One parent described this *stress* in her comment:

> LaRhonda and I went from doctors' appointments to school evals. to speech evals. It really took us 6 months to get her diagnosis. I really thought I wanted to know … that I could have peace once I knew … but … I still haven't gotten to the peace. I really wish we didn't have the diagnosis sometimes. It seems so final.

Table 8.2 Frequency of emotive/crisis statements associated with disability identification

Emotive Category	f	%
Anger	3	7.7
Confusion	11	28.2
Guilt	6	15.4
Inadequacy	10	25.6
Vulnerability	9	23.1
	N=39	100

Source: adapted from Luterman, 1999, p. 67.

LaRhonda's parent described the feelings of many families as they attempt to navigate the systems associated with disability diagnosis. *Stress* continued to be a primary factor affecting home literacy experiences of the study participants (38.2%) even when attention in our interviews was shifted from descriptions of feelings about having a child with a disability to home literacy experiences. The parents linked their stress to limited reading opportunities for their child in addition to increases in *information seeking* reading for themselves as a means of coping and managing the diagnosis. The high level of family stress illuminates the scale of this crisis and explains the infrequency of child focused literacy experiences in addition to the change in nature of described home literacy interactions.

It is clear that the parents recognized a shift in literacy practice away from their child and toward their own *information seeking* as a consequence of the diagnosis. Table 8.3 represents the frequency distribution by type of home literacy experiences (Teale, 1986) reported by the families as well as the social structures associated with the experiences described during the parent interviews.

Interestingly, only thirty-four interview responses related to home literacy for the seven parent participants in more than eleven hours of discussion combined. Even when I deliberately focused the interviews on literacy, the

Table 8.3 Frequency of reported statements related to literacy experiences/structures

Literacy Structure	f	%
Child Alone	2	5.9
Information seeking	11	32.4
Parent Alone	6	17.6
Parent–Child	2	5.9
Reference to stress when discussing literacy practices	13	38.2
	N=34	100

Source: adapted from Teale (1986).

parents continued to discuss *stress* and other emotions in their discussions of literacy in their homes. As an example, Lauren's mom commented:

> I would love to read more with her. Here's what I do. I'm so stressed out that I mostly look up everything I can about being deaf on the internet. There are wars about what to do out there with a deaf kid. Do you sign to them? Do you put the hearing aids on? Do you give em surgery? I don't know. It's freakin' me out. No matter what I do it'll be wrong for someone.

Reports of *stress* were frequent during the interview discussions describing the families' home literacy experiences. This excerpt provides a taste of the dilemmas that the parents encountered post diagnosis. This mom discussed the Deaf Culture wars and parental *stress* accompanying them. Additionally, she referenced her efforts of using literacy to cope with the identification and the changes in practices that she engaged in resulting from receiving her daughter's diagnosis.

Changes in Patterns and Practices in Home Literacy

In analyzing the frequency and distribution of types of literacy descriptions provided by the parents, I noted distinct patterns. Thirteen out of thirty-four (38.2%) literacy-referenced responses were related to *stress* in the parent interviews. The coping skill, *information seeking*, was also prevalent with total percentages of interactions reported accounting for 32.4% of the total responses. The high incidence of *stress* and *information seeking* supports the perspective that parents shift their practices away from their child directly in favor of solo experiences associated with *information seeking* post disability diagnosis, a strategy identified by Dunst and Dempsey (2007) as a mechanism for coping with the identification of child disability. I also noted a dominant occurrence in the parent interviews related to *stress* over concerns that the parents had for their newly diagnosed child. Parents described their feelings in terms of *vulnerability, guilt, confusion, anger* and *inadequacy*. The *stress* theme persisted during the parent interviews even when the parents described changes in home literacy experiences. This speaks to the importance of *information seeking* as a viable coping strategy during disability related crises.

Seeing Their Stories in Action—Home Literacy Practices Post Diagnosis

While it was important to hear the parents describe their crises associated with disability identification via the parent discussions, it was also necessary to witness the families' literacy practices in action post disability diagnosis as a means of verifying their responses. In observations, I noted much *information seeking*

Table 8.4 Comparison of total number of literacy events by family constellation

Child's Name	Total Number of Observed Literacy Interactions	Number of Adults	Number of Siblings	Total Number of People	Extended Family Visits
Christiano	15	3	1	4	Yes
Karly	6	2	0	2	No
Kelly	12	1	2	4	No
Kevin	10	1	0	1	Yes
LaRhonda	12	1	0	1	No
Lauren	11	2	0	2	Yes
Michael	9	2+1	1	4	Yes

occurring in the families' homes. *Networking* (particularly via email) was also prevalent. I noted significant diversity in the home literacy experiences of the seven participant families. Their experiences varied greatly in structures, frequency, and types of literacy artifacts during the home observations. Table 8.4 reveals the total number of literacy events observed in each home coupled with the number of people who either cohabited the family home or visited it regularly. (Pseudonyms were used to protect the anonymity of the participants.)

Again, as I did with the parent interviews, I quantified this data to illustrate patterns and structures that the parents exhibited in their homes. Interestingly, the number of adults in the family home was directly connected to the frequency of literacy interactions observed. Based on calculated total, the greater the number of adults found in the home, the more frequent the literacy interaction. In particular, the single-parent households had lower incidences of literacy interactions than the two-parent households. The child, Christiano, with the highest occurrence of literacy events had extended family members living in his home. Christiano's parents and grandmother co-resided with him. During the home observations, this triad of adults offered support for one another, which by observation appeared to lessen their observable stress. The three adults acted as a team, providing care and assistance to Christiano and to each other. Interestingly, this family demonstrated great diversity in social structures associated with literacy-mediated interactions. Of special consideration is the fact that this family found time to read for *entertainment* and for *storybook reading*. Most exemplary for this family is the fact that one book that the family read regularly with Christiano had a main character in it with a disability. This may have provided an important example of typicality for Christiano.

Storybook reading and reading for *entertainment* were rarely observed in the remaining six families' homes. In addition, all three family members in Christiano's household expressed interest in literacy and described growing up reading in their homes, suggesting a multi-generational value of literacy, to the point that it was an everyday routine in the household. This family was observed to engage in joint *information seeking* for the sake of mutual support

Table 8.5 Total frequency distribution of literacy events related to disability diagnoses found in all seven family homes compared with Purcell-Gates' data

Social Structure Associated with Literacy	Frequency Distribution		
	f	% Current Study	% Purcell-Gates
Work	3	4.9	0.8
Religion	7	11.5	2.1
Daily Living Routines	4	6.5	32.3
Entertainment	2	3.2	25.8
Participation in Information Network	15	24.5	1.5
Storybook Time	5	8.2	5.8
Interpersonal Communication	8	13.1	10.5
School/Program-Related Activity	9	14.8	12.3
Literacy for the Sake of Teaching and Learning Literacy	8	13.1	9.1
	N=61	100	100

Note
N= Total events recorded across all seven participant families.

of one another and attempts to understand Christiano's disability. The family used technology-mediated print including email and web searches in addition to hard copy print materials as explicit forms of *information seeking*. Interestingly, all of the observed families used the internet for *information seeking* during the observations. However, the amount of *information seeking* observed and described by Christiano's family far exceeded the other families in my study sample.

Table 8.5 reveals the frequency distribution of each social structure related to literacy events found across the seven families. Additionally, in an effort to describe potentially atypical patterns in literacy practices, I compared these literacy patterns to those in Purcell-Gates' study (1996) in the table. The comparison indicates significant differences in patterns between the families in my study and those in Purcell-Gates' study. The socio-demographics were comparable in the two studies, however the families in my study had an additional variable of a childhood disability.

In reviewing Table 8.5, it appears that the two categories *Entertainment* and *Daily Living Routines* were dominant structures in the homes of the typically developing children (Purcell-Gates, 1996). This is very different for the families targeted in my study. The data were disbursed with greater variability in the families that I observed. Literacy was very much a part of the families' lives in both the Purcell-Gates study and in my study. *Participation in Information Network* was the dominant category that emerged in my study with a frequency of 24.5%. This finding is supported by my interview data as the dominant category found in interview data was *Information Seeking*. This appears by comparison to be much higher than the "typical" families portrayed in

Purcell-Gates' study. Accordingly, Purcell-Gates' families had greater incidence of literacy for *Daily Living Routines* and *Entertainment* than *Participation
in Information Network*. In contrast, it was noted that all families in my study had
busy lives and were preoccupied with the disability diagnosis through the
parents' report as well as through observation during my home visits. I infer
that families without crises are more likely to engage in *entertainment* related
literacy practices. This is demonstrated in the literature with typically developing preschoolers and primary age students across home literacy studies
(Purcell-Gates, 1996; Teale, 1986).

A different phenomenon exists for families engaging in special education
services as a result of their child's diagnosis. It appeared during observations
that the families in my study had such busy lives that they had little time for
storybook reading with their children (8.2%) or for reading for *entertainment*
(3.2%). The busy lifestyle of the families decreased the frequency of literacy
activities in the households overall. The observed home experiences either
focused on adult related *information network* (24.5%) or *school/program-
related activities* (14.8%). The high incidence of *school/program-related activities*,
while it does not mirror that of *information network*, may be accounted
for by the parents' introduction to special education services as a result of their
child's disability diagnosis. Additionally, these results imply that parents
attempted to be proactive in addressing their child's disability related
educational needs.

Discussion: Meanings for Families

Key findings in this study reveal that families shift their reading practices from
reading for pleasure to a mode of *reading for information* when their child receives a
disability diagnosis. I found that informational texts (brochures, web based
information sheets, therapeutic related materials, etc.) were dominant literacy
artifacts used during the crisis of disability identification, centered primarily
on accessing information related to the diagnosis in addition to reading
help-seeking information. Reading shifted from hard copy text to internet-
based text post diagnosis. A shift in the dynamics of literacy experiences was
also noted. It appears from the frequency distribution in my data that engaging, child-centered, interactive experiences were replaced with soloist information gathering reading activities, coupled with literacy experiences in which
the child learns vicariously from observing the parent and then imitates the
reading behavior. Additionally, parents reported a decreased interest in books
by the child during the identification process. Parents noted that siblings were
affected by these experiences in similar ways, indicating the scale of the impact
of the diagnosis.

It became clear during my study that the lives of families of children
with disabilities are much more complicated than those of families with "typically" developing children. I noted that families' lives in my study were complicated by stress associated with having a child made vulnerable by disability.

These families lived in constant worry during the first several months post disability identification causing them significant stress. Uncertain and unexpected futures complicated the families' lives, and stress associated with new, time consuming, complicated services related to their child's disability abounded. The literature on family stress and support (Dunst & Dempsey, 2007) documents that high levels of family stress can adversely affect the development of a healthy child. Ironically, the interventions prescribed by professionals that are meant to stimulate the child's development and to alleviate developmental compromise, such as reported by my families, added stress to their lives. From this, I infer that if the parents have social capital (Portes, 1998), they may be better able to navigate the medical and educational systems, however the finality of the diagnosis nearly always results in expressions of loss and stress. Figure 8.2 presents a visual model of the interconnected nature of the phenomena that were documented during my study as they relate to family stress and their affect on home literacy experiences post child disability diagnosis.

The model in Figure 8.2 provides a strong rationale for increasing the fully available information and related support provided to families during the time that they are coping with their child's new diagnosis.

Interestingly, the exemplary family in my study, Christiano's family, appeared via observation to have reared a highly stable child, developmentally.

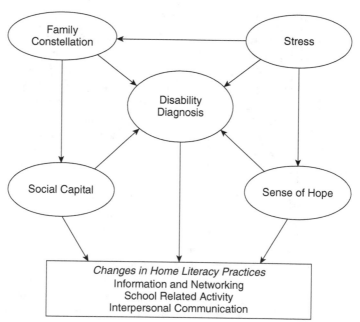

Figure 8.2 Interconnectivity of factors affecting literacy experiences for the newly diagnosed disabled child.

This family demonstrated significant resilience in spite of the challenges associated with Christiano's diagnosis. They banded together and sought information about the disability in addition to engaging with literacy activities in a natural and consistent way. The addition of the extended family members to their constellation not only provided additional support during high stress, it also provided an additional set of hands that were much needed with a potentially compromised child. Christiano's supportive and multi-generationally literate family was able to fully enable his literacy development immediately post diagnosis because they embedded teamwork and a natural approach of building literacy into his daily routines even with his hectic schedule. Christiano's literacy experiences involved his disability and his family made his disability a part of his daily life rather than a special circumstance. An additional pair of hands and strong values related to literacy were key elements in Christiano's post diagnosis success and his family's observed resilience. These elements were missing in some of the other participant families, causing them additional stress and less than optimal home literacy environments post disability diagnosis. In this study and in my previous disability study (Ragusa, 2007), I observed that most of the parents shift from reading books to their children to literacy practices associated with information seeking and a search for causal rationale for the disability, both of which are coping strategies identified by Behr and Murphy's (1993) cognitive coping research.

The study presented in this chapter indicates that during times of crisis, family literacy practices are dramatically altered. Some families halt reading related practices while others shift their reading practices from child-centered pleasure reading to parent-centered information seeking. Families who are resilient during crises seek information about the cause or rationale for the crisis they are experiencing using literacy as a medium for information seeking behaviors in efforts to cope and manage their crises (Ragusa, 2007).

Recommendations and Implications for Researchers and Practitioners

The results of the study described in this chapter have implications for future educational and family support interventions for children with newly diagnosed disabilities. As a consequence of the findings, I recommend that professionals view intervention as a supportive experience for families rather than an intrusive "intervening" experience. Practitioners should work in teams supporting newly diagnosed families and providing fully accessible interventions that are focused on child strengths rather than deficiencies. Practitioners should support naturalistic, typical infant, preschool and K-12 experiences rather than discrete and decontextualized, aggressive interventions for children with disabilities immediately post diagnosis to alleviate family stress. My study supports the importance of providing written, easily understandable information for parents so that their stress may be alleviated as they navigate the diagnosis processes. In addition, families should be supported in working as fully participating team members in designing and determining effective services for their child and themselves (Turnbull & Turnbull, 1997).They should be encouraged to enjoy their children and to engage in activities that are germane to all children rather than highly structured and skill specific remediation activities immediately post diagnosis. Interventions should focus on child and family strengths rather than child deficit (Dunst & Dempsey, 2007). Extended family support should be encouraged and facilitated to alleviate family stress. When extended family assistance is not available, respite and additional caregiver support should be offered. The fact that parents engage in much networking as a literacy practice leads me to believe that parent-to-parent support may be a useful substitute for extended family support. This process has been found to increase parents' coping abilities and ultimately their social capital and sense of hope (Behr & Murphy, 1993; Dunst & Dempsey, 2007; Turnbull & Turnbull, 1997), all factors that have positive effects on child outcome.

This study opens the door for additional family literacy studies on children with disabilities as it reinforces a well known assumption for typically developing children that home literacy experiences affect literacy development throughout the child's school years. This phenomenon is well known for typically developing children, but is not often considered for children with disabilities. I believe that intervention studies that increase literacy activities in children's homes as a strategy are noteworthy and should be supported with disabled populations. Longitudinal research related to long-term academic success of children with disabilities receiving home literacy support is warranted. Additional studies should be conducted that qualitatively document literacy experiences for all special populations.

This chapter offers insights into what may influence children's and adult's interest in various reading genres in homes, classrooms, and public libraries. First, diverse genres and literacy topics can serve children in difficult times in schools and in community libraries. Informational genres appear to be a natural support and coping strategy for parents and children in crisis post disability diagnosis. Books with characters with disabilities are helpful in assisting children in understanding the "normalcy" of disability in society. From my study findings, it appears that parents seek information from internet sources post diagnosis. In order to be certain that all families with disabled children have equal access to this electronic information, it is important that disability related information on the web and in schools and community agencies be fully accessible, continuously updated, and that it include a current and positive picture for families of children with newly diagnosed disabilities.

References

Alexander, P. A. (2007). Bridging cognition and socioculturalism within conceptual change research: Unnecessary foray or unachievable feat? *Educational Psychologist, 42*(1), 67–74.

Behr, S. K., & Murphy, D. L. (1993). Research progress and promise: The role of perceptions in cognitive adaptation to disability. In J. M. Patterson, A. P. Turnbull, S. K. Behr, D. L. Murphy, & J. G. Marquis (Eds.), *Cognitive coping, families, and disability* (pp. 151–163). Baltimore, MD: Brookes Publishing Company.

Chen, J., & Simeonsson, R. J. (1994). Child disability and family needs in the People's Republic of China. *International Journal of Rehabilitation Research, 17,* 25–37.

Colobro, J. (1990). Adjustment to disability: A cognitive-behavioral model for analysis and clinical management. *Journal of Rational-Emotive & Cognitive-Behavior Therapy, 8*(2), 79–102.

Dunst, C. J., & Dempsey, I. (2007). Family-professional partnerships and parenting competence, confidence, and enjoyment. *International Journal of Disability, Development and Education, 54*(3), 305–318.

Hartshorne, T. (2002). Mistaking courage for denial: Family resilience after the birth of a child with severe disabilities. *Journal of Individual Psychology, 58,* 263–278.

Horton, T., & Wallander, J. (2001). Hope and social support as resilience factors against psychological distress of mothers who care for children with chronic physical conditions. *Rehabilitation Psychology, 46,* 382–399.

Luterman, D. (1999). Grief: A parent's perspective. *American Annuals for the Deaf, 29*(3), 249–252.

McCubbin, H. I., & McCubbin, M. A. (1987). Family stress theory and assessment: The T-Double ABCX Model of Family Adjustments and Adaptation. In H. I. McCubbin, & A. I. Thompson (Eds.), *Family assessment inventories for research and practice* (pp. 3–34). Madison, WI: University of Wisconsin-Madison.

Moses, K. (Spring, 1987). The impact of childhood disability: The parent's struggle. *Ways Magazine,* 7–10. Retrieved September 1, 2009, from http://www.dsact.com/images/docs/theimpacts08.pdf

National Center for Health Statistics (NCHS). (2004). *Centers for Disease Control and Prevention.* Hyattsville, MD: NCHS.

National Institute of Health (NIH). (2008). *Medline plus.* Washington, DC: Pubmed. Retrieved March 27, 2008, from http://www.nlm.nih.gov/medlineplus/divorce.html

Portes, A. (1998). Social capital: Its origins and applications in modern sociology. *Annual Review of Sociology, 24,* 1–24.

Purcell-Gates, V. (1996). Stories, coupons and the TV guide: Relationships between home literacy experiences and emergent literacy knowledge. *Reading Research Quarterly, 31*(4), 76–82.

Ragusa, G. (2007). Born too soon: What can we expect? Nature of home literacy experiences for children with very low birth weight. *Early Child Development and Care, 24*(1), 1–18. Retrieved January 22, 2008, from http://www.informaworld.com/10.1080/03004430701491762

Rahman, A., Harrington, R., & Bunn, J. (2002). Can maternal depression increase infant risk of illness and growth impairments in developing countries? *Child: Care, Health and Development, 28*(1), 1–12.

ResearchWare Inc. (2006). HyperResearch version 2.7. Randolph, Runtime Revolution LTD.

Singhi, P. D., Goyal, L., Pershad, D., Singhi, S., & Walia, B. N. S. (1990). Psychosocial problems in families of disabled children. *British Journal of Medical Psychology, 63*(2), 173–182.

Smith, T. B., Oliver, M. N., & Innocenti, M. S. (2001). Parenting stress in families of children with disabilities. *American Journal of Orthopsychiatry, 71,* 257–261.

Teale, W. (1986). Home background and young children's literacy development. In W. Teale, & E. Sulzby (Eds.), *Emergent literacy: Writing and reading* (pp. 173–206). Norwood, NJ: Ablex Publishing.

Turnbull, A. P., & Turnbull, H. R. (1997). *Families, professionals, and exceptionality: A special partnership* (3rd ed.). Upper Saddle River, NJ: Merril/Prentice Hall.

Vygotsky, L. (1962). *Thought and language* (pp. 124–139). Cambridge, MA: MIT Press.

For Further Exploration

Cornell University (2007). *Cornell University Law School Divorce Resource Center.* Ithaca, NY: The Legal Information Institute. Available at: http://topics.law.cornell.edu/wex/divorce

Johnston, J., Roseby, V., Gentner, B., & Moore, E. (2005). *A safe place to grow: A group treatment manual for children in conflicted, violent, and separating homes.* New York: Routledge.

Part II

Crises Arising from Literate Practices

9 Finding Husbands, Finding Wives

How Being Literate Creates Crisis

Loukia K. Sarroub

> Creativity does not happen inside people's heads, but in the interaction between a person's thoughts and a sociocultural context.
>
> (Csikszentmihalyi, 1996, p. 23)

Introduction

Literacy and immigration scholars have not considered how refugees and immigrants negotiate the subtle and important connections between marriage, literacy, and migration to the United States. This chapter attempts to move these understudied connections to the forefront and does so by examining the ways in which young Iraqi and Yemeni immigrant and refugee women and men strive to become literate and simultaneously search for husbands and wives. Investigating these social connections involved in finding the appropriate spouse inevitably brings researchers to the field of education, as those young immigrants considered find themselves in a crisis that brings educational, economic, political, and religious factors into play. And, in order to understand these interconnections we have to take seriously the issue of how transnationalism, the phenomenon of living locally with global connections, demonstrates both the local and global tensions of refugees and immigrants as they interact in shared cultural sites. Moreover, transnational literacy, as described in this chapter, is evoked as a means to sort through particular literacy practices that simultaneously foster status and knowledge and explain the youths' sense of powerlessness and desperation as well as their perceptions of their success. The tension, between literacy as success and literacy as threat to marriage fosters crises of "glocal" proportions (see Robertson 1995; Sarroub, 2008). Measures taken by the young people to combat their own desperation by mobilizing literacy practices in the milieu of unfamiliar and often alien(ating) American cultural norms are the features that best express how glocalism can be understood.

The working definition of literacy in the context of marriage and transnationalism is that of a social event that accounts for communication with and through print as well as talk and rituals. Thus, literacy is broadly conceived to encompass local activity such as reading and writing that can be tangibly documented in addition to the communication norms with which people convey meaning and communicate with others. "Situated" and "local" literacies are now commonplace names in the research literature (see Alvermann, Hinchman, Moore, Phelps, & Waff, 2006; Barton, Hamilton, & Ivanic, 2000; Lewis, Moje, & Enciso, 2007; Rush, Eakle, & Berger, 2007), but they also serve as an important reminder that in everyday life, people often do not distinguish among different types of literacies, such as school vs. home, print vs. oral communication, in the same ways that scholars of literacy do in relation to achievement in schools. For example, in transnational contexts that mix the oral rituals of Muslim weddings with the print literacies of U.S. visa and citizenship forms, literacy takes on more ambiguous and fluid roles. Young people engage in the literacy practices necessary to achieve certain expected ends (such as travel to find a spouse) and sometimes, as in the case of some young Muslim women, being literate and educated reduces their chances of finding a spouse from the homeland.

Background

Spanning several years and drawing on a series of semi-structured and ethnographic interviews (Spradley, 1979) with Yemeni women (1997–2002) and Iraqi and Kurdish women and men (2001–2007), and on field work in two cities in different states of the Midwest, Dearborn, Michigan, and Lincoln, Nebraska, the analysis of the interviews offers a comparative perspective of immigrant and refugee youth attempting to live and thrive in the United States. In particular, three cases illuminate how marriage both empowers and mitigates social and academic success. The notion of marriage is further examined as it is constructed through various literacy practices, such as passing reading and writing exams in high school and community colleges or communicating with prospective spouses in the "homeland." Similarly, local marriage processes such as finding a prospective spouse, marrying the spouse, and living in a marriage with one's spouse are mediated by the global marriage market, which, in current times, is woven into a war economy.

Approximately 2 million Iraqis fled their country during the First Gulf War, and although many returned at the end of the conflict, a greater number remained in countries of first asylum, including Syria, Jordan, Turkey, and Saudi Arabia. In 2006 alone, an additional 1.5 million Iraqis were displaced from Iraq and traveled to neighboring countries, such as Syria. The Iraqi refugees are part of a larger permanent, global refugee population, approximately 19.8 million, 40% of whom were living in camps by 2001, according to the Office of the United Nations High Commissioner for Refugees (UNHCR). However, from 2003–2007, only 464 Iraqi refugees were allowed into the United States; and during the fiscal year 2008, 13,000 were admitted, and as many as 17,000 will be allowed to seek refuge in the United States during fiscal year 2009, following international criticism that the government has not sufficiently participated in facilitating resettlement. It is estimated that 30% of the displaced Iraqi refugee youth have not attended schools in the camps, which means that the children of thousands of families who resettled in the United States prior to the war in 2003, and after long stays in refugee camps, arrived in the United States with a variety of school experiences. Many lack preparation for formal schooling at primary and secondary levels. Literacy is therefore of paramount importance in the lives of these young people, who creatively find ways to negotiate the crises of texts, power, and identities in relation to marriage in the United States and the Middle East.

Examining transnational literacy in relation to gender, ethnicity, religion, and socioeconomic status contributes to our knowledge of new populations in public school and communities in the United States. The chapter explicates the ways in which literacy serves as the "imagined home" for individuals and families who deal with the "crisis" of marriage and whose daily American lives are governed to a great extent, by conceptions of their country of origin's normative values.

Literature that Informs the Study

The examination of the lives of refugees and immigrants from the Middle East is informed by literature associated by the study of language and power, a field of inquiry that has a home in philosophy, sociology, semiotics, and linguistics. The philosophical perspectives of Barthes (1972), Foucault (1970; 1977), Butler (1997), and Fairclough (1989) have shown that language is more than arbitrary symbols. It is a system of signs that we place between us and the world to make sense of reality and communicate our ideas about it. However, signs not only reflect or represent reality, they shape both the objects they point to and ourselves as sign users. Throughout history, discourse has imposed its order and its ideology on the way we know and talk about the world. The sociological and anthropological perspectives of Bourdieu (1991), de Certeau (1984), Goffman (1959), Street (1995), and Collins and Blot (2003) advance that language is a marker of our place in society in relation to social class, ethnicity, and level of education, among other factors. Language categorizes the world and is a carrier of ideology that creates in us durable dispositions that both structure and are structured by dominant discourses. We use language and literacies to position ourselves favorably vis-à-vis others, or to acquire a symbolic "profit of distinction" to gain advantage over them. At the same time, as Bakhtin (1986; Holquist, 1992) notes, no word is ever lost. Every utterance is always a response to other real or potential utterances, past or present, to which there will be a response in some way in the future. There is no sharp distinction between Self and Other. "Our speech, that is, all our utterances (including creative works), is filled with others' words . . . ," writes Bakhtin (1986, p. 89), and language has power precisely because it is heteroglossic, intertextual, conflicted and conflictual, and always open to question.

Much literacy and language research explores micro-level phenomena and dialogical encounters in everyday life (Cameron, 1998, 2000; Lakoff, 2000; Sarroub, 2002b; Scollon & Scollon, 2001; Tannen, 1994). This literature, informed by linguistic analyses, focuses on how encounters, discourse (utterances, speech acts), and Discourse (ideologies, worldviews) intersect to create instances of (mis)communication across people from different cultures, generations, genders, and social class. Communication itself has become a shibboleth of a culture of fast capitalism in the name of individual "empowerment" (Gee, Hull, & Lankshear, 1996), impacting the transnational texts of marriage and crisis.

Finally, an important aspect of literacy in the lives of the immigrant and refugee youth from the Middle East is that literacy is created and mastered. Csikszentmihalyi (1996) argues that creativity is a process by which a symbolic domain in the culture is changed. He notes that creativity "results from the interaction of a system composed of three elements: a culture that contains symbolic rules, a person who brings novelty into the symbolic domain, and a field of experts who recognize and validate the innovation" (p. 6). I argue that the creativity with which individuals become transnational, local experts as they learn new literacy domains through which they are then judged as successful (or not) is as significant, if not more so, as the publicly acknowledged cultural and social creative works of our society. This is so because youth and their families must master cultural and linguistic domains while sustaining and reproducing a commonness in their own "home" cultures. This entails a complex web of creative energy that changes, even if it is not immediately apparent, not only the local place but also the host country (in terms of national and international policy) and individual lives.

A Brief Synopsis about the Research Methodology

My research is based on seven years of fieldwork and a systematic comparative inquiry that includes procedures and strategies derived from ethnographic and anthropological methods (Erickson, 1986) and qualitative research methods (Wolcott, 1994). Overall, the research is guided by procedures grounded in sociolinguistic processes, such as symbolic interactionism (Blumer, 1969; Goffman, 1959; Spradley, 1979), to understand how people perceive and enact meaning in different contexts.

Since September 2001, I have followed 16 (8 female and 8 male) focal students as they progressed through high school (grades 9–12) and as they moved into jobs or post-secondary educational institutions. Supplemented with audio and/or video-taping whenever possible, I wrote field notes of school and classroom life, home learning, literacy and religious practices, and work and community. I also mapped demographic changes in the Midwest over time.

Methods of analysis include ongoing traditional ethnographic techniques such as constant comparative analysis, triangulation, and, if warranted, negative case analysis. Discourse and narrative analyses (Cazden, 2001; Coulthard, 1985; Gee, 1999) refine some of the sociolinguistic processes observed in classrooms and in the home. I employed a comparative and ethnographic analysis of the interviews including audio-taping, transcription, and coding based on domain, taxonomic, componential, and theme analyses (as elaborated by Spradley, 1979). Observation field notes were examined through a process of open and focused coding in which I paid particular attention to the participants' use of culturally relevant terms and meaning making (Emerson, Fretz, & Shaw, 1995). Analysis software such as Nudist, Nvivo, and Atlas were used as analytic tools for both the interviews and field notes. Part of the interpretive process of analysis included the creation of analytical memos that serve two functions: (a) they relate the data to the formulation of theory, and (b) they help me gain analytical distance from the field itself (Miles & Huberman, 1994; Strauss & Corbin, 1990). In addition, a case study design (see Bogdan & Biklen, 1992; Creswell, 1998; Erickson & Shultz, 1992) was used to document the discourse and language practices of each of the focal young people. Attention to the particulars of each case illuminated construction of their identities as readers in different contexts. Triangulation of codes and themes was applied across interviews, field notes, and various artifacts. A constant application of member checks (with teachers, students, parents, and community members) across time was conducted. I did this by sharing analysis reports with administrators, teachers, and the focal students.

The research culminated in comparative and multiple within-case and cross-case studies (Miles & Huberman, 1994) of the focal young people, descriptive statistics of school and district reading and writing assessments, and an ethnography of the school culture and the literacy classroom language and cultures. I also wrote within-case and cross-case study reports and discourse analyses of family and work literacy and language practices. Documents, records, images, and cultural artifacts were interpreted through a systematic content analysis that includes discourse analysis of printed texts, content analysis of material culture with particular attention to the symbolic and pragmatic meanings embedded in this data. Archival research was documented in analytical reports delineating the geopolitical, international, and historical factors that impact the lives of youth in American public high schools.

For the purposes of this chapter, I present two cases from this current research as well as a third case from my primary site of field work in Dearborn, Michigan. Together, the three cases illustrate how crisis can be created as youth become literate. Literacy, then, implicates a set of practices that are conflictual in their transnational locality and in their glocality.

Three Cases of Marriage, Crisis, and Creativity

Team Up and Scrabble as a Way of Learning

In the case of Sabrina, a young Yemeni American woman I interviewed in February 2002, crisis, in her words, describes everyday life as she helps her young Yemeni husband navigate being in the United States after 9/11. Reading and writing take on new meaning as the young wife takes charge of her husband's institutional identities while simultaneously fulfilling her roles as mother and worker. Negotiating transnational literacies locally in the United States necessitates a sojourner stance in order for Sabrina to successfully be American.

During one interview, Sabrina, an American citizen from the Southend of Dearborn whom I have known since 1997 (see Sarroub, 2001, 2002, 2005), described her journey to her family's village in Yemen, where she married her husband, a first cousin whom she describes as eventually also becoming her friend. The interview suggests that Sabrina's marrying a non-English speaker from Yemen rather than a Yemeni American in the United States does not make for an easy transition into motherhood or adulthood. Her responsibilities, which had earlier included negotiating various print texts for her parents and siblings, tripled when her husband also became part of the household. In adapting to the crisis of socializing a Yemeni subsistence farmer into the American auto factory, Sabrina dealt creatively with literacy learning at home when she found that her husband was not print literate in English.

Loukia: What, what kinds of, and the other issue is your husband, too, if he's learning English, what, what kinds of, you mentioned family time includes watching TV and playing, what kinds of activities do you do that are literacy oriented?

Sabrina: I love to play Scrabble.

Loukia: You do?

Sabrina: Yes.

Loukia: Is that a family thing?

Sabrina: It's a family thing.

Loukia: And you play it in English?

Sabrina: And we play it in English. So, but we like team up.

Loukia: Uh huh.

Sabrina: So, my husband and I will team up and my brothers will be like on their own, but the girls [two young children] will sit and watch us. They won't play because obviously they won't be able to get the words but that's one thing I like to do. And I felt that by playing Scrabble, my husband *will* learn the letters and words and things, even though he doesn't, *by working as a team*, I'll say oh, that's the word. We can do this. This means this and that's the letter. He can identify letters but when we have game time, it would be definitely, we play *Scrabble as a way of learning*. He's very, like if I was to sit and give him worksheets and do stuff like that, it wouldn't be an interest to him.[1]

Loukia: Is he taking English classes?

Sabrina: No. With his work schedule—

Loukia: It's hard—

Sabrina: Cuz he works from seven til eight, so it doesn't, doesn't, it just, the weekends, and there's nothing offered on the weekends. seven in the morning til eight in the afternoon, nothing's really open by eight. And then he's, by the time he's done taking a shower, getting ready to eat and stuff, it'll be like nine.

Sabrina has found a way to engage her husband in a literacy activity that her Yemeni American family enjoys. "Scrabble as a way of learning" and "working as a team" both offer an opportunity for her to teach her husband English, allowing him access to letters and words which she helps him remember. On his own, her husband is not likely to find ways to learn English during his 12-hour work shift or during the weekends, so Sabrina models "making words" for her young daughters and husband with a game that she and her brothers (three families live in the house) clearly enjoy. The "team up" approach further facilitates their unusual partnership, in which she, an English literacy expert does exert more power that she willingly shares with him in the game competition, thus preserving to some degree, male status and dominance in the household.

The next interview excerpt illustrates that the power dynamics are more complex in this marriage, for the husband also willingly gives his time for social occasions in which Sabrina wants to participate. Having a husband allows her more freedom to socialize with community members, to travel and drive faraway to places. Later in the interview excerpt, Sabrina returns to the topic of literacy learning and the impact her husband's print illiteracy has on her.

Sabrina: Yeah. They're gonna, we're thinking of driving there [Florida], too. We wanta like forget the plane, forget the bus, wanta enjoy the country. He's very like . . . you know, most, most, like when I talk to friends, they're like you're kidding? Your husband? Like yeah, he likes to, he always says *I only do it for you*. Like when we go to events, and dinners and stuff.

Loukia: He must love you very much.

Sabrina: He's a really great guy. You know, and he always says like *I only go because of you*. Or we stay for an hour or two, then we leave.

Loukia: Does he talk about returning to Yemen?

Sabrina: He always talks about going home. Cuz he just, what tires him is work.

Loukia: It's a hard job.

Sabrina: Yeah, it's a hard job. And it's 12 hours.

Loukia: I wonder if there's a way for him to get some minimal education so he can do a non-factory—

Sabrina: The point is that he's, *he doesn't want to.* I mean, I teach him at home. *And he goes in and he doesn't want to.* I go why don't you take classes? I mean, they offer night classes.

Loukia: Can he, yeah, or once they start the family literacy program, or the ESL—

Sabrina: I wish they'd do weekends.

Loukia: Well, you're here, Sabrina. You have a little bit of power.

Sabrina: But he's *so stubborn about learning*. He just wants to learn as he goes because he's learned a lot. Just his writing, he needs.

Loukia: Tell him it's for the sake of, tell him it's for the sake of his children so he can help them in school when they grow up.

Sabrina: *He always relies on me to do all of that*. I do the financing the house. I do the budgeting in the house. I do the shopping when he doesn't feel like doing it. *He, he likes to enjoy life but he ignores all the other stuff*. Like I take care of the bills. I take care of appointments. I take care of this for the girls, that for the girls, get this for the girls, that for the girls.

It's hard. It's really hard nowadays. It's really hard for, I mean, I know it was hard for my brother-in-law [also from Yemen and who married her younger sister]. It took him practically, he was here in November. He worked like for a few weeks and then he was like two months until he went back to work, like recently. So it's hard for, especially for immigrants. You know, the language barrier.

Sabrina finds herself in a partnership that paradoxically gives her power because she does have access to the literate world, and at the same time increases her responsibilities to an extent that she is overwhelmed by them. As a part-time working mother with a full-time home life, Sabrina not only fulfills all the parental roles and is the English teacher in her small family, but she also continues to support her parents and her younger sister's family. Sabrina noted that "every day there's a crisis" in relation to her husband's attitude that he would eventually learn English on the job. While she wanted to speed up the process so that their home life responsibilities could be more balanced and shared, she found that her being literate caused the opposite reaction. Her husband did not actively pursue venues in which he could become literate when Sabrina could do it all—work outside the home plus household tasks—as a mother, wife, daughter, and sister.

Love and Marriage in a Time of War

The cases of Hakim and Amina, young refugees from Iraq, illustrate how the credential of having passed a U.S. high school reading exam enables Hakim to make the dangerous journey back to Iraq in pursuit of the ideal wife. School literacy practices along with savvy travel-know-how through Iraq, Jordan, and back to the United States, in Lincoln, Nebraska, and Dearborn, Michigan, demonstrates the challenges faced by young people whose national status is in crisis.

In her analysis of the impact of immigration on Lincoln, Nebraska, Mary Pipher (2002) notes in her best-selling book, *The middle of everywhere: Refugees come to our town,* that Lincoln, Nebraska includes children from over 50 nationalities. What is more unusual is the fact that the immigrants to Lincoln from predominantly Muslim countries arrived in the city not voluntarily but at the behest of the U.S. government. We know little about their education in their home countries, or their experience of assimilation and concomitant language and literacy learning in English and their native language(s). Pipher's book is the first "popular audience" narrative to examine refugees chosen by the U.S. government to apply and seek refugee status. The refugees, some 20,000 a year admitted to the United States prior to 9/11, are brought to refugee-designated sites, such as communities in Nebraska, North Dakota, Virginia—states with relatively stable economies and low unemployment rates—and are expected to make new lives for themselves.

I met Hakim at Central High School in 2002 as I was shadowing his sister, Amina, who at the time was in a Level 3 English Language Learning class and in tenth grade. Amina and Hakim had spent ten years in the Rafha camp of Saudi Arabia after fleeing from Iraq during the First Gulf War. Known for its non-humanitarian conditions, Rafha camp, for Amina and her family, was a living hell, with no toilets, no schools for the thousands of children, and very little hope of ever getting out. In high school in Lincoln, Hakim was identified as a student with Special needs in reading and writing, so after failing the reading and writing graduation exams several times, he was allowed to bypass the exam requirement because of this Special education status. Once he earned his diploma, he and his family made plans to travel to Iraq during the current Gulf War for him to meet and marry his first cousin. Amina told me the story of her brother's journey while I helped her to read and understand her textbook and do her geometry problems. Her talk is peppered with affectionate insults for her brother as she explains what happened.

Loukia: OK, Amina. Let's read this textbook together. I have to tell you that it's been a while since I last saw a geometry textbook, but it was my favorite subject when I was in high school, so I hope I'll remember something that will help you.

Amina: I understand the problems. I don't get the text, the textbook, what it says. Mrs. S says we have to read the directions and I don't.

Loukia: OK. This is about isosceles triangles. What do you know about them?

Amina: Umm, that *I can't say that word?*

Loukia: Funny. It's iso-sceles, but don't worry about saying the word. What do you remember about these triangles from class? What's interesting about them?

Amina: Did I tell you that my brother married our cousin?

Loukia: Really, when did he do that?! The last I heard, you said that your family was thinking about that.

Amina:	They're in Jordan right now and he's trying to get back to Lincoln. Can you believe my dumb brother got married? *How is he supposed to take care of a wife? He can barely take care of himself. He doesn't even have a job. I do everything at home and I even found the house we're living in now.* He just finished high school, he's not ready to have a wife.
Loukia:	So, what happened? Did he go to Iraq?
Amina:	Yea, he went to Jordan first and then he and my uncles drove to Baghdad to my other uncle's house and he got married to my cousin there. I don't know how he's going to support her, what they'll do when if they have kids. She doesn't know English.
Loukia:	Why is your uncle's family still in Baghdad? Did they stay during the Gulf War?
Amina:	We had to leave cause Saddam was going to kill my dad [a car mechanic with little formal education] so we went to Saudi, but my uncle was quiet and he could stay.
Loukia:	So, tell me more about Hakim's trip so far. How is he managing all the paperwork in Arabic and English?
Amina:	I don't know. *He can't read nothin.* My mom's back is hurting her a lot – she's worried about Hakim.
Loukia:	Well . . . if your uncles are helping him, he'll be OK. I'm just trying to imagine how he'll be able to get out safely and then how he'll deal with all the immigration forms for his wife and himself.
Amina:	He got out of Baghdad—he's in Jordan now with her and they have people who help refugees get out. I'm the only one who doesn't have citizenship yet. He's an American citizen now, so it's easier for him, especially if there's someone there to help him with the reading.
Loukia:	Oh.
Amina:	But what'll they do when they get here. Hakim has no job and she don't know English. *I can't believe my stupid brother got married.*
Loukia:	What do your parents say about this?
Amina:	Nothing. They like having more family here, and my dad talks about going to Dearborn for more opportunities. Hakim could get a job there. Remember my cousin? The one in the picture?
Loukia:	Ye—
Amina:	My mom really wants me to marry him, *but I don't want to get married.* But if he came from Baghdad, he could get a job in Dearborn. Yea, she said the sides of the triangle are the same.
Loukia:	What? Oh, the triangle . . . what do you mean by the "same?"
Amina:	This side is as long as this side.
Loukia:	I want to talk more about your brother's trip, but you're right, let's finish this math homework and talk more later.

Amina and Hakim successfully negotiated their ELL (English Language Learner) program at Central High School with the help of excellent teachers (see Sarroub, 2007; Sarroub, Pernicek, & Sweeney, 2007). Amina, the most print-literate member of her family (she tested at a fifth grade reading level) helped her family move to Dearborn and rent a house when her brother returned from Jordan with his new bride. Our conversation illustrates the interplay of several relevant texts in Amina and Hakim's lives. First, there is the context of geometry and the textbook narrative with which Amina struggled. Texbooks took on a life of their own when Amina worked with them, becoming the backdrop of dramatic life stories such as this one, almost disappearing from the significant literacy events that pervaded her everyday refugee life. What is clearly emphasized in the conversation are her worries about her brother's (and parents') decision to let Hakim travel to Iraq and marry their cousin. Her use of "dumb" and "stupid" reflect her brother's status as a Special education student during high school and her lack of confidence in his ability to be responsible for his own new family. In addition, Hakim's successful entry and exit into Iraq during the war spell impending doom for Amina, who is not interested in marrying her cousin (or anyone). Her foci on geometry, reading, and school life have, to this point, made life happy for her. The year after high school, during which time she took classes at the local community college, she complained that now that she was home and more visible to the Iraqi refugee community, everyone in the neighborhood was watching her, and someone had even reported to her parents that she was in a car with a strange man, who turned out to be her brother giving her ride to her classes (see Sarroub, 2005). Life outside of public school for Amina meant restraint and lack of freedom. She thought of marriage as further limiting her options, and as she observed the transnational ease with which her brother, a Special education student who did "nothin," traveled to Iraq and Jordan to marry, Amina found herself in an identity crisis. She failed her immigration test on purpose in order to avoid becoming a citizen, not because she did not want to be a citizen, but because her literacy skills would inadvertently bring a future for which she was not ready. Amina is not yet a citizen and continues to struggle with the marriage crisis, using her ameliorating literacy skills with savvy and creativity and as a form of resistance.

"I'm too old" and "I want to marry a virgin man"

Loukia:	Hello?
Marstan:	Miss Loukia?!
Loukia:	Yes, hi Marstan!
Marstan:	Miss Loukia, hi. It's Marstan.
Loukia:	Yes, I know, Marstan. It's nice to hear from you. How are you?
Marstan:	Miss Loukia. How's your family? Your husband? Your children? Your mother and father? Your sister?
Loukia:	Everyone is fine, Marstan. Sef and Sofia had bad colds last week, but they're much better this week.

Marstan:	Oh good. Miss Loukia. I miss you so much. Come to my house this weekend.
Loukia:	I will, Marstan. You tell me what would be a good time.
Marstan:	OK. I clean at the hospital on Saturday, but Sunday I'm home and you see my mom and sister, Shaima.
Loukia:	That would be great!
Marstan:	Miss Loukia?
Loukia:	Yes?
Marstan:	I passed Level 7 at Southeast Community College.
Loukia:	That's wonderful, Marstan!! I am so happy for you. Does this mean you're finished with ELL?
Marstan:	Yes. I'm studying for nursing, Miss Loukia. I want to marry too. I'm too old.
Loukia:	Marstan, why do you say you're too old? You just finished high school recently.
Marstan:	Miss Loukia, I'm 22 and my sister Kurdistan, *no one wants to marry us if we're old.*
Loukia:	Is there someone you would like to marry?
Marstan:	I would like to go back to Iraq, to Kurdistan, to my country, and find someone there.
Loukia:	When will you do that?
Marstan:	I hope next summer. Miss Loukia?
Loukia:	Yes?
Marstan:	*I want to marry someone good, someone from my country.* The Kurdish men are bad here. They do bad things with women. *I want to marry a virgin man.* It's safe now in my country. It's friends with America. Did you see the news about Turkey?
Loukia:	About Turkey? Oh, you mean that the Turks and the Kurds don't get along and the United States supports Kurdistan? I did read about that. But wait, I thought last time we talked you said that you wanted to marry someone from here.
Marstan:	No. Miss Loukia? *I need your help.*
Loukia:	Tell me.
Marstan:	Do you know a good lawyer for immigration? We have to wait five years to becoming citizens. *I read all the questions for the test,* but five years is a long time and we want to go to our country to find husbands. Can you help me find a lawyer? I looked in phone book but there are many names.
Loukia:	Marstan, I don't know any immigration lawyers in Lincoln, but I know someone who does and as soon as we hang up, I'll call and find out and call you back.
Marstan:	Thank you, Miss Loukia. You always help when I call. Thank you.
Loukia:	You're welcome, Marstan. Now tell me about the immigration test. I know that the questions were changed recently.

Marstan: Miss Loukia. *The questions are hard!* But I want to pass so that I can marry.

Loukia: But Marstan, if you're not a citizen, you have to wait three more years before you can even take the test and only after that can you actually bring someone to the United States from another country—

Marstan: Miss Loukia, my sister, she too old, and I'm too old. *We can't wait three more years.* She wants to marry a Kurdish man who is in Greece now, a refugee—our cousin, but he has no papers.

Loukia: I think it would be a good idea to talk to an immigration lawyer. He knows more than I do about these laws.

Marstan: Miss Loukia, *I want a good man. In my country they're good.*

Marstan, the third case I explore, focuses on a young Kurdish Muslim woman that I shadowed in high school and who arrived in the United States print-illiterate and successfully graduated from high school five years later. Her successful academic experiences are part and parcel of the social and emotional upheavals her teachers dealt with as they taught her to read and write and to pass the writing and reading demonstration exams. Her goals of becoming literate, graduating from high school, and becoming a nurse were motivated by a real and desperate desire to be married to someone from her culture and religion.

Of the 37 telephone conversations that Marstan and I had had to this point, 31 were devoted to the subject of marriage and finding a "good man." The conversations typically followed the same pattern. Marstan inquires about each member of my family, then gives me some news about her literacy progress, and finally focuses on a problem with which she and her family need help. This was the first conversation that gives a clue as to whom a "good man" might refer to: someone from Kurdistan and someone who is a "virgin man." This was also the first conversation in which Marstan clearly spells out the dilemma she faces as her prospects for marriage become slimmer in her twenties. Her friends and acquaintances married between the ages of 14 and 22, and the fact that she is not married casts suspicion on her and her family. As such, Marstan's school literacy learning has been both magical and full of anguish, and more space devoted to her story is necessary than can be accommodated by this chapter. However, like Amina, Marstan wants to make a life for herself in the United States. She works in a hospital as a cleaning woman and takes classes in preparation for entry into a nursing program. In a family of ten children, ranging from their early thirties to teens, all the older children do service work entailing cleaning in Lincoln hospitals, hotels, or cafeterias. Marstan views literacy as her ticket to success, tackling the immigration test questions early, helping her non-English speaking mother with household literacy tasks, and constantly telling/showing her supervisors at work that she is becoming a more fluent reader so that she can get better cleaning jobs, when clearly, literacy is not the significant issue in her work place (see Hull, 1993).

However, unlike Amina, Marstan uses her literacy skills to be more successful on the marriage market. She thinks she has a better chance of finding a husband (and keeping him) if, similarly to Sabrina in the Yemeni case, she sponsors (see Brandt, 2001) and supports his literacy learning and life financially in the United States. The dilemma she faces is that of access to the type of husband that, in her view, is only available in Kurdistan. Marstan's glocal dilemma is in direct conflict with U.S. law. She cannot marry someone who is not a U.S. citizen until she herself is a U.S. citizen, and an older one at that, thus further limiting her chances of finding someone from Kurdistan who will marry her.

Literacy, Ordinary Lives, and Creativity

> Literacy is a curious thing. It seems to envelope our lives and be central to modern living, yet most of humanity has done without it for most of human existence.
>
> (Collins & Blot, 2003, p. 1)

Curiously, print literacy was not a significant part of Sabrina's husband, Amina and Hakim, and Marstan's lives prior to their arrival in the United States. They each come from places—Yemeni and Kurdish villages as well as refugee camps—where success is not measured against one's facility with print literacy. Crisis is evoked when one's identity (an ordinary life) becomes embedded in institutional texts, where every desire and form of communication must be visibly met through an endless array of sanctioned print forms whose language must be mastered. In the Bakhtinian sense, these young people are speaking through the words of American institutions (see Rogers, 2003 and Varenne & McDermott, 1998, for a good analysis of this through the lens of adult literacy in conjunction with the Special education discourse). At the root of these textual identities are competing notions of power.

In each of the situations described the young people adopt a set of institutional literacy practices, thus mastering domains of power in order to fully participate and expand possible boundaries for legitimacy and agency. For example, playing Scrabble at home as an alternative to worksheets enables participation, even from the margins. Butler (1997) enjoins her readers to "expand the domain of linguistic survival" (p. 7). Butler's analysis is focused on speech acts in relation to injurious speech and how individuals might try on and use, so to speak, the injurious speech, such as calling someone a taboo name, in order to expand one's range of linguistic survival tools. At the heart of this recommendation is the resolution of the tension between "the agency of language" and the "agency of the subject" (p. 7). This means that one cannot underestimate people's potential for adapting language practices to surmount political, social, or religious obstacles. Marstan's inquiry into what is possible under immigration constraints is an affirmation of her understanding that in the United States she can ask these questions and seek help to do so. Similarly, I argue that learning various forms of literacy can also expand power and agency vis-à-vis the textual identities that individuals master as they react to crises stemming from such texts and interactions with texts.

Crisis denotes an unstable moment in which a decisive change is impending, and it also connotes an emotionally significant event or radical change of status in a person's life (*Merriam-Webster's Online Dictionary*). The glocality of marriage situated in transnational and textual identities certainly qualifies as a form of crisis for these young people, and while literacy may have been of little significance in their pasts, mastering literacy in the present and then creating new identities with it invokes what Butler (1997) calls "insurrectionary potential" (p. 145). Sabrina and her husband, Amina and Hakim, and Marstan, with and through their new literacies reinvoke and restructure the conditions of their own possibilities in the United States, creating hope out of crisis and becoming literate, thus sharing a common set of perceptions about what it means to succeed transnationally. Finding husbands and wives as refugees and immigrants from the Middle East and elsewhere is, along with everything else, a creative process that calls for the mastery of powerful literacy domains that are transformative. Literacy in such a context is both a hindrance and a potent form of liberation.

Note

1 Italics denote both the speaker's emphasis and a theme (evidenced through patterns) in the data.

References

Alvermann, D., Hinchman, K., Moore, D., Phelps, S., & Waff, D. (2006). *Reconceptualizing the literacies in adolescents' lives* (2nd ed.). Mahwah, NJ: Lawrence Erlbaum.

Bakhtin, M. (1986). *Speech genres & other late essays*. (C. Emerson, & M. Holquist, Eds.), (Vern W. McGee, Trans.). Austin: University of Texas Press.

Barthes, Roland. [1957](1972). *Mythologies* (Annette Lavers, Trans.). New York: Farrar, Straus & Giroux.

Barton, D., Hamilton, M., & Ivanic, R. (Eds.). (2000). *Situated literacies: Reading and writing in context*. London: Routledge.

Blumer, H. (1969). *Symbolic interactionism: Perspective and method*. Englewood Cliffs, NJ: Prentice-Hall.

Bogdan, R., & Biklen, S. (1992). *Qualitative research for education: An introduction to theory and methods* (2nd ed.). Boston: Allyn & Bacon.

Bourdieu, P. (1991). *Language and symbolic power*. Cambridge, MA: Harvard University Press.

Brandt, D. (2001). *Literacy in American lives*. Cambridge: Cambridge University Press.

Butler, J. (1997). *Excitable speech. A politics of the performative*. New York: Routledge.

Cameron, D. (1998). 'Is there any ketchup, Vera?': Gender, power and pragmatics. *Discourse & Society 9*(4), 437–455.

Cameron, D. (2000). *Living and working in a communication culture.* London: Sage.

Cazden, C. (2001). *Classroom discourse: The language of teaching and learning* (2nd ed.). Portsmouth, NH: Heinemann.

Collins, J., & Blot, R. K. (2003). *Literacy and literacies: Texts, power, and identity.* Cambridge: Cambridge University Press.

Coulthard, M. (1985). *An introduction to discourse analysis* (2nd ed.). Harlow, Essex: Longman Group.

Creswell, J. W. (1998). *Qualitative inquiry and research design: Choosing among five traditions.* Thousand Oaks, CA: Sage Publications.

Csikszentmihalyi, M. (1996). *Creativity: Flow and the psychology of discovery and invention.* New York: HarperCollins.

de Certeau, M. (1984). *The practice of everyday life.* Berkeley: University of California Press.

Emerson, R., Fretz, I., & Shaw, L. (1995). *Writing ethnographic fieldnotes.* Chicago: University of Chicago Press.

Erickson, F., (1986). Qualitative methods in research and teaching. In M. C. Wittrock (Ed.), *Handbook of research on teaching* (pp. 119–161). New York: Macmillan.

Erickson, F., & Shultz, J. (1992). Students' experiences of the curriculum. In P. W. Jackson (Ed.), *Handbook of research on curriculum* (pp. 65–96). New York: Macmillan.

Fairclough, N. (1989). *Language and power.* London: Longman.

Foucault, M. (1970). *The order of things. An archaeology of the human sciences.* New York: Vintage.

Foucault, M. (1977). *Discipline and punish.* New York: Vintage.

Gee, J. (1999). *An introduction to discourse analysis: Theory and method.* London: Routledge.

Gee, J., Hull, G., & Lankshear, C. (1996). *The new work order: Behind the language of the new capitalism.* Boulder, CO: Westview Press.

Goffman, E. (1959). *The presentation of self in everyday life.* Garden City, NY: Doubleday Anchor Books.

Hammersley, M., & Atkinson, P. (2007). *Ethnography: Principles in practice,* (3rd ed.). London: Routledge.

Holquist, M. (1992). *Dialogism: Bakhtin and his world.* London: Routledge.

Hull, G. (1993). Hearing other voices: A critical assessment of popular views on literacy and work. *Harvard Educational Review, 63*(1), 20–49.

Lakoff, R. (2000). *The language war.* Berkeley: UC Press.

Lewis, C., Moje, E. B., & Enciso, P. (Eds.). (2007). *Reframing sociocultural research on literacy: Identity, agency, and power.* Mahwah, NJ: Erlbaum.

Miles, M., & Huberman, A. (1994). *Qualitative data analysis* (2nd ed.). New York: Sage.

Pipher, M. (2002). *The middle of everywhere: The world's refugees come to our town.* New York: Harcourt, Inc.

Robertson, R. (1995). Glocalization: Time-Space and homogeneity-heterogeneity. In M. Featherstone, S. Lash, & R. Robertson, *Global modernities* (pp. 25–44). London: Sage Publications.

Rogers, R. (2003). *A critical discourse analysis of family literacy practices: Power in and out of print.* Mahwah, NJ: Erlbaum.

Rush, L. S., Eakle, A. J., & Berger, A. (Eds). (2007). *Secondary school literacy: What research reveals for classroom practice.* Urbana, IL: National Council of Teachers of English.

Sarroub, L. K. (2001). The sojourner experience of Yemeni American high school students: An ethnographic portrait. *Harvard Educational Review, 71*(3), 390–415.

Sarroub, L. K. (2002a). From neologisms to social practice: An analysis of the wanding of America. *Anthropology and Education Quarterly, 33*(3), 297–307.

Sarroub, L. K. (2002b). "In-betweenness": Religion and conflicting visions of literacy. *Reading Research Quarterly, 37*(2), 130–148.

Sarroub, L. K. (2005). *All American Yemeni girls: Being Muslim in a public school.* Philadelphia: University of Pennsylvania Press.

Sarroub, L. K. (2007). Seeking refuge in literacy from a scorpion bite. *Ethnography and Education 2*(3), 365–380.

Sarroub, L. K. (2008). Living "glocally" with literacy success in the Midwest. *Theory into Practice 47*(1), 47–66.

Sarroub, L. K., Pernicek, T., & Sweeney, T. (May 2007). I was bitten by a Scorpion: Reading in and out of school in a refugee's life. *Journal of Adolescent and Adult Literacy 50*(8), 668–679.

Scollon, R., & Scollon, S. (2001). *Intercultural communication: A discourse approach* (2nd ed.). London: Routledge.

Spradley, J. P. (1979). *The ethnographic interview.* New York: Harcourt Brace Jovanovich College Publishers.

Strauss, A., & Corbin, J. (1990). *Basics of qualitative research: Grounded theory procedures and techniques.* London: Sage.

Street, B. V. (1995). *Social literacies: Critical approaches to literacy in development, ethnography, and education.* Harlow, Essex: Longman Group.

Tannen, D. (1994). *Gender and discourse.* Oxford: Oxford University Press.

Varenne, H., & McDermott, R. (1998). *Successful failure: The school America builds.* Boulder, CO: Westview Press.

United Nations High Commissioner for Refugees (UNHCR). Retrieved June 3, 2009, from http://www.unchr.org/cgi-bin/texis/vtx/home.

Woolcott, H. F. (1994). *Transforming qualitative data: Description, analysis, and interpretation.* Thousand Oaks, CA: Sage Publications.

For Further Exploration

Arab Community Center for Economic and Social Services, Dearborn, Michigan: http://www.accesscommunity.org/site/PageServer

Classroom windows 06/17 Episode 05: Culturally responsive teaching: http://video.google.com/videoplay?docid=-6066894268476055581

Esposito, John L., & DeLong-Bas, Natana, J. (2001). *Women in Muslim family law* (2nd ed.). Syracuse, NY: Syracuse University Press.

10 A State Takeover

The Language of a School District Crisis

Rebecca Rogers and Kathryn Pole

Introduction

"The Public Schools are in a state of crisis," asserts Francis Slay, the mayor of St. Louis, in his blog on December 15th, 2006, in the context of deliberations around tax-credits, vouchers and a state takeover of the provisionally accredited city school district. During the months between December 2006 and February 2007, politicians, the media, and citizens on all sides of the issues repeatedly referred to the St. Louis Public Schools (SLPS) as in "crisis." As the story of St. Louis shows, this atmosphere of a "crisis" provides the pretext to suspend democratic policies and usher in solutions that otherwise would be deemed unacceptable.

As two literacy educators and researchers concerned with issues of educational equity and democracy, we watched as event after event unfolded in the developing crisis of SLPS. Our story here represents a form of problem-based praxis where we were both inside and outside the problem. As insiders to education, we had a stance; we were against the takeover of SLPS, and attended public hearings, wrote letters to the editor, and spoke out against takeover plans. As outsiders to the city of St. Louis, some of the politics and history were not as transparent as they might have been. As educators and citizens who believe education is vital to a healthy democracy, we embarked on this work as a form of praxis—theory, practice, reflection, and action (Croteau, Hoynes, & Ryan, 2005). Using the tools of critical discourse analysis (e.g. Fairclough, 1992; Scollon, 2008) and critical policy analysis (Lipman, 2004, 2007; Woodside-Jiron, 2004), we asked, "How was this crisis constructed through public discourse and literacy practices?" We explored the interplay of interests, social roles, and traditions that contributed to the construction of a crisis as we examined the use of language and literacy circulating around a crisis in the SLPS.

We collected and examined various texts produced in the debate over the state takeover. The discourses around the crisis occurred within a larger set of literacy practices (e.g. the production and dissemination of official reports, transcripts of public hearings, speeches, news reports, blogs, letters to the editor, emails circulated by activists, protests, and songs). As such, the discourses and literacy practices expand our reading-speaking-writing definition to the ways in which people critically access and assess the multiple genres, texts, and discourses that constructed and were constructed by the "school crisis."

We focus on the pivotal date of February 15, 2007, the date that the State of Missouri Board of Education voted to set in motion a plan to transfer control of the SLPS system to a politically-appointed three-member board, disempowering the urban school district's elected school board. From this pivotal date, we trace back to significant other texts that led to the vote, and follow threads of post-vote discourse, ending with the actual political naming of the Special Administrative Board.

Background on SLPS in Crisis

St. Louis has been described as having a Southern segregation legacy with a Northern political geography that completely separates the city and county (Heaney & Uchitelle, 2004; Wells & Crain, 1999). The city has been characterized as maintaining the status quo with regard to inequities in education, housing, and employment despite reform efforts such as school desegregation (e.g. Morris, 2001; Wells & Crain, 1999). The history of race and public education in St. Louis is interwoven with the history of residential segregation. Public schools are affected by changing demographics that leave inner cities with significant proportions of the very poor, manifested by high drop-out rates, poor attendance, and low test scores (Portz, Stein, & Jones, 1999). Not all urban school districts responded to the challenges the same way; St. Louis was found consistently to lag behind other urban districts in addressing these challenges, for reasons such as: a legacy of systemic racism, a "machine-politics" city government where personal rewards count more than policy (p. 111), a "calcified, inbred, and resistant to change" school bureaucracy (p. 113), and the low-tax low-service approach of the State of Missouri's government. A great deal has been written about the educational and political landscape of St. Louis, Missouri (e.g. Ayres-Salamon, 2004; Heaney & Uchitelle, 2004; Morris, 2001; Portz, et al., 1999; Wells, 2002). Because of space limitations, we review only selected portions of this history.

In 1967, at its peak enrollment, SLPS served 115,000 students (Wilson, 2003). However, due to issues that faced many urban school districts at that time, the district began a decline as affluent residents moved to the suburbs, and other residents withdrew in favor of a strong parochial school system. Shifting demographics eventually led to one of the largest desegregation agreements in the nation. Part of the 1981 desegregation agreement established a voluntary transfer program between the city and county schools; thousands of black city parents enrolled their children in county schools. At the same time, a few hundred white county parents enrolled their children in the new city "magnet" schools. The desegregation agreement brought a complex funding formula designed to minimize the impact of the loss of enrollment in city schools.

In 1999, with all parties weary of the continuing agreement, the desegregation case was finally settled. The State of Missouri agreed to distribute $180 million to SLPS, to be paid over 11 years, for the construction of new schools to accommodate students returning from the voluntary transfer program. However, many of the suburban schools continued to voluntarily accept city students, and there was no need to build new city schools. This money is currently in an SLPS account, designated for new construction.

The settlement also provided a school funding formula that would ensure SLPS enough money for annual operations. For the first year, the state provided money according to that formula. However, soon after, the state began changing the formula and decreased funding several times, often in the middle of school years, after budgets had been set and expenses committed. The superintendent of SLPS, Cleveland Hammonds, announced in early 2003 that he was leaving his position, acknowledging that the district was $55 million in debt. Later in 2003, SLPS filed a lawsuit against the state. The judge ruled in favor of the school district, and the state appealed. The case was sent back to the same judge, who then reversed his initial decision. The dramatic decrease in funding following this judgment had a serious impact on the budget of SLPS.

Coincidentally, provisions within NCLB at the national level, and the difficulty of many urban districts including St. Louis to meet Adequate Yearly Progress requirements, created a sense of increasing academic failure. At about the same time, the mayor of St. Louis, supported by a group of influential businessmen representing the largest businesses in the area, became interested in urban revitalization; new sports venues were built, and old factories and warehouses were bought and converted to condos and office space.

With an eye on the four open seats on the seven-member elected school board, the mayor announced and promoted his team of four candidates. Backed with funds borrowed from the mayor's own election campaign and donations from major area corporations, these candidates easily won, and the new majority assumed control of the board in April, 2004. They wasted little time before looking outside district, community, state, and national educational expertise in the hiring of the New York City-based corporate turnaround firm, Alvarez & Marsal, for a one-year term at a cost of $5 million, despite the fact that the firm and its SLPS CEO, William Roberti, had no experience in education. The Missouri Department of Elementary and Secondary Education granted Roberti a waiver, allowing him to lead the fragile urban school district without educational administration credentials or experience.

In a *PBS Online News Hour* report aired on August 17, 2004 called "Turning around," reporter John Merrow (Lehrer, 2004) examined the hiring of Alvarez & Marsal. To correct a district deficit and systems that were not working, school board member Vince Schoemehl explained, "We've tried to take private sector practices and blend them with a public sector institution." The continued instability of the district was integral to the imposition of unpopular policies that mixed public resources with privatization of services. Yet, there continued to be resistance. For many reasons, including the closing of some schools, the selling of district property, and a sense that the reforms based on cost-cutting philosophies weren't working for students or the community, the next two years of school board elections resulted in the defeat of mayor-backed candidates. The mayor decried the decisions of the voters, and vowed to "seek alternatives to the St. Louis Public Schools," (Slay, April 7, 2006). He became increasingly public in promoting charter schools (ex. Slay, Nov. 15, 2006). The mayor lobbied lawmakers for increased opportunities to bring charter schools to the city, and made no secret of his belief that for-profit educational management companies would produce better student-products than the current public school system. One of his strongest allies was a state senator who was already the co-founder of three St. Louis charter schools run by Edison, a for-profit Educational Management Organization.

Coupled with changing alliances on the elected school board, SLPS also had a series of short-term superintendents. In the years between 2004 and 2007, the District was under the leadership of five different superintendents, some lasting just months. Finally, in 2006, the superintendent's office saw its first hint at stability with a superintendent who survived a complete calendar year with no plans to leave the position.[1]

Related to the mayor's campaign for more authority over the SLPS, in late July 2006, the State of Missouri Department of Education Commissioner appointed a five-member "blue ribbon committee," referred to as the "Special Advisory Committee" (SAC), "the Freeman-Danforth Committee," and "Danforth," and charged them to gather information about the district, and specifically "consider possible state law concerning the state's involvement with the school district" (SAC, SLPS, Aug. 31, 2006b). The committee was given three months to investigate and make recommendations that would change the direction of SLPS. One of the emergent "guiding principles" charting the direction of this committee stated, "Management of the SLPS with 92 different schools with varying missions spread throughout St. Louis is difficult, complex, and challenging" (SAC, SLPS, Oct. 9, 2006b, p. 3). This could have been an early signal of future developments—the closing of existing schools and the push for individually managed charter schools. On October 19, 2006, the SAC held a Parent Assembly meeting, and reported that, "overwhelmingly, the audience opposed State takeover" (SAC, SLPS, Nov. 2, 2006b, p. 2). In contrast, a month later, the mayor reported that "majorities of every group of major stakeholders—parents, teachers, taxpayers, administrators" believe that the "last hope for the tens of thousands students (sic) enrolled in the City's public school district is a change of governance" (Slay, Dec. 4, 2006). Oppositional statements from cooperating entities made it difficult for people to know what to believe.

The culminating report of the SAC was released on December 4, 2006. The report concluded with the statement:

> It is undoubtedly obvious from the above that we believe the SLPS is in crisis and that the crisis has been building for some years. We believe that this crisis continues to have great impact on students, their families, their teachers and the City of St. Louis and the region. We believe that the community should not accept the status quo, but rather make the most of current opportunities. We believe that the State should not "takeover" the district, but that the State can, if it acts wisely, help the community stabilize the SLPS so that it can move forward to improve its ability to educate all students. We recommend steps toward that goal. We have confidence that whatever course is taken, St. Louisans can put aside their old quarrels, can look forward and not back, and can come together to support the communities most valuable resource, its children.
>
> (SAC, SLPS, 2006a)

The conclusion left us wondering what, exactly, the committee was recommending, but it was clear that they didn't endorse a state takeover. Nevertheless, the mayor greeted this report with his own statement:

> Because the next several weeks are likely to be contentious ones, I want to be very clear about my position. I support the Danforth recommendations; and I support a return to local control when the SLPS has stabilized.
>
> (Slay, Dec. 15, 2006)

In that entry he provided a hyperlink to an earlier entry explaining what he referred to as "my position."

> As I said ... a State takeover of the district is a needed first step. The State Department of Elementary and Secondary Education should put the district in the hands of a strong administrator with a mandate to stabilize the district and start it on the long road to recovery. If legislation is needed to make the law clear and to protect a takeover from legal challenge, the Missouri General Assembly should pass a bill the first month it is in session—and the Governor should sign it.
>
> (Slay, Nov. 25, 2006)

In January, 2007, the State of Missouri's Department of Education invited citizens to speak about the "crisis" and proposed solutions at a public hearing. Approximately 1,500 people appeared at this hearing, many wishing to speak in three-minute turns. About fifty attendees, chosen by random drawing, were permitted to speak. The overwhelming majority of attendees and speakers opposed state intervention. Only two citizens stood to support intervention, one of them the then-president of the school board—who had been appointed by the mayor to fill a vacated position and was actively engaged in efforts to dismantle the elected board.

Despite the opposition, in February, 2007, the State voted to strip the district of accreditation, which led to another vote later that spring that installed a three-member politically appointed board in place of the elected SLPS school board. Once the public was removed from decision-making around the school system, the merging of the state and business interests could proceed.

Discourse Analysis as a Tool for Public Engagement: A Note on Methods

We chose our research methods based on our need to understand the situation in the public schools as it unfolded. We sifted through mountains of publicly available texts from different sides and different perspectives, including the city newspaper, email notices, official reports, blogs, and transcripts of public hearings. To more closely analyze the discursive themes and linguistic strategies used in these texts, we used the tools of critical discourse analysis (Fairclough, 1992, 2003; Lakoff, 2004; Scollon, 2008; Wodak & Meyer, 2001). We spent more time with parts of the texts that were at once problematic and provocative. We asked questions of the texts such as "Which types of genre (reports, public testimonials, letters to the editor, etc.) tended to be associated with the different groups of people?" and "How were messages distributed?" We also attended to the themes, or discourses, that arose in the text and how the discourses both constructed and represented the social world. For example, we asked, "Are some voices more easily heard than others?" and "How does the social or political position of the speaker affect the distribution of the message?" Finally, we attended to the ways in which the people's position about the crisis was encoded at the syntactic level of the text. Were sentences in the active or passive voice? Were the agents of the actions implicit or explicit? How were words used to identify people and their actions? What kind of vocabulary dominated the text? We then examined the intertextual relationships between discourses, genres, and texts as well as connections between local and global contexts.

We regularly bounced our developing interpretations off people in the community. As we participated in public events, we deepened our understanding of the connections between people and what was happening in the district. We also recognize the limitations in our analysis. There are many resources that provide overviews on issues raised (but not fully addressed) in this chapter—issues such as mayoral control of schools, privatization, the history of SLPS, and charter schools. What we offer here is a window into one point in time—a point in time in which we both observed the public use of literacy and used literate practices ourselves to make sense of the crisis as it unfolded around us. We recognize that there are certainly blind spots in our analysis, points left out, and perspectives not included.

Interpretations: Making Sense out of the Crisis

We identified two distinct networks and functions within the SLPS crisis—pro-state takeover, and anti-state takeover of schools. Within those networks, there were various stakeholders, including the local and state political systems, teachers, parents, students, community advocates and activists, and the business community. We also identified an overlapping of networks that enabled expanded participation and distribution of some discourses.

One of the first things we noticed was the sheer number of texts circulated by the anti-takeover side—those with the least material capital but the majority of human capital. These texts were represented through informal genres—letters to the editor, emails, leaflets, and short comments at community events, almost all written by the person sharing the message rather than by professional writers. In contrast, the pro-takeover side, the side with the official state-sanctioned power, circulated texts in a much more calculated manner—using things like official reports, surveys, and media spots, many written by professionals. In addition, messages were spread through the mayor's blog. Unlike many blogs, where readers have the ability to leave comments, the mayor's blog didn't allow for public response, nor did it provide a link to reply directly to the mayor's office, effectively providing a forum for the one-way distribution of important political messages without opening the door to public debate.

The pro-takeover voice used the formality of the genres to strengthen the credibility of their arguments. Further, the way in which they framed the argument led to a more stable discourse—one in which it was less possible to intervene. They constructed this stability, ironically enough, by using ambiguous terms such as "partial" state takeover and a "transitional" or "appointed" school board. Such terms left many people unclear of what, exactly, was transpiring, and positioned people as passive bystanders in the process.

We have organized this story into three sections—sections that tell a story about public education in St. Louis and also provide insight into the discursive and material construction of a school district in "crisis," insight made available to us through texts and social practices found in the public domain. In each section we share major themes that circulated during this time period: defining and framing the crisis, voting and democracy, and the intersection of finances and achievement. Each section includes the perspectives of the pro- and anti-takeover sides set against the backdrop of the history of SLPS.

Defining and Framing the Crisis

A crisis is an unexpected negative event or series of events. Sometimes crises are sudden, such as natural disasters, coups, and invasions. Other times, crises are built through a series of events that last over a longer period of time. Regardless of the type—crises result in collective shock and awe, and prepare the groundwork for the solutions that follow (Klein, 2007). The problems in SLPS have been decades in the making but when it became advantageous to frame the situation as a crisis by the pro-takeover side, it was. Ironically, the pro-takeover group referred to the situation as a crisis, but did not often acknowledge the historical context of the situation. There had been pressure on the school district for decades to improve the same conditions that the pro-takeover side spoke of in their declaration of the schools as in crisis.

NCLB provided the policy backdrop for the state takeover. "NCLB is organized to induce school failure and promote reorganization around market designs" (Shannon, 2007, p. 196). Further, Missouri state law provides for state takeovers—for financial or political instability, for example. While the sense of "chaos" had been introduced earlier, effectively giving the public the feeling of crisis within the district, the discourse of state takeover was not brought to the front until the pro-takeover side had social structures in place—the right legislators, the visible, tangible, and, we believe, orchestrated instability in the district, and pressure to fix the mounting crisis. Suddenly, not unlike the unfolding of other educational crises, the pro-takeover side simultaneously named the crisis and proposed the solutions, in calculated and precise ways of releasing information. Within months, the newly elected State Senator from the city introduced legislation that could make all of this happen.

On January 14, 2007, a televised video report titled "School Solutions" announced, "Democratic and Republican leaders in the senate will meet in St. Louis to discuss the crisis facing the St. Louis Public School District and the possible take over by the state" (Fox News, 2007). The language of the report effectively conflated the existing elected school board, the proposed appointed new school board, and the proposed state takeover. The report began with ambiguous tenuous language, stating the meeting would take place "to discuss the crisis" but then reported that state leaders have "already concluded the existing, elected St. Louis School board must go." The language moved quickly to future-tense statements that affirmed the likelihood of the "decision." For example, the reporter stated, "the mayor, the president of the board of aldermen and the governor *will* (emphasis ours) each appoint a new board member." Similarly, comments by the President of the City Board of Aldermen made around the same date stated, "I'm not going to pick someone who is going to be an obstructionist," again signaling that the decision to take over the schools had already been made.

While both sides engaged in the discourse of "crisis," each side defined and described the crisis differently. The pro-takeover side listed financial misman-agement, declining academics and political turmoil as the main reasons, and evoked individuals and small groups such as an appointed school board, the mayor, and business leadership as saviors and solutions to the crisis. Racism or profit-making in the "education sector" were not discussed. In contrast, the anti-takeover side had more complicated and nuanced arguments that drew on history and context. For instance, the anti-takeover voice called on a complex set of social relations such as racism, politics, funding, control of the budget, social contracts, NCLB, school closings, the history of the district, the relationships between social services and education, school district and the city, tax abatements, and flaws in the process such as the manipulation of data. This side was more likely to evoke networks and groups of people (e.g. unions, parent groups, politicians, teacher activist groups) working together to find solutions rather than sole individuals.

On the anti-takeover side, the overall sentiment was that the state should give the district the millions of dollars it felt was owed, and that the now relatively harmonious, non-mayoral-support dominated, elected school board should be allowed to do its work. In reply to the message from a mayor-backed elected school board member's demand for a state takeover, a local activist stated that if elected officials (i.e. school board members) can't do their jobs, "they should quit." His point was that the people of the city who want to run the schools should be running the schools, rather than abdicating responsibility and turning resources over to outsiders. A St. Louis teacher's union spokesperson stated, "Local 420 must be a partner in the solution. It's going to be hard work . . . ." She outlined the union's Five-Point Plan, ". . . research based and has worked to raise achievement in other urban districts" (AFT, 2006). This plan included zero tolerance for violence, smaller class sizes, high-quality professional development, a program to educate the whole child, and current accurate data about the school district. Interestingly, those things that the anti-takeover side identified as necessary to the improvement of the district are the same things that frame the vision of charter schools—but were denied in the existing public schools.

In the years preceding the state takeover, the mayor regularly discussed charter and private schools as the solution to the education and economic problems of St. Louis. He called on St. Louis to become a global city, and asserted that the "key to the city's renaissance is to provide more and better educational choices for families . . . . , I focused on two areas: state funding for SLPS schools and charter schools" (Slay, May 11, 2005). This foreshadowed at least ten later statements in which he asserted his support of charter schools. A blog entry revealed more in the timeline of events in the city's road to state takeover. The mayor wrote:

> I also lobbied lawmakers to pass legislation to allow us to create more quality charter schools in the City of St. Louis. Charter schools are certainly not fool-proof. Several current charter schools have failed children/parents/backers/employees badly. But, I am supporting two new charter schools in South St. Louis and I would like to see a new workforce charter school open Downtown.
>
> (Slay, May 11, 2005)

The mayor's blogs were regularly punctuated with statements that link charter schools with the economic revitalization of the city—statements that were peppered with language such as "choice," "competition," and "growth"—the linguistic precursor to the charter school movement which would appear less than two years later, in full swing.

During this time, the mayor clearly laid out his plan for SLPS, explaining how he worked with the state legislature to "create more quality charter schools." What was not stated was that in order to create these new schools, existing schools needed to be closed—something the management company running the school district did during this timeframe. The mayor recognized the limitations of charter schools but then quickly looked beyond this, leaving the failure of charters a real possibility. He gave no explanation for why the charters failed or how the new charter schools that would open would be different from the ones that failed.

Throughout all of this was the language of the markets—that choice, competition, and alternatives—would aid the city. The discourse of choice was used repetitively throughout the entries. So, too, was the rhetorical strategy of using collective pronouns to insinuate that everyone agreed with this logic and these decisions.

Without surprise, on November 9, 2007 the front page headline of the *St. Louis Post-Dispatch* read "[Mayor] Slay's answer to city school woes: Charter Schools." This article allowed the mayor to publicly announce his plan to open thirty new charter schools in the coming ten years. The mayor, despite having no authority to sponsor a charter school himself, then sent invitations to the largest Educational Management Organizations in the country— corporations such as Can! Academies, KIPP Academies, Imagine, and Edison Schools—asking them to bring their programs to St. Louis.

Voters and Democracy

In the deliberation over the state takeover of the district, voting and democracy surfaced as central issues. The pro-takeover side discounted the importance of citizens directly electing school board members, and argued that elected officials would appoint the state-appointed school board, thus giving voters a voice in the governance of the school district via other elected officials. The anti-takeover side felt strongly that because the city and the school board were separate entities, with separate funding, accountability, and missions, the citizens had a right to directly elect those who would lead the school district, just as they had a right to elect city leaders.

The pro-takeover voice rarely entered the discourse on voting, and when they did, it was to discredit the system of elected school boards. Interestingly, to the pro-takeover side, "almost everyone" already agreed that the system of elected school boards didn't work, and used low voter-turnout as evidence of that agreement. In contrast, democracy was a theme of the anti-takeover side, and, most often, this theme related to aspects of voter rights and responsibilities. A common argument for the pro-takeover side was that in St. Louis there has been a long-time trend toward low voter turnout, so taking away voting rights was really not an issue. As printed in the city newspaper, the *St. Louis Post-Dispatch*:

> Opponents of the transitional school district have argued that it disenfranchises voters. It's true that under the plan, the elected school board would be stripped of its decision-making power . . . As for all the sturm and drang at the meeting this week, where was that passion and concern last spring when there was a school board election? We hope interest remains high and that future elections attract more than the scant, scandalous 12% of voters who turned out last time.
>
> (*St. Louis P-D Editorial* Feb. 2, 2007)

The mayor spoke to low voter turnout in his blog:

> The problems are so numerous and so deeply entrenched that many people have given up: their involvement is limited to signing a tax check and does not extend to voting. Nearly nine out of ten registered City voters stayed away from the polls on April 4th.
>
> (Slay, April 7, 2006)

The mayor also created a dichotomy—one can either be for elected school boards, or for educated children, but not both. He claimed that nearly everyone agreed that the direct citywide election of school board members cannot solve the District's problems, which he identifies as thirty years in the making.

> I expect the state Board to come to the same conclusions that almost everyone else has: that the school district is mired in a crisis decades in the making, and that the current system of governance (direct citywide election of seven board members) cannot undo the damage of thirty years of decline. Those conclusions will place two competing values—elective school boards and educated children—at odds with each other. As much as I cherish the notion of direct elections, I hope the State Board puts children ahead of ballots. It is clear to most people that the status quo is untenable . . . . Most people won't notice the difference: more than 80% of the City's voters skipped at least one of the past three school board elections.
>
> (Slay, Jan. 9, 2007)

It is important to note that St. Louis elections have notoriously low voter turnout. In any given election over the past decade, less than 15% of all registered voters turned out. This not only applies to the school board; the mayor of St. Louis won his position in an election with a voter turnout of about 12%.

The anti-takeover side evoked the discourse of voters' rights and that an appointed school board is a violation of voters' rights. They talked about disenfranchised voters, the history and struggle of gaining the right to vote for African-American people, the difference between elections and appointments, rights and the U.S. Constitution, and evoked a discourse of civil rights.

One determined voice on the anti-takeover side was that of a group of high school students from the city schools who created a multimedia video that documented their struggle for public education. Central in their efforts was the creation of a socially conscious rap song (Weinstein, 2007) called "The Democracy Anthem" that spoke to their frustration with voting issues, racism, corruption, and democracy. They brought their message to public forums, City Hall, and a State Legislative session.

Democracy Anthem
It's all about democracy
See, y'all don't see what we be sayin'
We're not a bunch of puppets,
So, Dirty, no we ain't playin'.
Just tryin' to get our point across
But before we vote, we already lost.

It feels like you mocking me
It's all about Democracy.
Democracy is who we with
Education is what we get.
Y'all trying to take it away
Y'all just don't understand
We, the people, elected
So now we gonna stand!

(The full song may be heard, in its entirety, at http://web.mac.com/debbiemac1/iWeb/DEBBIE1/Movie.html)

At the time of the takeover, the Superintendent, who was hired by the elected school board, was speaking out in opposition to the takeover. In support of students who attended the public hearing and adults who addressed democratic, civic, and voter rights, she issued this statement:

Most importantly, the hearing was a lesson to the numerous students who attended. They learned about the importance of democracy, civics, and the right of the people to vote. The right of the people to a free public education is one of the tenets upon which this country was founded. The number of lessons that could be derived from this one hearing is overwhelming.

(Bourisaw, 2007)

A middle-school student at the hearing addressed voter rights as well.

> Giving the power to . . . three politicians in the SLPS, giving them power,
> giving them the power to override . . . people's votes, it's just—it's as
> logical as feeding a baby to the group—it's just not logical.
>
> (DESE, 2007 p. 80)

Several adults on the anti-takeover side addressed the nullification of votes.
One participant suggested that since no one would elect this board, the board
would not accountable to anyone. A retired teacher spoke about several issues
related to voter rights as follows:

> Gentlemen and women . . . please do not nullify my vote . . . . The mayor
> of the city has no regard for the citizens of this city, even though he would
> deny it. When he can't have his way, he slithers up to Jefferson City like
> a snake to get you and others to change the free will of the people and to
> punish them to satisfy himself and those power brokers in the city to get
> their fangs into the money of education . . . .
>
> (DESE, 2007 p. 54)

Despite this resistance, the pro-takeover side was able to effectively undermine
one of the largest issues in a state takeover of a public school system—voter's
rights. They did this through a series of strategic moves including: the use of
ambiguous language, timed public announcements, public forums which did
not inform decision making and control of the media. This has long-term
implications, for as Lubienski (2006) argues, diminishing citizen participation
in the public sector reconfigures "the internal logic" of public schools—thus
setting the stage for the complete privatization of schools (p. 12).

The Intersection of Finances and Achievement

There were times in the public deliberations over the state takeover of public
schools when both sides used the same frame—finances and achievement, for
instance. Despite the agreement, however, each side used different discursive
strategies to address the issues.

Finances

Cleveland Hammond, the Superintendent of SLPS from 1996–2003, first
noted the $55 million deficit, created in large part by the unanticipated change
in the state level of funding, as he announced his retirement. William Roberti,
the corporate turn-around CEO who replaced Hammond for a one-year term,
ushered in drastic cuts including: employee layoffs, privatization of district
services, transportation changes that created havoc, the borrowing of money
from the construction fund that subsequently required hefty annual debt

repayment, and the axing of the professional development budget. The crisis around finances was picked up by the local press:

> Education officials are acting responsibly by stepping in and taking decisive action when they see a school district in crisis. It is their duty to do so . . . [considering the] looming financial crisis.
>
> (*St. Louis P-D*, Feb. 2, 2007)

The timeline of events showed a circulation and reproduction of the term "financial crisis," which led to a logic that touted the need for "quick and decisive action" with regard to finances. The pro-takeover side used the financial health of the District differently at different points in time, depending on political aims.

In a December 15, 2005 blog entry, the mayor declared "an immediate financial crisis." This was just three days after his recognition that the "district is much better off financially today than it was when institutional reform [began] . . . . " (Slay, Dec. 12, 2005). By using time in a confusing manner, the pro-takeover side was able to hedge and avoid responsibility. It was interesting to note who was positioned as the culprit of the District's financial troubles. "SLPS has wasted billions of dollars," (Slay, April 7, 2006). Agency and responsibility of State and mayoral decision-making around finances was absent from all of the pro-takeover artifacts, despite the City and State's roles in funding problems. In all of the documents, the mayor is positioned as if he was on the sidelines, as a passive observer versus an active decision-maker.

Also in his blog, he called on his familiar rhetorical strategy—listing the poor qualities of the district—"broken systems, run-down facilities, bloated non-teaching bureaucracies, unengaged parents, ill-trained teachers, and an immediate financial crisis" (Slay, Dec. 15, 2005). It should be no surprise that these qualities were those called on to support the state takeover of the SLPS. Left out of the mayor's blog and most other texts represented in the pro-takeover side in the discourses around finances was the idea that SLPS was under-funded. The Special Advisory Committee report does mention the under-funding of the SLPS and connects SLPS to a national scene. The following was written:

> The committee believes that K-12 education in the US in general and in the SLPS in particular is under-funded given its importance. However, we realize that the SLPS, like other school systems, must balance its budget or it will run out of money to pay its bills. It is not for profit, but it is also not for loss.
>
> (SAC, SLPS, 2006a)

Also missing is the history of tax abatements to businesses and individuals who are given incentives and tax-breaks. The report states that since 2001, "the financial reserves of the SLPS have declined drastically." Again, the State, the mayor, the school board members he supported, and the management corporation and its CEO, Roberti, are left unmarked.

The anti-takeover side recognized that the State owed the District money, that there was a history of financial mismanagement, and that the decision to take over the schools was politically motivated. The pro-takeover side evoked the discourse of privatization, while the anti-takeover side talked about the perils of merging public and private interests—big corporations making money off of public education; the State wanting to control the budget of SLPS; and privatizing services.

Achievement

During the years after the 2004 hiring of Alvarez & Marsal, SLPS saw a rapid decline in accreditation points, mostly tied to student achievement. During those years, in an effort to save money, the District closed and consolidated many schools, almost all of which were in lower income neighborhoods on the northern side of the city; cut professional development from the budget; and invoked other methods aimed at cost-savings. In addition, the District implemented a standardized curriculum that required teachers to remove "non-approved" teaching materials, including books, from their classrooms. The State Department of Education began requesting new accountability information—and wanted some of this information retroactive to five years. While the average citizen seemed to believe accountability was directly related to test scores, it actually was a much more complicated formula that changed over the course of our analysis.

The pro-takeover side used an argument that evoked academics and achievement more so than the anti-takeover side. The pro-takeover side discussed the racial achievement gap, graduation rates, and test scores as measures of success. It was interesting to note that many of the documents on the pro-takeover side discussed student achievement without much evidence. The Special Advisory Committee report—considered to be an important and official document in the proceedings—made statements about achievement without supporting evidence, using the term "academic achievement" without a definition. The report stated, "Academic achievement has not met the expectations of children, parents, SLPS leadership .... " The contradiction around claims for evidence appeared stark when the State Board of Education questioned the data submitted by SLPS about graduation and college enrollment rates. The discourse of achievement was linked with both a state and a national definition based on test scores used to measure the success and failure of children and, by extension, school districts under NCLB. No questions were raised or asked about the validity of the test scores, the complexity of achievement, multiple forms of evidence to represent achievement, changes in curriculum and assessment that may influence the results of the test scores, or the flawed nature of drawing conclusions from test scores about district and school performance.

There is an irony around the definition of achievement. That is, achievement was defined in terms of narrow indicators (test scores and state standards) by both pro- and anti-takeover sides, and was used to determine the vitality of a school district. The frame was established and neither side attempted to break the frame. Much of the discourse around academics/achievement focused on flawed reporting of data rather than a critique of the frame itself.

The mayor's discourse around achievement shifted in importance from before to after his slate for the school board lost elections. Throughout, the discourse of achievement is defined through comparison, test scores, point systems, levels, and other indicators at a system level. In general, the mayor's blogs before he lost control of the elected school board represent cautiously optimistic statements about achievement at the elementary level. The mayor seemed to carefully disaggregate the data per grade level and show achievement rates in a complicated manner. After the anti-takeover school board was elected, the mayor's blog entries made more general statements about the lack of achievement in the District, without the same attention to disaggregated data. For example, his blog entry on September 3, 2006 was written, it seems, as if it is in dialogue with past entries—"another set of disappointing achievement test scores," (Slay, Sept. 3, 2006) asking the reader to call on other disappointing test scores. Suddenly all of the test scores were lumped together, and none were disaggregated to show the areas of most success as had been done before his candidates lost the election.

For the anti-takeover side, the discourse of achievement is defined in much the same way—through "standards," "test scores," "accreditation," and discussion of the flawed process in which the District is being asked to produce data. However, there was a reactionary and defensive tone in anti-takeover texts. For instance, in a memo written by the SLPS Superintendent, Diana Bourisaw, on September 23, 2007, she noted that the district was on the defensive to "validate our college placement numbers back to 2001" (Bourisaw, 2007). Achievement/academics were discussed in terms of the State standards and other discourses including "the district's annual performance," "provisional accreditation," "data," "college placement standard," and the general "standards." Achievement was discussed at the systems level, not at an individual level, and set up an "us-them" dynamic, with SLPS as "us" and "we" and the State as "they" and "them."

In this memo, achievement was associated with "loss of accreditation." The Superintendent extended her analysis beyond the school district to her concerns for the city of St. Louis. She cited the numbers of students who left the city for county schools or who enrolled in charter schools. She introduced the discourse of choice; "We are already a district of choice." This statement held an intertextual connection with the discourse of choice that had been circulating on the pro-takeover side; specifically as seen in the mayor's blog. She discussed the ramifications of being an unaccredited district. "State law requires us to open our school doors and allow students to leave the city if they so desire," pitting the District and State against each other. She called on the metaphor of "school doors" to make her point about declining enrollments, which, in turn will impact finances, achievement, and academics.

Shocked into Educational Change

The discursive stage for the "crisis" in the SLPS was set through a combination of the widespread circulation of one-sided official texts, orchestrated rhetorical strategies, and the confusing use of educational concepts (e.g. choice, takeover, charter schools). Through sharing the discursive construction of the "crisis" from the points of view of the pro- and anti-takeover voices, we have highlighted the way in which the discursive landscape unfolded alongside material and policy changes. What is clear is that a few representatives of the state and the business community set the frame, while parents, educators and community activists responded. It was difficult for average citizens to put the pieces together, because there was no unified way of disseminating information. Further, the language that was used to describe the dismantling of the district was chosen in a way that made the solutions sound viable.

What is happening in St. Louis is but one example of the gradual erosion of public education. Across the country, school districts are taken over, schools closed, and for-profit schools take their place (e.g. Howell, 2005; Lipman, 2007; Viteritti, 2005; Wells, Slayton, & Scott, 2002). Preceded by years of standardized tests, scripted curriculum, and calls for stronger accountability, this wave of neoliberal educational and economic policies designed to gut the educational system has effectively laid the groundwork for a crisis in our public schools (Tracy, 2007). Neoliberal social policies emphasize the deregulation of the market and shrinking of the public sector. Neoliberalism restructures relations in society—not just between people and the market but away from the "common good" to an emphasis on competition and personal responsibility (Chomsky & McChesney, 2003; Hursh, 2007).

The solution is proposed by the collective wisdom of the state and the free market—a solution that opens the door to the privatization of education. Klein (2007) points out the way in which natural disasters (tsunamis, hurricanes) as well as terror attacks (e.g. September 11th attacks) result in people who are traumatized and ready for solutions. Governments and corporations partner up to provide free-market solutions—a series of interventions that Milton Friedman referred to as "economic shock treatment."

> Only a crisis—actual or perceived—produces real change. When that crisis occurs, the actions that are taken depend on the ideas that are lying around. That, I believe, is our basic function: to develop alternatives to existing policies, to keep them alive and available until the politically impossible becomes the politically inevitable.
>
> (Friedman, 1982; quoted in Klein, 2007, p. 6)

During these times of crisis, governments swiftly intervene to impose free-market programs—such as handing out vouchers for children to attend private schools in the case of New Orleans after Hurricane Katrina, or selling off the coastline of Sri Lanka to entrepreneurs after the 2004 tsunami. This is now "the preferred method of advancing corporate goals: using moments of collective trauma to engage in radical social and economic engineering" (Klein, 2007, p. 8).

Sustained crises, such as we have reported in SLPS, result in putting people into a prolonged state of collective vertigo, reeling from misinformation, years of instability, and carefully framed discourses. The takeover, the school closings, and the firing of the superintendent are but three examples within a year of what Klein would refer to as "shocks" to the parents, teachers, and citizens of St. Louis. As Klein's (2007) "shock doctrine" argues, shocked societies give up things they ordinarily would not. As we have seen with the SLPS, the continued instability of the schools is integral to the imposition of unpopular policies of a state takeover, school closings, and the ushering in of for-profit charter schools. The public yearns for stability and the only foreseeable stability for the district lies in the merging of the public sector with the private, in treating the school system as a market.

Spaces for Resistance

There is a long history of the struggle for educational rights in St. Louis, Missouri. Where there are assaults on democracy, there is also resistance and collective action (Rogers, Mosley, Kramer, & LSJTRG, 2009). Parent groups, educators, and the greater community organize to protest school closings, personnel changes, and other decisions made by the appointed board. The resistance to neoliberal policies and the privatization of public education is being fought in other cities as well. A national Teacher Activist Group (TAG) is working to build a broad base of support and mobilization around public education.

The story we have presented is part of the story of the changes in the landscape of public education in St. Louis. It is also our story of making sense out of the construction of a school district crisis. In our work as university professors, this story found its way into our teaching, and we became part of public discourse about the state takeover. It kept us engaged and up-to-speed with the construction of the crisis and its impact on public education. As we moved between local and national patterns and trends we found new and different ways to share information in public places. In our work as public intellectuals we draw on tools of critical policy analysis and discourse analysis to more fully understand the complexity of the situation and—as importantly—to find ways to intervene and act with others to preserve public education.

Note

1 However, in February 2008, the appointed Special Administrative Board kick-started their "reforms" of the school system by announcing their plan for a national

search for a new superintendent. The current superintendent, Diana Bourisaw, was invited to reapply for her position. She declined to do so. Orchestrated or coinciden-tal—the revolving door of superintendents in the district achieved the same outcome, a prolonged set of shocks to an already devastated group of parents, teachers, and community members.

References

AFT 420. (2006). *Five-Point Plan.* Retrieved February 2, 2007, from www. mo.aft.org/local420

Ayres-Salamon, M. (2004). *A recipe for failure: A year of reform and chaos in the St. Louis Public Schools.* Victoria, BC: Trafford.

Bourisaw, D. (2007). *From the desk of Diana Bourisaw, Superintendent.* Retrieved February 2, 2008, from http://www.slps.org/superintendent/weekly_message.html

Chomsky, N., & McChesney, R. (2003). *Profit over people: Neoliberalism and global order.* New York: Seven Stories Press.

Croteau, D., Hoynes, W., & Ryan, C. (2005). *Rhyming hope and history: Activists, academics, and social movement scholarship.* Minneapolis: University of Minnesota Press.

Department of Elementary and Secondary Education, State of Missouri. (2007). Public meeting on the status of the St. Louis Public Schools, January 31, 2007, Harris Stowe State University, St. Louis, MO. Transcript provided by DESE.

Edmonson, J. (2004). *Understanding and applying critical policy study: Reading educators advocating for change.* Newark, DE: International Reading Association.

Fairclough, N. (1992). Intertextuality in critical discourse analysis. *Linguistics and Education, 4*(3–4), 269–293.

Fairclough, N. (2003). *Analyzing discourse: Textual analysis for social research.* New York: Routledge.

Fox News. (Jan. 14, 2007). School solutions. KTVI, St. Louis, MO.

Heaney, G., & Uchitelle, S. (2004). *Unending struggle: The long road to an equal education in St. Louis.* St. Louis, MO: Reedy Press.

Howell, W. G. (Ed.). (2005). *Besieged: School boards and the future of education politics.* Washington, DC: Brookings Institution.

Hursh, D. (2007). Assessing No Child Left Behind and the rise of neoliberal education policies. *American Educational Research Journal, 44*(3), 491–518.

Klein, N. (2007). *The shock doctrine: The rise of disaster capitalism.* New York: Henry Holt & Company.

Lakoff, G. (2004). *Don't think of an elephant: Know your values and frame the debate.* White River Junction, VT: Chelsea Green Publishing.

Lehrer, J. (2004). "Turning around." *Online News Hour.* Retrieved February 20, 2008, from http://www.pbs.org/newshour/bb/education/july–dec04/stlouis_8–17.html

Lipman, P. (2004). *High stakes education: Inequality, globalization and urban school reform.* New York: Routledge.

Lipman, P. (2007). From accountability to privatization and African American exclusion: Chicago's renaissance 2010. *Educational Policy, 21*(3), 471–502.

Lubienski, C. (2006). School choice and privatization in education: An alternative analytical framework. *Journal of Critical Educational Policy Studies, 4*(1), 1–25.

Morris, J. (2001). Forgotten voices of black educators: Critical race perspectives on the implementation of a desegregation plan. *Educational Policy, 15*(4), 575–600.

Portz, J., Stein, L., & Jones, R. R. (1999). *City schools and city politics: Institutions and leadership in Pittsburgh, Boston, and St. Louis.* Lawrence: University of Kansas Press.

Reinhard, B. (1998). Racial issues cloud state takeovers. *Education Week, 17*(1), 1.

Rogers, R., Mosley, M., Kramer, M. A., & LSJTRG. (2009). *Designing socially just learning communities: Critical literacy education across the lifespan.* New York: Routledge.

Scollon, R. (2008). *Analyzing public discourse: Discourse analysis in the making of public policy.* New York: Routledge.

Seder, R.C. (2000). *Balancing accountability and local control: State intervention for financial and academic stability.* Policy Study No. 268. Prepared for the Reason Public Policy Institute, Los Angeles (ED 451 261).

Shannon, P. (2007). *Reading against democracy: The broken promises of reading instruction.* Portsmouth, NH: Heinemann.

Slay, F. *From the Mayor's Desk.* Retrieved February 20, 2008, from http://www. mayorslay.com/desk.

> Better educational choices. May 11, 2005. deskID=36.
> SLPS, Part 1. Dec. 12, 2005. deskID=265.
> SLPS, Part 2. Dec. 15, 2005. deskID=261.
> What's next for SLPS? April 7, 2006. deskID=377.
> SLPS. Sept. 3, 2006. deskID=516.
> Charter choices. Nov. 15, 2006. deskID=578.
> A state takeover of SLPS. Nov. 25, 2006. deskID=585.
> SLPS survey. Dec. 4, 2006. deskID=590.
> Danforth Report. Dec. 15, 2006. deskID=596.
> Ballots or children. Jan. 9, 2007. deskID=617.

Special Advisory Committee, St. Louis Public Schools. (2006a). *Final report.* Missouri Department of Elementary and Secondary Education, St. Louis, MO. Retrieved February 20, 2008, from http://www.slps-committee.org

Special Advisory Committee, St. Louis Public Schools. (2006b). *Minutes* August 31, October 9, November 2. Retrieved February 20, 2008, from http://www.slps-committee.org

St. Louis Post-Dispatch. (2003–2007). *Letters to the Editor* (multiple). Retrieved February 2, 2007, from www.stltoday.com

Tracy, K. (2007) The discourse of crisis in public meetings: A case study of a school board's multimillion dollar error. *Journal of Applied Communication Research, 35,* 418–41.

Vitcritti, J. (2005). The end of local politics? In W. Howell (Ed.), *Besieged: School boards and the future of education politics* (pp. 308–323). Washington, DC: Brookings Institute.

Wells, A. S. (Ed.). (2002). *Where charter school policy fails: Issues of accountability and equity.* New York: Teachers College Press.

Wells, A. S., & Crain, R. (1999). *Stepping over the color line: African-American students in white suburban schools.* New Haven, CT: Yale University Press.

Wells, A. S., Slayton, J., & Scott, J. (2002). Defining democracy in the neoliberal age: Charter school reform and educational consumption. *American Educational Research Journal, 39*(2), 337–361.

Weinstein, S. (2007). A love for the thing: The pleasures of rap as a literate practice. *Journal of Adolescent and Adult Literacy, 50*(4), 270–281.

Wilson, D. J. (2003). Demolition man. *Riverfront Times,* St. Louis, July 9, 2003.

Woodside-Jiron, H. (2004). Language, power and participation: Using critical discourse analysis to make sense of public policy. In R. Rogers (Ed.), *An introduction to critical discourse analysis in education* (pp. 237–254). Mahwah, NJ: Lawrence Erlbaum Associates.

Wodak, R., & Meyer, M. (Eds.) (2001). *Methods of critical discourse analysis.* London: Sage.

For Further Exploration

Dingerson, B. M., Peterson, B., & Walters, S. (Eds.). (2008). *Keeping the promise? The debate over charter schools*. Milwaukee, WI: Rethinking Schools.

Literacy for Social Justice Teacher Research Group: http://www.umsl.edu/~lsjtrg.

Teacher Activist Groups: http://www.teacheractivistgroups.org.

11 Brewing a Crisis
Language, Educational Reform, and the Defense of a Nation

Susan Florio-Ruane[1]

How Is a Crisis Brewed?

This chapter is about the language of national crisis—especially how crisis functions as a powerful metaphor in public discourse about educational reform. Leaders attempt to influence citizens' beliefs and actions in order to effect change, often in terms of "crisis." Such crises have personal consequences but are presented or perceived as problems of large scale and broad impact. They do not arise within, nor are they expressed by individuals. The characterization of a problem as a national crisis is a sociolinguistic transformation of that problem into an urgent call for organized response. The crisis is situated in a particular time, place, and social context. It is described in terms of the problem, its cause, the urgent need for decisive change, and the nature and content of that change.

A problem of authenticity in educational change exists when crises are not experienced or acknowledged directly and locally. If such is the case, persuasion is needed to convince educators that, indeed, a problem of practice has reached proportions threatening the national welfare. The cyclic appearance of an urgent call for reform in education is sometimes referred to by practitioners as the inevitable "swinging of the pendulum." However, identification of a national crisis sometimes illuminates problems in disparate locales, thus raising them to national significance. In addition, (inter)national crises may affect U.S. society in ways that call for response in education policy and practice. This chapter offers examples of the varied contexts for and negotiation of crises in 20th Century U.S. education.

Who Brews Crises in Education—How and Why?

As noted above, the metaphor of the swinging pendulum is often used to characterize educational changes. Yet, if we look across the last century, the path of change seems circuitous. At intervals roughly approximating the political ascendancy of various parties or social movements, leaders have used crisis-laden rhetoric to attempt to change the nation's direction, and education has played a part in that process (e.g. the Presidential Report, "A Nation at Risk").

There have also been occasions when an unexpected national or international event has been interpreted as a moment of crisis in which education should play a central role (e.g. the Cold War launch of Sputnik by the Soviet Union). Thus, although they are neither as predictable nor as repetitious as the swinging pendulum, education-related crises are frequent and they alter our society's educational trajectory.

Regardless of their source, crisis calls are made by leaders and resemble one another in form and function. They depend on core narratives and make heavy use of metaphor to accomplish the following: (1) identify clear and present danger, (2) assert the decisive changes to be made (typically framed by leaders and the experts who advise them), and (3) call citizens to action. Notwithstanding their variety, the rhetoric of national crises tends to reinforce the structural features of public institutions even as it calls for changes in their activities. This is because in the national crises of the last century we typically sought to regain order, not to create new order. However, as we will see in the examples below, since crises and their narratives are of human creation and proportions, they can, in Elbow's terms, be "believed or doubted" (1986, passim). Moreover, we can tell new and different stories of change and respond to them in novel ways (Florio-Ruane, 1997).

One of the most powerful figures of speech we use to accomplish change in times of crisis is *metaphor*. When orators use metaphor to move readers and listeners, they are using a heightened form of the ordinary human capacity to make and share experiences by means of figurative language. In Lakoff and Johnson's words, "Our ordinary conceptual system, in terms of which we both think and act, is metaphorical in nature" (1980, p. 3). Thus, metaphors can shape consciousness in an individual life history and in a nation's shared history. In an analysis of the role of experience in the education of literacy teachers, Rosaen and I (2008) wrote that, "metaphors are . . . central to how we explore and understand the world because they provide an experiential framework for making sense of abstract concepts" (p. 706).

Since the entwining of language, thought, and culture happens as part of ordinary experience, we come to hold and share tacit meanings passed on within cultural groups. We often do not recognize how our interpretations and actions have been shaped by powerful social rhetoric. We can see evidence of this in the ways that we readily assimilate ideas and situations into our vocabulary and take them for granted as "the way things are." This is a decidedly mixed blessing. It enables us to develop a working consensus with one another quickly and with relative ease, but it also enables us to take shared understanding for granted. This can close off inquiry and authentic dialogue in our personal and professional relationships as well as in our response to problems (Florio-Ruane with deTar, 2001).

In the past decade, for example, in my practice as a teacher educator, I have noticed how even the greenest of newcomers to literacy teaching readily pick up and use acronyms associated with education policy in the nation and my state (e.g. NCLB, AYP, GLCEs). Along with this shared fluency comes the assumption of common knowledge of what these acronyms mean, belief in their objectivity, and expectation of their durable reality in a teacher's career. Thus, if asked, "Why are you teaching that literacy strategy?" the newcomer may reply, "Because it's a GLCE." (This acronym is pronounced, "glick," and refers to Michigan Grade Level Content Expectations.) When asked, "What is a GLCE?" the response is typically, "It is a strategy I am expected to teach."

As a teacher educator, I try to help my students risk breaking this sociolinguistic frame. Acknowledging the ubiquity of the GLCEs, I urge my students to put them aside for a while and to try their hand at designing curriculum. In this way, they begin to think about teaching literacy by asking such questions as, What do my students know? How can I find out? What do they need to learn? Why is it important for them to learn this? How will I help them learn it? How will I know that they have learned it? This shift centers on their practice, students, and local context. It highlights the need for their thoughtful action as educators. We will return to this idea at the end of the chapter.

Crises in Education and the "Nation as a Family"

A fundamental metaphor by which we understand ourselves as a society is that of "the nation as a family" (Lakoff, 2006, p. 49). This metaphor is tapped—implicitly or explicitly—in times of crisis. Lakoff notes the depth and durability of "the nation as family" as a cultural metaphor by pointing out, for example,

> We have Founding Fathers, The Daughters of the American Revolution. We "send our sons" (sic) to war. This is a natural metaphor because we usually understand large social groups, like nations, in terms of small ones, like families or communities.
>
> (ibid., p. 5)

When we think about something large in terms of something small, or something "experience distant" in terms of something "experience near" (Geertz, 1973), we are not *de facto* exercising reductionism. Both the familiar and the unfamiliar (or the small and the large) are complex. It is the association of the two in metaphor that permits us to contemplate complexity—as Pinker (2008) says, metaphor "efs the ineffable." What Pinker means is that something we otherwise would find difficult to contemplate or comprehend becomes easier to understand when we think about it in terms of something more familiar, immediate, or concrete. Thus, for example, we can contemplate the history of our kinship relationships with the familiar image of the "family tree."

There are two problems associated with such "effability." First, the small is not the large—they are schematically related. If we confuse one with the other, we will distort rather than illuminate aspects of the complexity of each. This problem is a serious one if we are trying to theorize, predict, or control what is happening in one context based on our understanding of it by analogy to another. Second, the power to use the human capacity for metaphor to move large groups of people to a shared sense of meaning and collective action is socially consequential.

In Classical times, it was thought essential to master the skills of oratory, especially the rhetorical skills of persuasion by means of using figurative language, in order to lead (Lentriccia & McLaughlin, 1990). It is important but difficult to apply checks and balances to such power precisely because of its transparency, its use of ordinary sense making to shape ideology and its enactment. Pursuing the complexity of the nation as family metaphor, for example, Lakoff wonders, "If there are two different understandings of the nation, do they come from two different understandings of family?" (2006; the information referred to here draws on Lakoff's text, pp. 50–66). He suggests that how you view the nation as a family depends on your sense of the safety of that family in the context of world events—both those directly experienced and those about which you are told. This, in turn, influences the kind of parenting you value.

A dangerous worldview, Lakoff suggests, calls for a "strict father" who can: (1) protect the family in a dangerous world, (2) support the family in the difficult world, and (3) teach his children right from wrong. In contrast, a view of the world as a safe place invites nurturance rather than vigilance. In Lakoff's terms, such a nurturing national family would value the following: (1) If you want your child to be fulfilled in life, the child has to be free enough to do that. Therefore, freedom is a value; (2) You do not have very much freedom if there is no opportunity or prosperity. Therefore, opportunity and prosperity are values; and (3) If you really care about your child, you want your child to be treated fairly by you and by others. Therefore, fairness is a value.

Teachers Reading the Rhetoric of Crisis

Multiple calls to national crisis have characterized education as problem, solution, or both. The crisis-driven rhetoric of educational reform tips toward the strict parent. However, even in crisis, teaching must balance discipline with nurturance of the child's developing intellect, convention with invention (Bruner, 1960/77). Rosaen and I argue that it is a particular aspect of the educator's professional identity to be acutely sensitive to words and meanings in context and to

> avoid confusing naming (e.g. the "struggling reader") with knowing how to enact practices (e.g. that support all learners to become successful readers). Educators must take the time to investigate meaning and pay attention to the rhetoric of teaching—what it is like, and what it reveals.
>
> (Paraphrased, 2008, p. 720)

Slowing down or stopping to look closely at our language and activity during a crisis is counter-intuitive. Yet it is precisely because national educational crises are rhetorical that we need not only to react to them, but also to "read" them. The remainder of this chapter "reads" three 20th Century crises involving educational reform in the United States that have had implications for all teachers and, in the case of the most recent, particular implications for teachers of literacy. They occurred in: (1) the inter-war years of the Great Depression in the 1930s; (2) the Cold War launch of Sputnik in the 1950s; and (3) recent era of reform under the law, No Child Left Behind, spanning 2001–2007. The chapter concludes with reflections on the need for educators, especially those who specialize in language and literacy, to be aware of how their pedagogy can be shaped, directed, or limited by the powerful rhetoric of crisis.

The Inter-War Years: All Hands on Deck!

Headlines of crisis rock the news. Reading reports of war, terrorism, and economic decline, we turn to the editorial page. There we find a highly charged essay turning on the metaphor of the "ship of state" in danger.

> The mariner blown out of his course by adverse winds and sailing long under clouded heavens among dangerous reefs seizes the first opportunity to get his bearings and chart his way by fixed marks of sky or land. Likewise, in the management of human affairs, although the analogy is not exact, it is often necessary for leaders of the State, the professions, and callings, amid great disturbances, to take their reckonings—to recur to first principles. This applies to education as well as to other branches of national interest and activity. None is independent of the others.
>
> (The Educational Policies Commission, 1937)

The essay identifies a crisis, rallies a collective response, and conveys what that response must be. The authors tell us that navigation of the ship to safety will be the interdependent effort. All must work together to figure out how to point the ship in the right direction. The language of this 1937 essay (published by the Educational Policies Commission of the National Education Association of the United States and the Department of Superintendence), as well as the crisis it names and the solution it offers, seems contemporary.

If you were to read this essay in today's news, its content, tone, or rhetoric would not surprise you. However, it was published at a time when the nation and the world were reeling from the shock of the First World War and struggling to survive an ensuing worldwide economic depression. The parallels in its rhetoric of crisis and those we have heard at times of reform in our own careers are striking. For example, the essay continues,

> Since the outbreak of the … war …, American society has faced disconcerting issues at home and abroad, has experienced storms of passion, and encountered the vicissitudes of a profound economic dislocation. The human and economic destruction of the war itself, the ensuing overthrow of governments and social systems …, the collapse of prosperity in the United States … have shaken American thought and practice from center to circumference.

To find our way, it asserts, we must return to "first principles" and, since educators are among the crew, teachers will have a major role to play in rescuing the ship of state in crisis—it is a role of re-asserting core knowledge. Reading on, however, we are told that education is not only a part of the solution, but is also implicated in the crisis. Failing to keep democratic principles strong, teachers left the nation unprepared to weather the storms of national and international events. The authors write that

> The war and the economic crisis accentuated the problem of the schools and added new cares to old burdens; but distracting issues arose. Their origins lie deeper than military events and economic stringency, and they will not be automatically settled by a guarantee of peace or a return of prosperity. Indeed, apart from immediate distresses, the chief effect of the financial shortage has been to make the teaching profession and the interested public acutely aware of the challenges and claims that had been dimly discerned years before the war and the panic broke upon the normal course of history.

Thus, the essay enjoins teachers to help save the nation, yet it also reminds them that they are part of a crew that let the ship drift. The essay evokes the image of teacher as both "vigilant father" and "indulgent mother"—strict yet also lax—in ways that have put both children and the nation at risk.

Blurring the metaphors of the nation as a family and the ship of state, we recognize a strict father/captain responsibly commanding a hierarchy of people who, themselves, hold official ranks, rights, and duties. It is a closed society marked by interdependence with explicit rules and meanings. The ship of state described in the 1937 essay was rocked not only on the stormy seas of worldwide conflict in ideologies, cross-national power struggles, and the rapid changes brought about by modern technologies, but also by immigration, a world war, and intense poverty. It cannot afford ignorance of core democratic values, lack of a common language and literacy, or internal moral lassitude. The captain shouts, "All hands on deck!" and educators are immediately summoned to action under the captain's command.

"Crisis" interrupts ordinary, chronological time ("chronos"). The interruption calls for a swift response that takes the form of decisive change of course. This is a moment of danger and of opportunity, what Biblical scholars and rhetoricians call *"kairos"* (Erickson, 2004). This state of change can reinforce hierarchies but it can also be revolutionary, opening up possibilities of new action. As such, crisis can be a powerful catalyst for the making (or re-making) of society and identity. But there is a difference between a crisis that is experienced as authentic (either by way of powerful events of a social or natural cause or by powerful persuasion by leaders) and the rhetorical act of calling a national crisis—using the language and images of crisis metaphorically to prompt a particular response or to define a situation and the identities of its participants in particular ways. The former will present a moment of decisive change, while the latter may call for change but be resisted.

For those of us who live within, wrestle with, and/or study such narratives in our practice as literacy educators, according to Whitebrook, "the process of narrative construction is relevant inasmuch as it makes the point that identity is narratively made, and shows what that means for an understanding of political identity" (2001, p. 5). The authors of the 1937 position statement were using the metaphor of the "ship of state" to tell a particular story about the role of education in a democracy authentically in crisis. Over the ensuing seventy years, powerful voices seemed cyclically to proclaim that the nation was in crisis—either by force of events or by effort at political persuasion. The results were mixed, but teaching and teacher identity would be located in the eye of every one of these storms.

The Cold War, Sputnik, and Educational Identity

The "Cold War" centered education in the struggle to protect both American ideology and values, and also its very existence and the security and safety of its citizens. The Soviet Union's launch of Sputnik, the first man-made satellite to orbit the earth, is widely viewed as the major U.S. crisis of the Cold War period. The launch disrupted ordinary time and expectations, evoked rapid and definitive response, and changed the course of American life. Sputnik's launch came at a low point in our own development of rocket technology. Americans were aware of the competition between our own and the Soviet Union's rocket development programs and the importance of success in launching a satellite into earth orbit in terms of both prestige and national defense.

Sputnik insinuated itself into Americans' public and everyday lives. With the naked eye, adults and children watched from backyards as it blinked across the night sky (Hickam, 1998). Amateur radio operators picked up its signal. Newspapers, magazines, radio stations, and television networks covered the event. Speeches were delivered, bills introduced, reports written, conversations held, curricula designed, and lessons taught about Sputnik. Literally and metaphorically, Sputnik brought the global and the local together. It caused knowledge systems to change rapidly to accommodate new reality (Cope & Kalantsis, 2000). Interest in science grew at the grassroots level even as experts in the military, Congress, and academy pondered a new science curriculum (Bruner, 1960/77). The first Federal legislation to fund state and local education initiatives was passed, largely in response to the Sputnik launch, and signed into law by President Eisenhower as the National Defense Education Act (NDEA). This act enabled the Federal government to help states build new schools to serve burgeoning baby-boom enrollments. It also enabled Congress to capitalize on an emerging relationship between the government and the academy in the form of the National Science Foundation (NSF) and step forward, with scientists and other academicians, to lead reform of U.S. high school science and mathematics curricula.

It took a momentous event of crisis proportion, indeed, for the historic and sacrosanct national value of local control of education to give way even slightly to Federal assistance and involvement—and the small Soviet orb, with all that it implied, provided such a moment. It created a powerful, enduring way of triangulating science, national security, and education. In Lucena's terms, "As language resonates with the image of the nation under threat, it acquires a legitimacy that allows policymakers to define problems and solutions in terms of scientists and engineers" (2005, p. 8). Sputnik's launch was appropriated by a collaborative of national political, military, and scientific leaders to call for educational reform. As such, it was the first occasion to embody the saving role of education called for in the National Education Association text of 1937.

No Child Left Behind and the Failure of a Crisis Narrative

Many literacy educators cannot recall a time when education reform was deliberated absent a sense of crisis. The narrative of national crisis has permeated educational reform for much of the 20th Century. As such, it is a part of everyday reality to expect that education plays an important role in our democracy, and that our politics influence education. We hold this knowledge tacitly, becoming aware of it only when policies fail to meet (or violate) our expectations. The re-authorization of the 1965 Elementary and Secondary Education Act (ESEA)[2] in 2001, as No Child Left Behind Act (NCLB), failed to meet expectations of education's stakeholders in numerous ways. These have been expressed in research reports, professional discourse, websites and blogs, university classrooms, and conversations in many teachers' lounges around the country. What these texts have in common is the sense that NCLB's call to reform of education—for our purposes, elementary literacy instruction—was wanting and disturbingly different from previous calls to crisis.

Among the reasons why NCLB did not effectively mobilize a supportive response are the following: (1) it lacked a clear, compelling crisis narrative; (2) it posed a solution that overstepped traditional, normative boundaries between Federal and state authority related to education; (3) it violated educators' customary local rights and responsibilities; and (4) it called for change that was limited in scope yet sweeping in impact on schools, teachers, and children. Sunderman, Kim, and Orfield (2005) argue that its micro-management of change via stringent regulation and accountability makes NCLB, "in many ways ... the most startling departure in federal education policy in US history." They go on to say that

> under NCLB, performance on state reading and mathematics tests determines whether schools make annual yearly progress (AYP). Schools failing to meet these achievement goals are subject to an escalating series of severe sanctions over time .... For the first time in the history of Title I, the federal government is dictating the pace of progress required of all schools, regardless of the students they serve and the resources they have,

and requires prescriptive standards for low-performing schools that fail to improve scores on standardized reading and math tests.

(2005, pp. ix-x)

The rhetoric of the nation's well-being as tied to education runs through NCLB as surely as it ran through the NDEA (and other precursors such as the 1983 Federal report, *A Nation at Risk*). For example, in a brief *Guide to Education and NCLB* available to citizens at no cost on the Internet, then-Secretary of Education Rod Paige wrote that

Education is one of the most important functions of government ... [and] satisfying the demand for highly skilled workers is the key to maintaining competitiveness and prosperity in the global economy.

(*A Guide to Education and NCLB*, 2004)

Note that Paige's statement describes education as a function of government, not of society, and that the rationale for its importance is related to national competitiveness and prosperity.

According to Secretary Paige, the purpose of education is to satisfy industry's "demand" for highly skilled "workers," yet neither their skills nor the nature of their work is described. In phrasing which oddly echoes the need for a continuous stream of young people to do the grinding labor of millwork (as in the novels of Charles Dickens, for example), contemporary schools apparently exist to meet the insatiable "demand" for workers, presumably in light industry, business, and service. In this case it is not their physical strength and endurance that must be tapped, it is their "skill." Therefore, the function of the school, delegated by the government, is the production of workers with the requisite skills to fulfill the demands of undisclosed, corporate enterprises.

We must teach all children "skills" because we are "competing" in a "global economy." The idea of a global competition is apocalyptic—especially since our competitors are unspecified and it is unclear what it is we are competing over. What will happen if we lose? How will we know if we are winning? Are we already behind? Ahead? If we teach our children skills, how will they help us win the competition? What will they do? Are corporations somewhat like the army, and are literate workers the foot soldiers? If not, why is the government directly responsible for ensuring the training of skilled workers for global competition? What will happen to the children who are behind? Will they hold us back? How should we save them?

In Secretary Paige's metaphor of a global "competition," we have the basis of a crisis narrative in which our nation's fate is tied to educating skilled workers. In order for this narrative to mobilize citizens for educational change, they must be persuaded that there is an imminent crisis, that educational change is needed, and that this reform should be aimed specifically at teaching skills of literacy and math to all students. As such, it has the generic structure of the Sputnik crisis narrative, yet it lacks the immediate and widely felt experience of a threat to national security and well-being that the Sputnik launch created. Moreover, it proposes a solution that is less obviously connected to the vague threat it poses—skill instruction in literacy and math, while very important to all of the nation's children and their future success as workers, seems the appropriate responsibility of our educational system, not a radical change in our ordinary commitments and practices.

Notwithstanding its focus on competence in reading (and math) at the elementary-school level, however, NCLB's reach is far and wide—creating a large and ready workforce to feed industry's demand for workers with skills. Our economic future depends on such skilled workers because they will replace laborers in our country (which has in the 20th Century not only shed its agrarian identity, but also its industrial one). And, in a sociolinguistic act of sleight of hand, the very architecture of NCLB mirrors that of the corporation, replete with standards, benchmarks, high stakes assessments, and outcomes-based awards or sanctions.

As was the case with the response to the Sputnik Crisis, when NCLB called for reforms in education, expert panels were convened to deliberate and produce reports. Expertise again resided in science and research conducted chiefly within the natural science paradigm. A select group of experts in the field of literacy learning and research were charged to conduct a sweeping review of extant research in literacy instruction, applying the highest standards of empirical research to identify the knowledge that must be taught if our elementary schools were to be able to achieve the goal of teaching all children to read at or above grade level by third grade.

The NCLB Act merged high standards, accountability by assessment, rigorous research to identify core knowledge, and Federal funds to insure that all youngsters achieve its goals. Its mandates focused on literacy skill development in the early years of schooling basing curriculum and instruction on research selectively reviewed and recommended by federally created commissions, most prominently the National Reading Panel. The law's mandates took a narrow focus on the nature of literacy and the preparation of children to perform as generically skilled workers. Yet the National Reading Panel's role as experts (whose authority strengthened NCLB's crisis narrative), meant that their reports and recommendations were interpreted by state and local educators as far more directive than had been the case in other crises (see, for example, the nature of scientists' recommendations in the 1950s reform of science curricula described by Bruner, 1960/77).

With governmentally sanctioned standards of performance, assessment, and accountability, and teachers playing minor roles in the development of policy, it was commonplace during the decade of NCLB to hear teachers ascribe the entirety of their literacy curriculum to the authority of the Federal government (Pardo, Highfield, & Florio-Ruane, in preparation; Sunderman et al., 2005). Gradually it became apparent that NCLB was tainted by an apparent conflict of interest built into the very nature of the law's design.[3]

The Department of Education (DOE) held a competition for states to win grants to raise the reading achievement scores in schools with large numbers of students deemed not to be making Annual Yearly Progress (AYP). The grants program was called Reading First and although states were not required to compete for these grants, only one state declined. Rich proposal development resources (reflecting the solutions implied in the reports of experts identified by the Federal government) were offered by the DOE to help the states develop their Reading First proposals and plan for their curricula, assessments, and professional development activities within those proposals. Yet the DOE did not—in fact legally could not—require that any state include in their proposed plan for improvement any of these particular resources. To do this would be to explicitly violate the limits set on the DOE at its inception and violate the legal limits the Congress had set on NCLB to promote products or promulgate particular methods. Yet from the perspective of many teachers, a clear line could be drawn from NCLB through their state department of education to their intermediate school district directly into their district, school, classroom, bookshelf—or first ninety minutes of their day.

Initially the rhetorical force of NCLB was sufficient to move states and districts to fall in line with the DOE beyond what was requested, required, or even legal. Yet sufficient public restiveness about NCLB in general, and Reading First in particular, prompted an investigation of the program six years into the authorization of NCLB. Its Reading First grants program was investigated by the Government Accountability Office (GAO) so that Congress could determine if there had, indeed, been conflict of interest in the ways the grants were awarded to states by the DOE. In the investigation and the follow-up recommendations for change, the GAO identified the DOE's failure to act, rather than its having acted inappropriately in implying that certain reading programs on the market, which had been used as examples in the Reading First grant preparation workshops, were implicitly preferable and hence more competitive. Henceforward DOE would make it clear orally and in writing that there were no such expectations or advantages. Quoting the report of the Government Accountability Office,

> Education officials made a variety of resources available to states during the application and implementation processes, and states were generally satisfied with the guidance and assistance they received. However, Education developed no written policies and procedures to guide Education officials and contractors in their interactions with state officials and guard against officials mandating or directing states' decisions about reading programs or assessments, which is prohibited by NCLBA and other laws
>
> (*Reading First*, 2007; In this quote Education refers to the U.S. Department of Education, and NCLBA refers to the No Child Left Behind Act).

However, in a system where there are historically shared assumptions about rights and duties and where familiar narratives are spun which underscore "who we are and what we are doing," we cannot assume objectivity, rationality, or "saying making it so." It is hardly surprising that the Department could remain silent on the issue of choice of programs and yet states would appropriately assume that particular programs were more highly valued and thus more competitive than others. This is an example of how members of a system tend to perpetuate that system in their language and thought. As part of tacit, cultural knowledge, the crisis narrative functions within an educational system that has a shared social history and discourse. Thus, participants will follow rules or norms for interpretation even to the point of limiting their range of options or opting not to act on the full range of their own authority and responsibility in order to maintain the system and their place within it. There are rewards and negative sanctions –explicit but also implicit—related to compliance with this unspoken but widely shared understanding.

Complicating the situation is the fact that notwithstanding the many layers of apparent surveillance in NCLB's structure, there was curiously little monitoring of the implementation of the Reading First grants, once received and disbursed by the states. Had there been more oversight, presumably this misunderstanding could have been identified early on (the audit was conducted six years into a seven-year appropriation) and rectified. Of this the GAO wrote,

> While Education officials laid out an ambitious plan for annual monitoring of every state's implementation, they did not develop written procedures during monitoring visits and, as a result, states did not always understand monitoring procedures, timelines, and expectations for taking corrective actions.
>
> (*Reading First*, 2007)

The mixture of: (1) high stakes assessment, (2) financial benefits tied to performance, (3) powerful Federal oversight, and (4) uncertainty and lack of predictability or clarity about when, how, and to what standard states were to perform reinforced the authoritative tone of the DOE's suggestions. Not surprisingly, if you were teaching in a low-income, non-AYP second grade classroom in a Reading First school and were told to teach a particular text or use a particular test, you might assume that you were required to by the Federal government under NCLB to do so.

However, more than a few state and local policy-makers and practitioners resisted the inevitability of the structure of education and its crisis narrative. Some states, as reported in the GAO audit, refused to assume the implied obligation to use federally sanctioned materials (one even refused to apply for the Reading First funds). Less visible, but as important, was the aforementioned restiveness among varied stakeholders in the change process in the academy, school administration, national professional organizations, and in teachers' local responses to the policy. The failure of NCLB to function as an effective crisis narrative is evidence of change in the landscape of American education. Its failure to persuade, its overreaching in its attempts to change practice, and the limits of its conceptual horizons as well as its support for lasting change have been noted.

The calling of a crisis where one is not apparent depends on persuasion—and those whom NCLB aimed to influence were ultimately not persuaded. Thus, what has happened over the lifespan of NCLB at multiple system levels is the making explicit of the limits of the policy but also the making use of the policy to more authentic, local ends. NCLB's failed "call to crisis" actually created an *authentic* crisis for educators calling for their immediate action "on the ground"—one in which powerful rhetoricians failed to control the terms of the narrative. Should they follow this limited yet high stakes path? How could they reconcile their values and professionalism with the force of governmental regulations pushing them to the margins of curriculum, instruction, and assessment? How could they "teach all children" if they were not sufficiently supported to do so? The stakes were enormous, and there was a felt need for decisive action to avert many "local" disasters. These are the dramas largely invisible to all but the teachers and children who experienced them, to the beginning teachers who witnessed and puzzled over them, to the teacher educators who worked at their periphery, and to those researchers who were able to chronicle them in descriptive studies (e.g. case studies, interviews, surveys).

Making Change by Making Do: Local Action to Solve Authentic Crises

It is reasonable to ask why a perennial problem of ongoing importance to U.S. education, that of equity in the preparation of students in basic skills of literacy and math, was elevated rhetorically to the status of a "crisis" in the late 20th Century. It is also reasonable to question the solution anticipated in the identification of the crisis—greater accountability by teachers for students' learning of the elemental features of written language. Teacher accountability was to be objectively measured by assessing students' learning chiefly by means of standardized tests. NCLB was hardly the first of such calls for teachers to respond to a crisis. Yet entailed within its identification of the crisis was an uncharacteristically intrusive solution: to regulate practice by the imposition of strict standards and high stakes pupil assessment. In a nation historically committed to the de-centralization of public education, and given a problem rather than a "crisis," the solution proffered by the DOE seemed draconian to many citizens.

Erickson (2004) has written about the ways practice is affected by large-scale political movements or organizing cultural narratives that are highly predictive of how people will think and act because they are part of common experience and norms within institutions. He is also interested in the local and immediate ways that people take action. What people do at the local level is not always predictable; it is less predictable when they lack a clear, compelling rationale for taking particular action. Especially in times when a major change in course of action has been mandated, it is in the local enactment that change happens—and various scholars have theorized about the ways that this change occurs and what it implies for social structure and the possibility of change within it. Of this Erickson (2004) asks, "How can change happen through practice that is local yet borne on the weight of history, as practitioners make use of prestructured tools for doing the work at hand in the immediate moment?"(p. 165).

Response to NCLB in terms of administrators' and teachers' local, decisive action can be described in terms of the metaphor of *bricolage*, in Erickson's words, "a metaphor for the process of evolutionary change in social practice" in "realtime work by social actors …." (ibid.). Reflecting the work of anthropologist Claude Levi-Strauss (1966), Erickson explains that, "the French all-purpose handyman … jack-of-all-trades, the *bricoleur* 'makes do' with what is available at hand, adapting prestructured materials to do whatever work needs doing" (ibid.).

In case-study research on urban teachers who responded creatively to the actual and presumed mandates of NCLB (Pardo et al., in preparation), we find that, in addition to more public, legal challenges such as the identification of implied conflict of interest, teachers have taken action daily in subtle yet powerful ways to make of NCLB mandates opportunities for their own creative practice. Like *bricoleurs,* they face authentic problems in their "realtime work" calling for immediate action, and they take what is available to them (in the form of the mandates, methods, and materials in their environment but also using their prior knowledge, experience, and the tools and artifacts of their classroom community) to make necessary changes and move on. These teachers innovate by turning the NCLB constraints with which they must contend into opportunities to: *widen professional dialogue* among their colleagues; *engage in practitioner research* on the effectiveness of the reforms to make a difference in the literacy learning of their students; *clarify values* for themselves as well as within their own classrooms by assessing the pre-packaged curriculum in relationship to their own knowledge and experience; *teach in tactical ways* that adopt the most useful requirements as "tools" which they can use not only in the ways they have been assigned, but also in ways that empower them and their learners.

In the NCLB call to crisis, the crew did not report immediately or unquestioningly to their battle stations—and although they did not mutiny, they challenged the orders they received and risked taking alternative, tactical, local action. They acted not merely to make the best of things, but to take ownership of the runaway change process and shape it toward more complex and authentic ends than were provided for or envisioned by the law. In Erickson's words, such making use of circumstance to one's own ends, or *"bricolage,* carries with it a sense of tactics employed within concretely opportunistic situation of work; of doing what it takes to get the necessary work done in real-time moments of *kairos"* (p. 167). Educators authentically responded to this crisis. If the purpose of the law was to transform teacher thought and action, it certainly succeeded— but perhaps not in the ways intended.

Conclusion

Literacy, as central to all education, is most heavily implicated when a crisis is called and educational reforms are introduced. Therefore, literacy educators bear both the burden and the responsibility of enacting change when a crisis is called. Yet, as professionals with expertise in language and literacy, they also have the specialized knowledge about language—its forms, functions, and contexts. As such, literacy educators are uniquely positioned to identify the dynamics at play when calls to national crisis serve to mobilize educational reform. They are able to examine discourse critically, and exercise leadership as professionals and as citizens to raise questions, frame problems, and pose alternative definitions of situations.

As practitioners, teachers must also take action in three areas: literacy education, preparation of literacy educators, and research on literacy teaching and learning. They are recipients of policies, practices, and materials not of their own design but with which they must work. However, they are also local problem-solvers who think, act, and respond moment to moment and in situations of complexity and continuous novelty. Thus, educators take creative ownership of the terms of their work, including the ways they make use of materials and mandates. Viewed this way, they are not the teacher-militia called to defend the nation. They are creative professionals who act according to law, knowledge of best practices, and their own professional judgment to educate the citizens of the democracy.

Notes

1 I thank my colleagues, Cheryl Rosaen and Paul Morsink, and the students in my graduate literacy seminar for helping me think about the topic of this chapter. The Michigan State University Literacy Achievement Research Center (LARC) sponsored my work on this chapter, a version of which was presented at the annual meetings of the National Reading Conference (2007) in Austin, TX. Its content is my sole responsibility.

2 It is beyond the scope of this chapter to provide even a brief history of ESEA, an Act of Congress arising out of educational reform during a previous period of crisis, the Civil Rights Era and the "War on Poverty." However, the purpose of the act was to provide Federal support to economically disadvantaged school districts to assist them in providing special services and compensatory education to the children attending schools in those districts. Title I of ESEA, the part of the act dealing with assistance to low-income schools, is re-authorized by Congress on a cyclic basis.

3 Websites and blogs abound discussing the ways that NCLB's implementation overstepped the bounds of Federal policy. Their titles are colorful and angry— "D-Ed Reckoning"; "The Ongoing Reading First Debacle"; "NCLB Outrages," and so forth.

References

Bruner, J. (1960/77). *The process of education*. Cambridge, MA: Harvard University Press.

Cope, B., & Kalantsis, M. (Eds.). (2000). *Multiliteracies: Literacy learning and the design of social futures*. London: Routledge.

Elbow, P. (1986). *Embracing contraries: Explorations in learning and teaching.* Oxford: Oxford University Press.

Erickson, F. (2004). *Talk and social theory.* Cambridge: Polity Press.

Florio-Ruane, S. (1997). To tell a new story: Reinventing narratives of culture, identity, and education. *Anthropology and Education Quarterly, 28*(2), 152–161.

Florio-Ruane, S. with deTar, J. (2001). *Teacher education and the cultural imagination: Autobiography, conversation, and narrative.* Mahwah, NJ: Erlbaum.

Geertz, C. (1973). *The interpretation of cultures.* New York: Basic Books.

A Guide to Education and No Child Left Behind. (2004). Washington, DC: US Department of Education. Retrieved May 2005, from www.ed.gov/nclb/overview/intro/guide.

Hickam, H. (1998). *Rocket boys.* New York: Random House.

Lakoff, G. (2006). *Thinking points: Communicating our American values and vision.* New York: Farrar, Strauss, & Giroux.

Lakoff, G., & Johnson, M. (1980). *Metaphors we live by.* Chicago: University of Chicago Press.

Lentriccia, F., & McLaughlin, T. (1990). *Critical terms for literary study.* Chicago: University of Chicago Press.

Levi-Strauss, C. (1966). *The savage mind.* Chicago: University of Chicago Press.

Lucena, J. C. (2005). *Defending the nation: US policymaking to create scientists and engineers from Sputnik to the "War against Terrorism."* Lanham, MD: University Press of America.

A Nation at Risk: Report from the US Secretary of Education to American People. (1983). Retrieved October 2005, from http://www.ed.gov/pubs/NatAtRisk/risk.html

No Child Left Behind. (2001). Retrieved May 2005, from http://www.ed.gov/policy/elsec/leg/esea02/index.html

Pardo, L., Highfield, K., & Florio-Ruane, S. (Eds.). (In preparation). The still point in the turning world of educational reform: Cases of powerful literacy teaching.

Pinker, S. (2008). *The stuff of thought: Language as a window into human nature.* New York: Viking.

Reading First: Status Report Improvements in Reading Instruction, but Additional Procedures Would Clarify Education's Role in Ensuring Proper Implementation by States. (February, 2007). Washington, DC: United States Government Accountability Office Report to Congressional Requesters.

Rosaen, C., & Florio-Ruane, S. (2008). The metaphors by which we teach: Experience, metaphor, and culture in education. In M. Cochran-Smith, S. Feiman-Nemser, D. J. McIntyre, & K. E. Demers (Eds.), *Handbook of research on teacher education: Enduring questions in changing contexts* (3rd ed.) (pp. 706–731). New York: Routledge/Taylor & Francis, & the Association of Teacher Educators.

Sunderman, G. I., Kim, J. S., & Orfield, G. (2005). *NCLB meets school realities: Lessons from the field.* Thousand Oaks, CA: Corwin Press.

The Educational Policies Commission. (1937). *The unique function of education in American democracy.* Washington, DC: National Education Association of the United States & the Department of Superintendence.

Whitebrook, M. (2001). *Identity, narrative, and politics.* London: Routledge.

For Further Exploration

Hickam, H. (1998). *Rocket boys.* New York: Random House.

Lakoff, G. (2004). *Don't think of an elephant: Know your values and frame the debate.* White River Junction, VT: Chelsea Green Publishing.

National Reading Panel. (April, 2000). *Teaching Children to Read*. Retrieved September 2007, from http://www.nationalreadingpanel.org/Publications/publications.htm.

Powell, A. (2007). How Sputnik changed US education: Fifty years later panel considers a new science 'surge.' Cambridge, MA: *Harvard University Gazette*. Retrieved October 11, 2007 from www.harvard.edu.

October Sky. (1998). Hollywood, CA: Universal Studios, Universal Pictures.

Part III
Reflecting on Crisis and Literacy

12 Commentators' Insights

**Tracy Sweeney, Early Career Teacher,
Rancocas Valley Regional High School**

> "I will be the first to write on the wall and say that was one hell of a landing sir . . . "
>
> (Posted to Captain C. B. Sully Sullenberger's Group Fan Page on Facebook, 8:44 p.m., January 15, 2009)

On January 15, 2009, my husband texted me "Turn 2 CNN. Plane down NYC." Immediately, my heart fell. New York City and planes incites negative connotation. Fortunately, there was no imminent national crisis; terrorism was not to blame. US Airways Flight A320, Charlotte, N.C. bound, struck a flock of birds during takeoff from LaGuardia Airport, and minutes later, Captain Chesley "Sully" Sullenberger safely landed the jetliner and all 155 passengers in the Hudson River. Globally, traditional media began reporting the "miracle on the Hudson." Electronically, social media coverage grew exponentially.

Within hours, a Facebook page dedicated to the captain was created. Originally, the page was sent to two people, but within 48 hours, it assumed 250,000 members with 200 members added per minute at the page's peak. The tens of thousands of postings on Sully's virtual wall articulate support and praise for the captain and crew's heroism. People from all over the world chimed in their printed thoughts, prayers, and reflections of the crisis that could have ended in tragedy. "You handled the crisis and kept your focus through the chaos and confusion," one member wrote. And "You have done what we all have the potential to do. In a moment of crisis we can choose to be completely present without fear. Call it God or not, this was a miracle of which you were the human instrument," another added.

Today, in times of crisis, we have the opportunity to express our feelings through mediums previously inconceivable. Electronic social networks abound and word spreads at supersonic rate. Considering MacGillivray and Brenner's six facets of crisis in Chapter 1, this potential averted disaster was global in scale, highly visible, uncommon, significant in impact (affecting everyone connected), unexpected, and, as the media images showed the passengers in real time standing on the wing of the plane in water, perceived as a crisis of urgency. As the authors in this volume have explored, individuals respond to crisis in various ways, and for some, a way to cope and to make sense of a situation that has personal effects, is to read and write to extend others' reactions. In this case, there was cause for words of celebration. Paradoxically, less than a month later, a similar crisis event ending in tragedy prompted language of sorrow and promotion of prayer.

"Sigh. Damn Sully, wish your grace and skill could have extended to those aboard Continental 3407. God bless those on board and on the ground." These sympathetic words posted on Sully's wall were in response to the devastating crash of a Colgan Air flight from Newark Liberty Airport to Buffalo Niagara Airport that went down on February 12, 2009, killing 50 people. This time, there were no fan groups, but Facebook prayer and memory groups. Crisis workers for the Red Cross listed contact information of trauma response counselors, witnesses wrote their accounts, community members named organized local prayer services, and members posted messages about and for the passengers onboard. The electronic world once again provided space for people to express themselves in a time of crisis.

The two aforementioned crises consider the place of new literacies in harrowing times. Bedford and Brenner discuss the new literacies that helped April during Hurricane Katrina. At the time, email served as a way to maintain social connections and provide friends and family with comfort and reassurance. Today, Facebook, MySpace, and Twitter function as social networks devoted to keeping friends abreast and "in the know." These sites grant members the opportunity to remain in contact and to contact through blogs, status updates, and postings. Traditional communication methods failed April in 2005 and she had to rely on new forms of literacies for support during her time of crisis. Bedford and Brenner explain, "One of the salient features of new literacies is the way they change rapidly. Changing technologies afford new ways of communicating and novel ways of using text to convey ideas" (p. 19). Finding new ways to communicate, to attach meaning, and to make connections is the foundation of my pedagogical beliefs. This leads me to consider the place of new literacies in my classroom and to answer the questions I originally posed in Chapter 2.

How are Students in Crisis Affected by Literacy Practices in My Classroom?

Bedford and Brenner (Chapter 3) acknowledge the importance of social networks like MySpace and Facebook as literacy practices for young adults despite their opposition in school settings. They do not suggest explicitly teaching how to use these new literacies, but rather, understanding and stating their value, especially for students in times of crisis. As the thousands of postings on the walls of group pages connected with the US Airways and Colgan Air flights attest, there is a relationship between new literacies and crisis.

Teaching students "the skills and strategies of adaptation and innovation" supports students in times of need. Thus, the literacy practices in my classroom need to be diverse.

In addition to the implementation of the valuing of new literacies, Bedford and Brenner suggest teaching students to read and write in a variety of ways to purposefully engage students in a mélange of literacy practices. Promotion of multiple reading and writing genres in the classroom adds to students' literacy practice repertoire and can function as consolation for students in crisis. This requires developing a broader understanding of text. In Chapter 4 MacGillivray explores the function of literacy in the lives of children in a homeless shelter and expands the definition of text. She discusses the importance of recognizing outside of school literacies which requires thinking beyond traditional text frameworks. MacGillivray cites literacy events within religious practices as supporting families during crisis. This requires assisting children in naming their literacy experiences in and out of school which can benefit the child and those involved in his/her educational welfare.

Often, tapping into students' out-of-school life is difficult. Students need to see their teacher as a trusting individual worthy of entry beyond the brick and mortar. In the case of Lo in Thompson's (Chapter 7) study, the poetry she wrote outside of school was personal, for her, not "them [teachers]." Even in supportive classrooms, students may not feel comfortable sharing their personal lives in front of other students. Thus, it is important for me to consider how my students, already in crisis, are affected when I am asking them to share their lives. Will they embrace the opportunity? Will they be honest? Will the literacy activity support or hinder their personal expression? To allow the student to engage in the event on his/her own terms, to make it meaningful, Ragusa (Chapter 5) suggests dialogue journals. In her study, journaling served as a communication strategy for mothers and children during divorce. However, the activity appropriately translates into the classroom setting as a teacher–student exchange. An interactive journaling structure, where the reader (teacher) can respond, offers students a therapeutic sharing safe haven and the teacher a place of opportunity to learn more about students' out-of-school lives and literacy.

What is My Role in Fostering Literacy Activities for Students in Crisis?

In Chapter 4, MacGillivray suggests self-selected reading and writing and family involvement as a way to suture in and out-of-school literacies. While I do allow students to select their own texts and writing prompts and genres, I have not previously considered involving parents in this quest. MacGillivray states, "This would mean that parent involvement goes beyond informing the teachers and curricula to include gathering information about how their family practices can be enhanced by the literacy practices which occur in schools" (p. 44). Thus, for those students in crisis, I can foster literacy practices by reaching out to parents or caretakers to find out what literacy looks like in their family under stressful conditions.

To specifically meet the needs of students in crisis, Lycke's (Chapter 6) study suggests the power of a curriculum aligned with students' future goals and interests. In her study of the changing literacy practices of teenage mothers, she found that Elaine's reading and writing was information focused. Elaine's interest in non-fiction escalated as she began to connect what she was learning in her psychology class to her future medical aspirations. In addition, Elaine's teacher, Rachel, adjusted the curriculum to provide the students with lessons pertaining to motherhood. Thus, for students, especially teenagers, connecting their literacy activities with their educational pursuits and possibly with their current crisis, may be one way to help students make sense of, cope with, or combat crisis situations from an academic scope.

If literacy activities match students' interests, goals, and aspirations, students are likely to be more engaged. In Chapter 7, Thompson explains, "Even though the stakes were high with senior high school the following year, Lo did not see the point in doing well when the things she was asked to do were in her words, 'silly things teachers make up cause they be mean'" (p. 91). Thus, connecting classroom curriculum can support literacy. My role is to help establish those connections through the inclusion of self-selection, parental involvement in furthering understanding of students' literacy practices, and crafting assignments related to student interests.

How Can School Literacy Communities Support Students in Crisis?

In Chapter 3, Bedford and Brenner explain how it was important for April to have an audience when writing during the Hurricane Katrina Crisis. While a more intimate experience like journaling may be appropriate for some students, writing for a specific purpose, for intended readers, may better meet the needs of some. School literacy communities can be supportive environments for students in crisis. I teach a Journalism II course that produces the school's literary magazine. The intimacy of the small class atmosphere creates a literacy community. In this course, students can take risks in their writing without fear of ridicule. Since the course is pass/fail, active participation is assessed and writing is ungraded. The emphasis is on creative and free writing. Thus, students pursue writing that is meaningful. In Chapter 6, Elaine expressed her enjoyment of creative writing class where she could "freely express herself." In contrast, Lo, in Thompson's (Chapter 7) study, did not have an in-school supportive literacy community, and her after-school poetry and fanfiction went unnoticed.

Thompson explains, "Lo's writing was meaningful in the after school context because it was collaborative, social, and purposeful" (p. 98). The classroom, for Lo, was a teacher-directed "thick space" that stifled her creativity, whereas her after-school space served as a literacy community supportive of her literacy practices.

Thus, finding ways to create school literacy communities provides students with "thin spaces" where students can determine their reading and writing agendas and pursue those genres and topics that are of interest to them. In this context, school literacy communities can serve as an outlet for students dealing with crisis.

As a teacher early in my career, I am still refining my instructional methods. I am constantly reflecting on best practices to meet the educational needs of my students. These empirical chapters answered the questions I outlined in Chapter 2, and helped me explore my teaching against a medley of times of crisis. School can support a student in crisis. However, it can also exacerbate a student's crisis situation. Acknowledging that the decisions I make regarding literacy activities in my classroom, my specific actions to foster literacy practices, and my involvement in literacy communities shape a student's educational path and consequently his/her evolving identity, I am reminded why I entered the teaching profession.

Jane Ching Fung, Veteran Teacher, Alexander Science Center School

My initial questions were:

- What literacy experiences are most helpful to young students during times of crisis?
- What strategies can I use to promote home literacy practices in times of crisis?

Reading *Literacy in Times of Crisis: Practices and Perspectives* has reaffirmed some of what I already do in my classroom as a practitioner. At the same time, it has brought to light the many other literacy experiences I can and should be providing to help students deal with times of crisis if and when they occur. After reading the entire collection, I found four themes which cut across the chapters and impact my teaching in different ways.

Learning about Cultural Practices

MacGillivray's Chapter 4 and Sarroub's Chapter 9 focus on literacy practices as embedded in cultural practices which are rarely acknowledged in schools. They both helped me understand the role texts can play in creating, maintaining, and controlling relationships. I was also reminded that literacy development doesn't always equal improved academic success or even quality of life.

Their chapters remind educators that we need to know our students; we need to learn what matters most to them. In schools, we introduce, promote, and focus on certain authors, pieces of literature, and genres we are passionate about, while we ignore the texts of the home. As MacGillivray suggested, schools can use literacy practices already established at home to support student growth at school. The practice of reading the Bible with their parents provided the children at the homeless shelter with a sense of identity and belonging when their environment was unstable and traumatic. When the children talked about this practice, they were passionate and opened up to one another. Can you imagine finding that same passion in a literature circle at school?

There may be some apprehension in highlighting the practice of reading typically not acknowledged in schools such as religious or cultural practices but if we did, it would validate the roles they play in a student's culture and home life, and better help us understand how families use literacy to cope with and explain crises. Last year I wanted my class to learn about the month of Ramadan. I asked the Muslim families in my class if they would share their cultural experiences with us, and they all happily agreed. What I discovered from Adullah and his mother was that reading from the Quran every night was part of their daily home literacy practice. The other Muslim students shared that they also practiced the same literacy practices in their homes. During this discussion, several other students equated the reading of the Quran with reading the Bible. This helped other students relate to and identify with the Muslim students' home literacy practice. Adullah and the other students' experiences with reading and interpreting religious literature at home will serve them well when they are asked to interpret and analyze literature read in the classroom. Many of the reading skills and strategies students use at home can transfer to school, especially if the connections are encouraged.

Sarroub (Chapter 9) captures the complexity of the relationship between home and school and literacy when she writes, "Families must master cultural and linguistic domains while sustaining and reproducing a commonness in their own 'home' cultures" (p. 124). The stakes are high for the young adults she writes about. Literacy practices are more than simply academic or cultural. The work of Sarroub and MacGillivray reminds me of the importance of literacy practices as situated in life, with ramifications beyond the classroom.

The Power of School Literacy Practices to Help Face Crises

Lycke (Chapter 6) captures how young women's literacy experiences in and after school served as "tools for negotiating, supporting, and mediating accompanying identity changes" (p. 67). Ragusa (Chapter 5) documents the way parents co-opted dialogue journals to use with their children during the crises of custody. These chapters remind me of the power of reading and writing as situated in supporting healing interactions. Creating literacy communities is essential to my classroom and prepares students for so much more than a test.

I have seen the essential nature of rich interactions in my own classrooms. In my first year of teaching, I used interactive journals. I was teaching a third grade class with the majority of the students working below grade level, and many were English Learners. I was introduced to interactive journals in one of my new-teacher workshops. The experience of reading and responding to interactive journals helped me get to know my students better and they got to know me, but more importantly, the journals were also a place where students were able to express themselves freely without fear. I will always remember reading an entry one day from one of the boys that simply read, "I want to die." As a new teacher, I wasn't sure how I should react, should I make a big deal out of it and call attention to the student? What I did was respond to him like I always did and wrote back asking why he felt that way (at the same time informing the school psychologist). On the outside, this student never appeared to be depressed or in trouble, but once a safe place was provided for him to write down his feelings, he was able to take more risk and share his inner crisis. With some counseling and continued written interactions with me, he was able to work out his emotions and slowly began to gain more self-esteem. His journal entry informed me, as his teacher, about his crisis, and I was able to help provide support and direct him to resources that would help him overcome this difficult time in his life.

When Ragusa (Chapter 5) writes about the role writing can play in coping with crisis, I fully understand. Having students write freely on a daily basis in class has been an activity I have incorporated over the years. Students look forward to writing down their thoughts, ideas, and stories. They know there will be time allotted in the school day where they will have an opportunity to express themselves in a safe place. What they write can be shared or kept private, they make the choice. I teach younger students, and I have come to the conclusion that what is written or drawn in a journal "needs" to be shared with others. It is rare for kindergarten or first grade students not to want to read their journal to peers. This practice of informal journaling provides a structure for students to seek support from others when a crisis occurs. I truly believe that when students write about and/or draw their personal crisis, they are developing not only writing skills, but coping strategies as well. When Whitney draws and writes in class about not having any friends or that her friend Michelle was mean to her at recess, she is writing for a purpose. Whitney is upset and wants others to read and respond to her discomfort. She is seeking answers and support from others to her anxiety of not having anyone to play with. By making her feelings public, she knows someone will acknowledge her feelings of loneliness and offer to play with her. Through writing she has communicated her needs and, as a result, was able to solve her problem without it causing her further stress.

New Out-of-School Literacies

When I started teaching 22 years ago, the term literacy in the classroom meant reading, writing, speaking, and listening. Although, I would define literacy in the same terms today, the literacy tools we have access to in the 21st Century give us the potential to do so much more with our students. Reading Bedford's account (Chapter 3) of the literacy tools she used to deal with her crisis with Hurricane Katrina made me wonder, are today's educators equipped to use the very same tools that Bedford did in handling her crisis? In today's world, our students are exposed to and have access to a world of unlimited information instantly at their fingertips. The days of reading the daily newspaper for a current event assignment are all but gone. We now have the capacity to get information in real time with the use of technology. We saw the parents doing this in Ragusa's (Chapter 8) work. She showed us how parents used the Internet when coping with crisis.

Students' texts, emails, blogs, and fanfiction "post" their status as fast as they can type. These new literacy tools are being utilized daily by our students to not only communicate, gather, and share information, but often, to express, reflect, and deal with crises in their life. In Chapter 7 Thompson documented the power of an array of technologies to cope with one teenager's life. In Chapter 3 Bedford used email and blogs to connect with people during the days after Katrina. Students and parents that I have worked with use those same tools to convey feelings of doubt, anger, and hurt. I have read students' posts related to personal reflections, poetry, and open letters expressing personal crisis. They seem to be searching for answers on how to deal with them.

The new literacy tools have a lot to offer students, but how many teachers know how to use them to teach? I agree with recommendations in Chapter 3 about the role of schools in "teaching the skills and strategies of adaptation and innovation." Teachers must know and be able to use the wide range of technology-based literacy practices that are available before they can teach students the skills to access them and adapt these practices to help them through times of crisis. If students have been taught to use and see value in the new literacy tools out there today, they will be more prepared to deal with crisis if and when it occurs. This relates to a quote from Thompson (Chapter 7) as she describes Lo's frustration with life at school, "She was limited and forced into a production model of activities and assessments" (p. 98). This quote makes me reflect on my own teaching practices and those of other educators. I know my students can do incredible things given the chance, and just like Lo, they need the classroom to be a safe haven for expressing thoughts and feelings through a variety of literacy activities.

High Stakes

Chapters 10 (Rogers and Pole) and 11 (Florio-Ruane) address how outside forces have an impact on what we do in the classroom. As teachers, it is easy to lose our moorings and forget what really matters. At times I have allowed reflective, community-based literacy practices such as journal writing and literature circles to get pushed aside by school, district, state, and national debates. I let the voices in the newspaper determine what I do in the classroom. Rogers and Pole and Florio-Ruane offer a look at the often ignored external pressures of public discourse which blames parents and teachers for low student achievement, when we all know that the problems are much more complex.

I am fortunate enough to currently be at a school where I am allotted freedoms to provide meaningful literacy opportunities for students, which I balance against preparing for the end-of-year test. Unless I get too distracted, I can craft meaningful teaching for my students. But what about the teachers that are trying to balance scripted programs, mass-produced grade-level activities, controlling administrators, a disgruntled public, and high stakes assessments? As our schools become more rigid, how can educators provide the safe space and time for our students to use literacy as a tool for knowing and reflecting on their lives and feelings, and more importantly, what will happen to students if they don't?

I plan to carry with me the ideas and issues discussed in this volume. It has offered me a new way to consider literacy practices by making the connection between reading and writing and crisis. I will work even harder than I have before to create spaces and experiences for students to use literacy in powerful ways both at school and at home. These new insights will shape my future teaching, connections with parents, and my professional inquiries.

Elizabeth Birr Moje, Teacher Educator and Researcher, University of Michigan

Literacy, Crisis, Learning, and Power

In my introductory essay at the outset of this volume, I presented a narrative written by a distant relative in a time of personal crisis. I used the narrative to illustrate how people turn to literate practice in times of crisis, both to solve problems posed by the crisis and to record events, experiences, and feelings. This two-pronged purpose for literacy in times of crisis is well-represented in the chapters that make up this volume. One set of chapters (e.g., Chapters 4, 5, 6, and 7) represents the use of literacy and text forms as a way of expressing and working through emotions associated with the trauma of a crisis. These chapters highlight the expressive functions of literate practice, particularly writing (Britton, Burgess, Martin, McLeod, & Rosen, 1975), and call attention to the important role of self-expression and comfort-seeking in the literate practices of people's lives. In brief, people often read and write not necessarily to solve a particular problem or gain information, but simply to talk a problem through—often after the fact—and to distance themselves from the problem by encapsulating it in the abstraction of language and print. That is, there appears to be some power in putting the experience down on a page and thus, at some level, gaining power over it by naming it, being able to reflect on it, and finally, even restricting it to its life on the page.

This focus on the value of expression through literacy reminds educators of the need to consider the lives and experiences of the people who populate their classrooms. As illustrated in the Thompson chapter (Chapter 7), a classroom teacher inadvertently elicited negative social behavior in one of her adolescent students by showing a film that evoked and highlighted several aspects of the crisis of the student's life. With no other means to express her trauma and no mediation on the part of the teacher (who showed the film with good, albeit uninformed, intentions), the youth turned to negative behaviors. Intentional literate instruction could have provided alternate forms of expression had the teacher only known more about who her student was or had stopped to consider the possible consequences of the representations embedded in the text she asked her students to watch. Similarly, the MacGillivray chapter (Chapter 4), with its focus on religious literacies, reminds us of the need to be aware of students' commitments, values, and subjectivities outside of school. Although religious commitments seem not to be the purview of school, many children's lives are mediated and sustained by their religious commitments. For the children featured in Chapter 4, children who live without the security of stable home spaces, religion and literacy become intertwined in the act of sustaining their lives and were brought to the fore whenever MacGillivray brought up the subject of literacy. Knowing the value of particular texts and literacy practices in children's lives can help a teacher make sense of their readings and choose texts that will sustain their emotional and academic, or affective and cognitive, development.

Several other pieces illustrated how literacy practices were used, adapted, or invented to address immediate problems of crisis (e.g. Chapters 3, 7, 8, and 10), in some cases to intervene on political moves made in the name of crisis and thereby constituting a new set of political moves. Finally, two chapters demonstrated how literacy education in and of itself can produce crises, while simultaneously providing the means to address the crises literacy creates or that are created in the name of literacy (Chapters 9 & 11).

In each case, these chapters help to address some of the questions I raised at the start of volume. For example, how do educators who face daunting demands on their time, including following pacing guides and accountability demands, learn how to make instructional space for the crises and trauma that children and youth may face? How might literacy instruction be designed to mediate life crises or to teach children and youth to cope with or challenge crisis conditions? These chapters demonstrate that literate skill affords people the power to respond in times of crisis, whether for purposes of healing the self and others or for purposes of fighting injustice. But teachers need to know who their students are and what they are experiencing if they are to help students address the crises in their lives through literate practice.

This point, unfortunately, raises questions difficult to address. How do we—teachers, researchers, youth counselors, and others involved with youth—prevent a focus on trauma and crisis in children's and youth's lives from becoming voyeuristic? It is easy to see the potential for a focus on the crises in people's lives garnering problematic attention. For example, what is the risk involved in knowing that a child's father committed a "heinous crime" (Thompson, Chapter 7, p. 83)? Would the teacher in the Thompson chapter have decided not to show the movie, *Smoke Signals,* had she known both Lo's ethnic background and her father's crime?

Similarly, what are the pitfalls of recognizing that women developing sophisticated literacy skill may threaten the fabric of their family lives (Sarroub, Chapter 9)? Is there a chance that teachers would lower their expectations of these women? More worrisome, it is easy to see the possibilities for teachers and researchers to slip from empathy and instruction to pathology and marginalization in their interactions with children and youth. Some crises in particular risk being pathologized. Lycke's chapter (Chapter 6) does an excellent job of demonstrating the productive and responsible literacy practices of two teen mothers, but how many teachers will see those pregnant young women in the same light? Similarly, would the children of divorced parents, as represented in Ragusa's Chapter 5, be treated with kid gloves and not pushed to high expectations if teachers saw them as stressed by the tensions of divorce?

Each of these chapters implicitly answers this concern. Specifically, the chapters illustrate the powerful ways that particular texts and particular literate practices served as channels for the trauma of crisis and expression of voice. Bedford and Brenner's Chapter 3, for example, illustrates not only the problem-solving tool that blogs provided, but also the supportive and comforting power of writing one's own experiences, and reading and sharing in the experiences of others. Bedford revealed the comfort she derived from her virtual stranger of a neighbor's offer to shelter Bedford's husband, even as his location and safety remained unknown. In other words, the communicative function of literacy served multiple purposes of information-gathering, nurturing, and healing. Similarly, Ragusa's Chapter 8 on parents dealing with their children's disabilities demonstrates the power of literate practice to intervene, even as it makes clear the sophistication one needs to make a difference in crisis situations. Rather than allowing the reader to merely gaze on or even pathologize these experiences of literacy-in-crisis, the chapters demand that the reader recognize the power of these practices in the lives of these children and youth.

Do the chapters go far enough in relation to the question of power, however? One question I raised at the outset of the volume was whether traumatized children and youth could feel empowered merely through the practices described herein. A refinement of that question, based on the chapters in the volume, is whether the opportunity either to work through issues or to speak back to the forces of trauma and crisis, is enough. What does it take to develop a sense of agency when everything is crumbling around a person? Does literacy confer power or is a sense of agency a necessary prior condition for one to employ literate skill in powerful ways? To some extent, these questions remained unanswered across the chapters. It is not possible to determine whether these particular instances of individually powerful literacy practice will sustain the children and youth throughout their lifetimes or even in their immediate futures. Will Lo (Chapter 7), for example, make it through high school or will her shame and rage consume her? Are literate practices of Bible reading enough to sustain children who lack fulfillment of the most basic needs of shelter or food? Furthermore, it is not clear whether the cultural and structural conditions highlighted in the chapters by Sarroub (Chapter 9), Rogers and Pole (Chapter 10), and Florio-Ruane (Chapter 11) will be changed or even tweaked by the literate practices in which their protagonists engage.

What is clear in each case, however, is that these practices are not merely romantic moments of self-expression and that they require support from teachers and other well-resourced adults and community members to make even the small impact they may make. Thus, although the chapters cannot address the question of sustained empowerment, they do illustrate that empowerment is not only a matter of individual agency; all people need support in times of crisis (and times of stability), and teachers and other adults can scaffold children's literacy learning and practice in ways that will sustain agentic and powerful literacy practices to speak back to trauma.

Finally, and most problematic, what is the role or *proper* place of work on literacy in times of crisis in the upper grades? Does this work matter in physics class? British Literature from 1900-1960? Pre-calculus? Should we assume that students in such classes do not experience trauma or crisis? Or are they "mature enough" to handle their own crises? Three of the chapters, in particular, speak to these questions in somewhat more general terms. Ragusa's Chapter 8 on disability, Rogers and Pole's Chapter 10, and Florio-Ruane's Chapter 11 each demonstrate the importance of the sophisticated literacy practices necessary to deal with crisis, especially "manufactured" crises generated for political purposes. Whereas Bedford and Brenner (Chapter 3) illustrate the powerful new literacies that can be generated with new media in intense moments of crisis such as Hurricane Katrina, these latter chapters illustrate the need to invest in teaching young people even more sophisticated skills for accessing and critiquing information; navigating both new and so-called "old" literacies and media; and writing, speaking, and reading for particular purposes. Rogers and Pole, in particular, point out that their own ability to critique the crisis of state attempts to control urban schooling was dependent on advanced skills in discourse analysis. Without such sophisticated skills, people can navigate crises on a limited basis and hope for only limited or local change, such as the crisis-inspired adaptations Bedford and Brenner described in response to Hurricane Katrina.

What we still need to learn, then, is how to intervene on these practices and to what extent the recognition of crisis and the teaching of literacy for addressing crisis belongs in secondary-school classrooms, particularly at the upper grades (my own area of interest). In both the Rogers and Pole and Florio-Ruane chapters (Chapters 10 & 11) it is possible to see evidence of the *need* for upper-level schools to address crises (and to produce them), but we need additional research to help educators at all levels understand how the consideration of literacy and crisis can be merged with the consideration of literacy in the disciplines to form meaningful "third space" (Gutierrez, 2008; Moje, Ciechanowski, Kramer, Ellis, Carrillo, & Collazo, 2004) literacy practices.

What this collection has taught me is the importance of recognizing the crises our children and youth deal with on a daily basis, valuing the ways they already employ literate practices and social strategies for addressing those crises, and teaching them additional—and more sophisticated—skills and strategies for rising above the crises and traumas of their lives and making positive change to prevent additional crises in the lives of others. As a teacher educator and researcher of secondary-school literacy teaching and learning, I will use these chapters to highlight the value and power in what children and youth already do and to help future teachers move them to new levels.

References

Britton, J., Burgess, T., Martin, N., McLeod, A., & Rosen, H. (1975). *The development of writing abilities*. London: Macmillan.

Gutierrez, K. D. (2008). Developing a sociocritical literacy in the third space. *Reading Research Quarterly, 43*(2), 148–164.

Moje, E. B., Ciechanowski, K. M., Kramer, K. E., Ellis, L. M., Carrillo, R., & Collazo, T. (2004). Working toward third space in content area literacy: An examination of everyday funds of knowledge and discourse. *Reading Research Quarterly, 39*(1), 38–71.

List of Contributors

April Whatley Bedford is an associate professor and Chair of the Department of Curriculum and Instruction at the University of New Orleans. Her research focuses on children's literature, early literacy, teacher development, and gender issues in curriculum and instruction. Her most recent publication is *Surviving the storm: Creating opportunities for learning in response to Hurricane Katrina,* co-edited with Dr. Judith Kieff and published by the Association of Childhood Education International.

Devon Brenner is Associate Professor of Reading and Language Arts at Mississippi State University in Starkville, Mississippi. As a member of the Higher Education Literacy Council she collaborates with other faculty in Mississippi to develop teacher education policy and strengthen pre-service teacher preparation. Her research focuses on the importance of the volume of reading practice, curriculum design, and literacy policy.

Susan Florio-Ruane is Professor of Teacher Education at Michigan State University. She has published widely on literacy education, ethnographic and sociolinguistic research, and teacher education. Her book, *Teacher education and the cultural imagination,* won NRC's Distinguished Book Award (2001). She is currently writing a book about the social history of educational anthropology. Susan is Co-head Editor of the *Journal of Literacy Research.*

Kara L. Lycke is currently an assistant professor of Education at Grinnell College in Grinnell, Iowa. For more than twenty years, as a teacher and researcher, she has worked with adolescents and their teachers connecting literacy perspectives and practices with critical social and self-awareness in and out of school contexts. She is interested in applications of critical pedagogy for linking adolescents' literate practices with local/familiar and distant/unfamiliar communities and cultures and for engaging with adolescents in literacy for social action and personal accomplishment.

Laurie MacGillivray is Professor of Literacy in the College of Education at the University of Memphis in Memphis, TN. Her research focuses on the literacy practices of families living in homeless shelters. She is currently working with community shelters to design meaningful after-school literacy-infused art programs.

Kathryn Pole is an assistant professor in the Department of Educational Studies at Saint Louis University, in St. Louis, MO. Her teaching and research focus on the teaching and learning of literacy, teacher decision-making, professional development, qualitative research methodologies, and education policy. She serves on the leadership team for the St. Louis-area Literacy for Social Justice Teacher Research Group, a professional development organization committed to literacy education and advocacy as it relates to equitable and just practices in classrooms and communities.

Gisele Ragusa is an associate professor and the Director of the Center for Outcomes Research and Evaluation at the University of Southern California, Los Angeles. She holds joint faculty appointments in the Rossier School of Education and the Viterbi School of Engineering at USC and has various federally funded research projects in K-12 and early childhood education. Her research interests include home-school literacy connections, literacy and special populations, and instructional practices in cognitively demanding STEMs content area literacy.

Rebecca Rogers is an associate professor in the College of Education at the University of Missouri–St. Louis. Her research focuses on language, power, and identity-work, particularly within the socio-political contexts of education. Her recent book (with M. Mosely, M.A. Kramer, & LSJTRG) is called *Designing socially just learning communities: Critical literacy education across the lifespan* (2009, Routledge).

Loukia K. Sarroub is an associate professor of Education and Anthropology with an emphasis in literacy, language, and culture at the University of Nebraska-Lincoln. She is the author of *All American Yemeni girls: Being muslim in a public school* and has published articles in journals such as the *Harvard Educational Review*, *Reading Research Quarterly*, *Ethnography and Education*, *Theory Into Practice*, *Journal of Adolescent and Adult Literacy*, and *Anthropology and Education Quarterly*. Currently, she is examining how young people struggling with reading negotiate literacy practices in and out of school.

Mary K. Thompson is currently an assistant professor at the University at Buffalo SUNY. Her current research is looking at vampire fanfiction online and how it relates to adolescents' view of authorship, multimodal composition, and identity work. She is also exploring multimodal composing in an after-school writing club for struggling third and fourth graders.

Index